THE
GREAT
HORIZON

To Highland Park with all good wishes

THE
GREAT
HORIZON

50 TALES OF EXPLORATION

Jo Woolf

SANDSTONEPRESS
HIGHLAND | SCOTLAND

First published in Great Britain by
Sandstone Press Ltd
Dochcarty Road
Dingwall
Ross-shire
IV15 9UG
Scotland

www.sandstonepress.com

The publisher acknowledges subsidy from
Creative Scotland towards publication of this volume.

Published in partnership with the Royal Scottish Geographical Society.

The RSGS is a charity registered in Scotland, No: SC015599

ISBN: 978-1-910985-88-5
ISBNe: 978-1-910985-89-2

Front cover image © Bengt Rotmo
Back cover image © Nick Hayes
Cover design and picture layout by Raspberry Creative, Edinburgh
Typeset by Iolaire Typography Ltd, Newtonmore
Printed and bound by CPI Group (UK) Ltd, Croydon, CR0 4YY

CONTENTS

LIST OF ILLUSTRATIONS

Black & White photo section

1. Sketch by W.A. Donnelly depicting the inaugural address by H.M. Stanley to the newly-formed Scottish Geographical Society at the Music Hall, Edinburgh, on 3rd December 1884.
2. Sir Ernest Shackleton's ship *Endurance* in London docks just before departure in July 1914. The ship was crushed by the Antarctic ice and sank in November 1915.
3. Sir Ernest Shackleton, Robert Falcon Scott and Edward Wilson on the *Discovery* Expedition in November 1902, pictured before their attempt to reach the South Pole.
4. Sir Ernest Shackleton (far right) showing Queen Alexandra around his ship *Endurance* in South-west India Dock, London, on 16th July 1914. The Queen's sister, Maria Feodorovna, Dowager Empress of Russia, can be seen in the background in a feathered hat, shaking hands with an officer. On the back of the photo Shackleton has written 'Saying goodbye to the officers'.
5. Map annotated by Sir Ernest Shackleton, showing his intended route across Antarctica on the Imperial Trans-Antarctic *(Endurance)* expedition of 1914-17. The crossing was never made, as fate led them on a different path.
6. Saltire embroidered with the initials SNAE (Scottish National Antarctic Expedition) carried by William Speirs Bruce aboard the *Scotia* (1902-1904).
7. Gilbert Kerr, piper on Speirs Bruce's Scottish National Antarctic Expedition, entertains a bemused Emperor penguin in the Antarctic.
8. Map showing the trawling stations of the *Scotia* during the Scottish National Antarctic Expedition, 1902-1904.
9. Members of Fridtjof Nansen's Greenland expedition, 1888-1889. L to R: Ole Ravna, Otto Sverdrup, Fridtjof Nansen, Kristian Kristiansen, Oluf Christian Dietrichsen, Samuel Balto. Ravna and Balto from Lapland are wearing traditional 'caps of the four winds'.
10. 'Carriage by bearers' - a lady's carrying chair, photographed (and probably used) by Isabella Bird in China. She noted that the bearers, 'patient, much-enduring people', would carry the occupant up to 25 miles per day.
11. 'A traveller arriving at an inn in Manchuria' by Isabella Bird c.1900.
12. A four-sailed boat on the Min River, a tributary of the Upper Yangtze. Isabella Bird travelled on one of these boats, which were used for running rapids; the high prow offered protection against rocks.

13. Sven Hedin, photographed at the Pamir Boundary Commission in the Wakhan Corridor, 1895.
14. Accompanied by his hosts, Sven Hedin prepares to lecture to the RSGS at St Andrew's Hall in Glasgow on 17th February 1909.
15. Fanny Bullock Workman in 1912, posing at 21,000 feet on the Siachen Glacier (Karakoram) with a paper headed 'VOTES FOR WOMEN'.
16. Frederick Marshman Bailey in Tibet, between 1904-09.
17. Leaflet advertising George Mallory's lecture to RSGS in November 1922. The photograph shows Everest from the Rongbuk Glacier base camp.
18. Isobel Wylie Hutchison in Alaska, signed 'Yours ever sincerely, Isobel W Hutchison and 'Whitie', an Arctic friend'. The dog is assumed to be one of Gus Masik's team. It rests on the letter written by Isobel to her sister, Hilda, on notepaper salvaged from the 'ghost ship', *Baychimo*.
19. Sir Alan Cobham and Sir Sefton Brancker with the de Havilland DH50 biplane used for the India flight in 1924.
20. Sir Alan Cobham landing his seaplane on the Thames in London on 1st October 1926 after his round trip to Australia.
21. Roald Amundsen by one of the Dornier flying boats used in his bid to fly to the North Pole in 1925.
22. N25 Dornier flying boat, flying up the Oslofjord on Roald Amundsen's return from the Arctic in July 1925.
23. Neil Armstrong receiving the Livingstone Medal from RSGS President, Lord Balerno, in March 1972.
24. First page from the RSGS Visitors' Book dated 4th and 5th December 1884. Among the first signatories are H M Stanley, Joseph Thomson, John George Bartholomew and Agnes Livingstone Bruce, daughter of David Livingstone.

Colour photo section
1. Map of Loch Lubnaig from the *Bathymetrical Survey of the Fresh-water Lochs of Scotland*, 1897-1909, undertaken by Sir John Murray and Laurence Pullar. The maps were produced by Bartholomews of Edinburgh.
2. Menu from RSGS celebratory banquet held in honour of Fridtjof Nansen in Edinburgh in February 1897.
3. Telegram to the RSGS from Robert Peary announcing his 'discovery' of the North Pole on 6th April 1909. His claim was later shrouded in doubt.
4. Tickets to a lecture by Robert Falcon Scott entitled 'Furthest South' in St Andrew's Hall, Glasgow, on 14th November 1904.
5. The Rainbow Falls in the Tsangpo Gorge, named by Frank Kingdon Ward who climbed the slope on the right bank and looked down over the Falls.
6. The Falls of the Brahmaputra: this thundering waterfall in the narrowest and deepest section of the Tsangpo Gorge was heard but not seen by plant collector Frank Kingdon Ward.

LIST OF IMAGE CREDITS

Chapter portraits

ICE
Nansen: Henry Van der Weyde*
Peary: NOAA Photo Library*
Scott: Unknown**
Evans: 1914, Bain News Service
Shackleton: Unknown**
Spiers Bruce: Messrs Thomson, London*
Amundsen: Unknown*
Herbert: Sir Wally Herbert on the Arctic Ocean, 1968. Copyright Herbert Collection, Polarworld www.polarworld.co.uk. Used with permission.
Fiennes: Liz Scarff
Ousland: Thomas Ulrich. Reproduced with kind permission of Børge Ousland.

VOYAGERS
Severin: Arthur Magan, from the Severin Archive. Reproduced with kind permission of Tim Severin.
Wylie Hutchison: Every attempt has been made to trace the copyright holder**
Bird: c.1899, photographer unknown*
Murray, J. 1923, William A Herdman *Founders of Oceanography and Their Work: an Introduction to the Science of the Sea*, Edward Arnold & Co.
Kingsley: Wellcome Images, via Wellcome Trust.
Hedin: Dated 3rd December 1897 and signed 'Yours faithfully, Sven Hedin, Edinburgh'.**
Stark: John Murray Collection.
Thomas: Reproduced with kind permission of Patricia Knowles.
Ballard: Courtesy of Titanic Belfast.
Palin: John Swannell.

HEAVEN AND EARTH
Lubbock: From a drawing by George Richmond RA in 1867, reproduced by courtesy of the Lubbock family.
Geikie: Reginald Grenville Eves (1913)*
Younghusband: 'A German staff officer in India', 1909*

Mallory: From a lecture programme (1922)**
Kingdon Ward: Undated studio portrait**
Murray, WH: J. Stephens Orr.
Hillary: c.1953, photographer unknown*
Bonington: Stuart Walker, Chris Bonington Picture Library.
Cobham: Bain News Service*
Armstrong: NASA publicity image*

MISSIONARIES AND MAVERICKS
Livingstone: Portrait by Frederick Havill*
Stanley: Unknown**
Thomson: Unknown*
Bullock Workman: Unknown*
Taylor: From *Travel and Adventures in Tibet* by William Carey (1902)*
Kitchener: Reproduced from De Guerville, A B, *New Egypt*, E P Dutton & Company, New York, 1906.*
Cable, French & French: Unknown*
Bailey: c.1934, photographer unknown*
Newbigin: Unknown**
Swale Pope: Bob Collins. Reproduced with kind permission of Rosie Swale Pope.

VISIONS FOR CHANGE
Bartholomew: Edward Arthur Walton*
Geddes: Unknown**
Wilkins: c.1922. Reproduced with kind permission of the Ohio State University, Byrd Polar and Climate Research Center Archival Program, Sir George Hubert Wilkins Papers.
Heyerdahl: Kon-Tiki Museet*
Maathai: Martin Rowe.
Balharry: With kind permission of Scottish Natural Heritage.
Attenborough: Courtesy of Mike Robinson, RSGS.
Hempleman-Adams: With kind permission of Sir David Hempleman-Adams.
Darke: Hannah Dines, reproduced with kind permission of Karen Darke.
Mathieson: With kind permission of Craig Mathieson.

Black & White photo section credits
1. Sketch by W.A. Donnelly**
2. Photographer unknown**
3. National Library of New Zealand, unidentified photographer.
4. Photographer unknown**
5,6. From the RSGS archives**
7. Unknown*

8. Reproduced from *Report on the scientific results of the voyage of S.Y. "Scotia" during the years 1902, 1903 and 1904, under the leadership of William S. Bruce.* Scottish National Antarctic Expedition 1902-1904
9. Siems & Lindegaard.
10,11,12. Reproduced from *Chinese Pictures - Notes on Photographs made in China* by Isabella Bird (1900)
13. Attributed to Thomas Hungerford Holdich**
14. *Glasgow Herald*, 18th February 1909**
15. William Hunter Workman.
16. The British Library Board, International Dunhuang Project 1083/18(170)
17. From the RSGS archives**
18,19,20. Unknown**
21,22. Unknown*
23. Unknown**
24. Artefact from the RSGS archive, photographed by Colin Woolf.

Colour photo section credits
1. Plate from *Bathymetrical Survey of the Fresh-water Lochs of Scotland* (1897-1909)
2–4. Artefacts from the RSGS archive, photographed by Colin Woolf.
5–7. Kenneth Storm Jr, reproduced with permission.
8. From the RSGS archives by kind permission of RSGS.
9. Douglas Scott, courtesy of Audrey Scott.
10. With kind permission of Sir David Hempleman-Adams.
11. Jim Fotheringham, Chris Bonington Picture Library.
12. With kind permission of Cornerstone, a division of Penguin Random House.
13. Roger Crofts, RSGS Chairman. Reproduced with permission.
14. Mike Robinson, RSGS. Reproduced with permission.
15. Kjell Ove Storvik, with kind permission of Børge Ousland.
16. Børge Ousland. Reproduced with permission.
17. Fiona Duncan, with kind permission of Karen Darke.
18. Bob Collins, with kind permission of Rosie Swale Pope.
19. With kind permission of Craig Mathieson.

* Public domain
** From the RSGS archives by kind permission of RSGS
Every effort has been made to trace the copyright holders.

Acknowledgements

THIS BOOK HAS been made possible through the interest, support and co-operation of many individuals and organisations. I have made lots of friends while writing it, and have been deeply touched by the enthusiasm of so many, both here in Scotland and around the world.

First and foremost, my heartfelt thanks go to everyone at the Royal Scottish Geographical Society, who supported this idea right from the start and believed in my ability to bring it to fruition. The RSGS is such a happy place to work and a lovely organisation to be a part of. In particular I would like to thank Mike Robinson, Chief Executive, and staff members Gemma McDonald, Susan Watt, Anne Daniel and Linda Davidson. Thank you all so much for your enthusiasm, encouragement and friendship.

My sincere thanks to RSGS Chairman, Roger Crofts, and the Board of Directors; to the Archive Collections Team comprising Margaret Wilkes, Kenny Maclean, Bruce Gittings, Pat Brown, Andrew Cook, Tony Simpson, Blair White, Cameron Ewen, and Michael Cairns; and all the other volunteers, both in the RSGS offices and in the Fair Maid's House, who have been so helpful and enthusiastic.

Grateful thanks to Professor Iain Stewart, President of the RSGS, for his warm support of this book and for writing the Foreword.

I wish to thank all the RSGS members and other benefactors who helped to make this book a reality with pre-orders and donations. What a huge vote of confidence, and greatly appreciated! The RSGS would like to acknowledge with thanks the support received from The Patron's Fund and RSGS Treasurer, Tim Ambrose.

This brings me to the explorers themselves. Special thanks to Børge Ousland, Craig Mathieson, Karen Darke and Sir David Hempleman-Adams who generously shared memories and images of their experiences while I was writing their chapters. My research has also brought me into contact with some relatives and descendants of past explorers. In particular I would like to thank Patricia Knowles, great-niece of Bertram Thomas; Kaye and Andrew Ridge, great-niece and great-great-nephew of Sir Hubert Wilkins; Oliver Tooley, grandson of Frank Kingdon Ward; the Lubbock family, in particular Lord Avebury; and Alexandra Shackleton.

For the generous supply of images, I would like to thank Frances Daltrey (for Sir Chris Bonington); Audrey Scott (for Bill Murray); Paul Bird (for Michael Palin); Joyce Burnett (for Sir Ranulph Fiennes); Rosie Swale Pope and James Swale; Tim Severin; Kenneth Storm Jr; and Kari Herbert. Many thanks to Bengt Rotmo, for allowing us to use his beautiful image on the front cover; for the fantastic artwork on the back I would like to thank Nick Hayes.

Members of organisations and institutions offered valuable assistance in my research, among them Håkan Wahlquist at the Sven Hedin Foundation; Sabine Kraus at Sir Patrick Geddes's Scots College, Montpellier; Olive Geddes at the National Library of Scotland; and Lucy Martin at the Scott Polar Research Institute. I would also like to thank Laura J. Kissel, Polar Curator, Byrd Polar Climate Research Center Archival Program, Ohio State University; Mark Pharaoh at the South Australia Museum; Dr Janet Owen at the Royal Society; Andrew Renwick and Nina Hadaway at the Royal Air Force Museum, London; Kenneth Cox of Glendoick; Ian Baker; staff at the British Library, including John Falconer; the Royal Botanic Gardens, Edinburgh; and the National Portrait Gallery.

I would like to thank Sir David Attenborough (via Michael Ridley of DLA Piper) for kindly permitting me to use quotes from *Life on Air*.

For their enthusiastic and professional support of this project, and for seeing it through to a happy conclusion, I would like to thank everyone at Sandstone Press, in particular Kay Farrell and Bob Davidson. My thanks also to Ruth Killick Publicity, Roger Smith and to Heather Macpherson of Raspberry Creative Type for her superb design.

From the bottom of my heart I thank my husband Colin for being an unfailing source of love and support; likewise Verity and Chris, Leonie and Andrew. You are my inspiration.

FOREWORD

A S WE PLUNGE headlong into the twenty-first century, it is tempting to think that the era of Earth exploration is over. After all, we are now in the 'Human Age' – the Anthropocene – an epoch in which humans have chemically if not physically touched virtually every corner of our planet, including its deep oceans and upper atmosphere, and the digital eyes of satellites, cameras and drones have scanned the entire face of the Earth. What's left to find?

In that light, globetrotting adventures of the kind chronicled here might seem like anachronisms from a bygone golden age of exotic discovery. Certainly, the Royal Scottish Geographical Society nurtured and encouraged many of those wild and wonderful nineteenth and twentieth-century expeditional forays. The archives and artefacts adorning its Perth home – the Fair Maid's House – evoke many of those past marvels and exploits, while its prestigious talks programme still gives public voice to first-hand accounts from the latest generation of wayfarers and voyagers. Indeed, the Society has three 'in residence' explorers of its very own, though they are more likely to be 'out of office' in the snowfields of the Arctic north.

For, as is clear from the final pages of this collection, there is a very real and vital need for modern adventurers of the type long celebrated by the Society. Many of the deep-seated signs of a planet under pressure from our modern industrial society are manifest most clearly in distant lands – amid the Arctic or Antarctic ice floes, on Alpine and Himalayan peaks, in deserts and drylands, and along tropical coralline shores. Highly tuned natural systems are subtly shifting, and with them the lives and livelihoods of those who depend on them.

Today, more than ever, we need daring and passionate explorers to venture out into the wilds to track, chart and document the transformations that are happening around us. Across the globe, people and place are changing at a quickening pace. Just as the Society championed past explorers who boldly went where none had gone before, so it seeks to excite and incite a new breed of adventurers to report back from the planet's front line.

Those frontline reports will, in turn, feed a broader appetite for armchair adventure among those who, for whatever reason, cannot journey far afield to indulge in their own escapades of derring-do. Perhaps someone like me, raised in the Scottish flat lands on a diet of David Livingstone, Mungo Park and James Bruce, and who assumed that 'explorer' was a standard profession that emerged out of school Geography lessons. Or perhaps someone who simply travels in the mind, infusing them with fascination for our remarkable world, past and present.

For whatever the motivation of those who read these pages, this is a collection of geographical grit designed to inspire.

Iain Stewart
President of the
Royal Scottish Geographical Society

INTRODUCTION

I N December 1913, when Sir Ernest Shackleton publicly announced his plans for the *Endurance* expedition to the Antarctic, he received nearly five thousand letters from hopeful applicants. Shortly afterwards, a friend noticed that these letters had been sorted into three large drawers in his desk, which he had labelled 'Mad', 'Hopeless' and 'Possible'.

Shackleton could only accept fifty of those applications, and it is tempting to wonder how many from each category were successful. I would love to believe those he considered 'mad' stood the best chance of all.

When asked to imagine an explorer, we likely picture someone muffled in furs and battling Arctic winds, or perspiring in the heat as they hack their way through an equatorial jungle. Exploration seems to be a basic human instinct; the Phoenicians and ancient Greeks, the Romans, the Vikings and the Polynesians all set sail in a quest for new territory. This questing spirit is also seen in the European Age of Discovery which inspired Christopher Columbus, Vasco da Gama and Ferdinand Magellan. In more recent centuries, explorers such as James Cook, Mungo Park and John Franklin staked their lives – and lost them – in the great unknown.

By the late nineteenth and early twentieth centuries, vast regions of the world still lay unexplored; there were, quite literally, blank spaces on the map. In the pure spirit of adventure, these attracted men and women whose curiosity spurred them to travel the unknown landscape, and tantalised the minds of scientists eager to expand and enhance their knowledge. Then there was political power; if a nation could plant a flag in these uncharted places, it could claim them as its own. Explorers often took on many roles, for example as scientists, cartographers, ethnographers, even negotiators and diplomats. Very often, therefore, their stories are linked with events in the wider world. In the late 1800s the 'scramble for Africa' saw European countries vying to claim slices of the continent for trade; meanwhile the 'Great Game' was playing out in Central Asia, as Russia and Britain manoeuvred for power in the Himalayas. This is true even of more modern figures; Neil Armstrong's first steps on the moon were arguably precipitated by the Cold War.

Some found themselves especially drawn to those inhospitable parts of the globe where the extremes of climate made human survival all but impossible. The Arctic and the Antarctic captured the imagination. The discovery of the Northwest and Northeast Passages opened up shorter routes for trading vessels, while the Antarctic was identified as a vast continent. For a growing band of explorers, the ultimate prizes were the Poles.

In more recent decades, our perception of exploration has undergone a subtle change. The euphoria that greeted new 'conquests' in previous centuries has gradually been replaced by a sense of responsibility. As we begin to understand the absolute dependence of human life on the survival of our natural environment, the efforts of modern-day explorers are focused on enhancing our awareness and encouraging us to look ahead for the welfare of generations to come. Although Sir Patrick Geddes warned us that 'environment and organism, place and people, are inseparable'[1] over a hundred years ago, we are only just beginning to appreciate the truth in his words.

The experience of the explorer himself has changed, too. From the time when voyagers would bid goodbye to their families and head off into the great unknown, with absolutely no contact for several years at a time, we have progressed into an era of digital technology which allows instant communication and precise global positioning. Increasingly, the feeling that those early pioneers must have known is going to be lost to us: their vulnerability, their total isolation. It took nearly eleven months for the news of Scott's death to reach the outside world. Admiral Teddy Evans, along with Tom Crean and William Lashly, was one of the last people to see him alive; as the two groups parted ways and Scott's men headed towards the South Pole, Evans watched them until they became specks on the 'great white horizon'.[2]

In 2014 I was invited to the headquarters of the Royal Scottish Geographical Society, to discuss writing about some of their medal recipients. The long list of names, stretching back to the late 1800s from the present day, reads like a *Who's Who* of exploration. Alongside the 'greats' of Scott, Shackleton and Amundsen were some unfamiliar names that invited further investigation. From that point I set out on my own journey of exploration.

The RSGS was established in 1884, the brainchild of a forward-thinking young cartographer named John George Bartholomew, whose influential friends included Agnes Livingstone Bruce, the daughter of David Livingstone, and Professor James Geikie of the University of Edinburgh. A meeting to constitute the newly formed Scottish Geographical Society was held in the Hall of the Chamber of Commerce in Edinburgh on 28th October 1884, and a little over a month later the inaugural address was delivered by the celebrated African explorer Henry Morton Stanley. In 1887 the Society was granted Royal status by Queen Victoria.

> Besides promoting geographical education, the Society will direct
> its attention to the encouragement and assistance of exploration
> in unknown countries...[3]

It was an auspicious beginning. Indeed, the RSGS was blessed with so much support, from both Council members and public subscriptions, that the newspapers wondered openly why a Scottish geographical society had never been thought of before. The nineteenth century had seen an explosion in scientific knowledge and the public's appetite for new discoveries was perhaps unprecedented at that time. The RSGS was welcomed as a champion of the newly emerging science of geography, setting the stage for explorers to share their stories of daring adventure with audiences throughout Scotland – which they did in their hundreds, year after year. Some sought purely to share their knowledge, while others also hoped to engage public interest in order to finance their next expedition.

It is hard to describe my excitement as their stories began to unfold, for the life of each person turned out to be a revelation. Mountains, deserts and oceans opened up for me as they had for the explorers themselves. I realised that these people were vulnerably human, with all the human qualities of fear and doubt. Diverse as the characters were, each had a connection with the RSGS, either as a medal recipient, a Fellow, a Council member or a guest speaker. I felt there must be a way of celebrating the Society's wholehearted support of these explorers and scientists throughout its 130-year history. That is how the idea for this book was born.

On the first page of each chapter you will find brief details about the explorers and their connection to the RSGS. This includes any medals or Fellowships they have received. The Society periodically bestows a total of eleven different awards, but here I have described only those that are relevant to these particular explorers.

The Gold Medal (renamed the Scottish Geographical Medal in 1933) is the Society's oldest gold medal, first awarded in 1890 'for work of conspicuous merit within the science of geography itself, e.g. by research, whether in the field or otherwise, or by any other contribution or cumulative service to the advancement of the science.'[4] The Society continues to present it periodically for 'conspicuous merit and a performance of world-wide repute.'[5] From its early years, the Society also bestowed Silver and Bronze Medals, which were often given to additional members of an expedition.

Struck in gold, the Livingstone Medal was endowed in 1901 by Agnes Livingstone Bruce in memory of her father, David Livingstone. Originally presented for 'outstanding public service in which geography has played an important part, either by exploration, by administration, or in other directions where its principles have been applied to the benefit of the human race'[6], it is now awarded 'for outstanding service of a humanitarian nature with a clear geographical dimension.'[7]

The Mungo Park Medal was introduced in 1930. Named in honour of the Scottish-born explorer, this medal is presented 'for outstanding contribution to geographical knowledge through exploration or adventure in potentially hazardous physical or social environments.'[8] The Geddes Environment Medal, introduced in 2009, celebrates the philosophy of Sir Patrick Geddes and is awarded 'for an outstanding contribution to conservation of the built or natural environment and the development of sustainability'.[9] Finally, Honorary Fellowships, first introduced in 1888, are awarded 'in recognition of services to the Society and to the wider discipline of geography'[10]; recipients may place the letters FRSGS after their name.

> The very bones of the pioneers became the stepping stones of knowledge.[11]

Wherever possible, I have used reference material from the RSGS archives. Of these, the *Scottish Geographical Magazine* (the academic journal of the RSGS) is the primary source. Newspaper cuttings, especially from the early days, are a goldmine of detailed observation, while other reference material includes lecture programmes, leaflets, invitations and even banquet menus. It is lovely to look through the lecture sheets and imagine the anticipation that preceded an appearance by Nansen, for instance, or George Mallory. How I would love to have been there in person!

In some cases, my investigations led me to make contact with descendants or family of the explorers, or the explorers themselves, all of whom have been very helpful.

With so many fascinating people to write about, it was a challenge to limit myself to fifty. Even with the scope defined by the timeline of the RSGS, what a vast array of stories can be found! I have deliberately mixed more famous characters with a generous scattering of lesser-known ones, in the hope that, while you are reacquainted with some of your lifelong heroes, you may find some more. Time after time, I have been astonished to discover that these 'quiet voices' have hair-raising stories to tell. Annie Taylor, for example, or Hubert Wilkins, or Frederick Marshman Bailey have been half forgotten by history, but they deserve to be brought back into the limelight.

From our present-day viewpoint, some of the choices are

undeniably controversial: Henry Morton Stanley, for instance, or Lord Kitchener. As I read about these potentially difficult characters, I began to think that there was more to appreciate about their nature, and wondered if history had required them to make the best of a situation they had created for themselves. Please understand, I am not attempting to justify prejudice or violence, but it was rewarding to try and glimpse the human spirit beneath the hardened shell.

Some of the most amazing stories are those of the women, who in the early days had an additional barrier to overcome: the prejudice attached to their sex. However, the RSGS was co-founded by a woman and opened its doors to women members from the very beginning, welcoming a large number of female speakers including Mary Kingsley, whose first ever public lecture was delivered in Edinburgh. The lives of these remarkable women, who usually travelled alone and revelled in the freedom and spontaneity, make an interesting contrast with the many military-style expeditions that are essentially the domain of men. There are exceptions, of course; Fanny Bullock Workman had the organisational capacity of an army general, whereas Frank Kingdon Ward could be lured down just about any precipitous gorge in the Himalayas if a rare and beautiful plant lay at the bottom of it.

As my research progressed, it seemed that some of these explorers fell naturally into groups. The polar explorers, of course, were the most obvious, and these are in the section called 'Ice'. Then there were those who set sail across oceans of sea or sand, and they became the 'Voyagers'. 'Heaven and Earth' is devoted to scientists, mountaineers, an aviator and an astronaut, while 'Missionaries and Mavericks' contains a colourful mix of characters, each a rebel in their own way. Finally, in 'Visions for Change', I have collected remarkable people from every era, whose messages challenge us to follow our own dreams, deepen our understanding and take steps towards a better future for the Earth and its inhabitants. Over the years, many of the place-names in this book have been spelled in a variety of ways. In most cases, for the sake of consistency I have chosen to use the form or spelling which would have been familiar to the explorers themselves.

The business of the discoverer is to leap into the dark – taking, of course, all the precautions he can to light softly.[12]

So what makes an explorer? The fur coats, the jungle heat? Is there some defining element in his personality which propels him towards that great horizon? Can you see it written in her face, along with the sunburn or the frostbite? And how many of them belong in Shackleton's 'Mad' drawer? These are the questions I found myself pondering while writing this book. Explorers are often described as inspirational, and indeed there is something to inspire in every story, especially those where the instinct for discovery is rooted in a heartfelt desire to care for fellow human beings and the environment in which we live. Is this what exploration is about, as the new generation succeeds the old? Are we not all explorers, after all?

Jo Woolf
Perth, July 2017

1. Patrick Geddes, quoted in *Patrick Geddes in India* by Jaqueline Tyrwhitt (1947)

2. *Dundee Advertiser*, report on lecture by Teddy Evans to RSGS in Dundee, 19th November 1913

3. *Prospectus of The Scottish Geographical Society*, 1884

4. Report of Council, *Scottish Geographical Magazine* (1930), 46:6

5. RSGS website

6. Report of Council, *Scottish Geographical Magazine* (1930), 46:6

7-10. RSGS website

11. *The Scotsman*, 5th June 1895, from an editorial about Franklin Commemoration, quoting W. Scott Dalgleish, RSGS Secretary

12. *The Scotsman*, 20th November 1885, report on Lieut Adolphus Greely's lecture to RSGS in Synod Hall, Edinburgh, 19th November 1885

ICE

Dr Fridtjof Wedel-Jarlsberg Nansen

Polar explorer, scientist, humanitarian, Nobel Peace Prize winner
BORN: 10th October 1861 (Oslo)
DIED: 13th May 1930 (Oslo)
§
RSGS Gold (Scottish Geographical) Medal, 1897
Honorary Member of RSGS

IN 1886, AT THE Royal Lyceum Theatre in Edinburgh, a twenty-five-year-old Norwegian man confided an astonishing ambition to a young Scotswoman as they watched a performance of *Hamlet*. One day, he told her, he would be the first man to cross Greenland, and in doing so would reveal to the world what lay in its unexplored interior. Marion Sharp, the vivacious and free-minded girl sitting next to him, saw no reason to dispute the claim. She knew the unyielding nature of Fridtjof Nansen well enough to believe he could succeed.

On 23rd May 1889 *The Scotsman* published a telegram which had been received by the Royal Scottish Geographical Society. It read: 'Copenhagen, 6.50 AM—Safely arrived. Hearty thanks. Greeting friends, Edinburgh. Fridtjof Nansen.'[1] True to his word, Nansen had made the first crossing of Greenland. In a short accompanying tribute the Secretary of the RSGS, Mr A. Silva White, acknowledged the remarkable feat, and added that the Society hoped to have a paper from Dr Nansen by the next session.

This was the first tangible proof that Nansen was a force to be reckoned with. What drove him on, and how did he hatch such an outrageous plan in the first place?

By the time he was eighteen, Nansen knew he was unlike his peers, although he could not explain why. He was the son of a lawyer in

12

Christiania (now Oslo), and with his brother and step-brothers would go away for weeks on walking and skiing tours in the vast Norwegian forest. He was a skilled hunter and sportsman, excelling in the winter competitions that were held regularly in the surrounding countryside. It sounds like an exhilarating life, but Nansen was aware of a darkness within himself. Once he came up against an obstacle – a terrifying ice-cliff, for example – it took hold of his mind until he was compelled to throw himself against it or down it, trusting to his athleticism and determination to survive. If the Norse gods were watching over Christiania, they must have held a special conference over his fate.

Despite his habit of courting death, the young daredevil had to think about temporal things, the most urgent of which was his choice of career. On the face of it, a degree in zoology offered many splendid prospects: a respectable profession, an academic post and the promise of a dependable income. The course of study would include field trips to far-flung places, allowing students to examine organisms in their natural environment. In his second year at the University of Christiania, Nansen responded to an invitation to study marine life in the polar regions. He had to make his own arrangements for travel, and in March 1882 boarded a vessel bound for the Arctic. This voyage awakened new desires that would change the course of his life.

> I got the idea one day in 1882, whilst on board a Norwegian sealing-ship [and] we were ice-bound for twenty-four days near the still unknown part of the east coast of Greenland, and from that time I could not get it out of my mind.[2]

Staring at unexplored terrain for the best part of a month must have played havoc with his brain. The crew, who were all hardened seamen, were focused on collecting seal skins and they were happy to ignore the challenge of geographical discovery. From the crow's nest, Nansen gazed over what is now Christian IX Land and he begged the Captain to put him ashore. The Captain refused on the grounds of safety, and when the ship broke free of the ice, Nansen watched the coast of Greenland melt back into the distance. He arrived home with a commendable haul of zoological specimens and a new sense of yearning that wouldn't go away.

Greenland, at that time, still held a special appeal in the minds of geographers. What lay in its interior? There had been several doomed attempts to cross it in previous centuries, and in 1886 the American explorer Robert Peary had ventured 100 miles east from Godhavn before turning back. Now Nansen saw a way of succeeding where others had failed. He was, after all, a master skier. Deciding that he would travel light and fast, completing the trek in just one season, he would take a small team of hand-picked men and, unlike all the former expeditions, he would travel from east to west. This choice of direction was governed entirely by logic. At that time, there were Danish settlements on the west coast of Greenland, whereas the east coast was virtually uninhabited. If they started from the west, Nansen argued, they would be leaving behind the only place of comfort, the 'flesh-pots of Egypt', with nothing ahead of them but the ice-desert. His men could easily grow dispirited and turn around. If, however, they started from the east and travelled west, they would be heading towards the promise of shelter and rescue. Nansen put it more brutally than that. 'They had no choice, only "forward",' he told the RSGS in 1889. 'Our order was, Death or the west coast of Greenland.'[3]

People muttered and shook their heads over Nansen's insane idea. He was not, however, blundering into it with his eyes shut: he had sought the advice of seasoned explorers such as Nordenskiöld and Holm, and was inspired by the legacy of Orkneyman John Rae. He was intensely practical, building lightweight sledges with broad runners, making sleeping bags out of reindeer hide, adopting a new layering system of pure wool garments and redesigning the heating stove so that it was more efficient. He tested them all rigorously on his own outdoor treks. The use of dogs as draught animals was virtually unknown in Scandinavia, and Nansen had no experience of dog-driving. Briefly, he considered taking a team of reindeer, but concluded that the animals needed vegetation on which to graze. He realised that his only option was to man-haul the sledges. It would be an exhilarating challenge. He could not attempt it alone, so he applied his mind to the choice of a team:

> I selected three Norwegians, viz. Captain [Otto] Sverdrup, Lieut. [Oluf Christian] Dietrichsen, and a peasant, Kristian Kristiansen Trana. From Lapland I got two Lapps, Samuel Balto and Ole Ravna...[4]

On 17th July 1888 the party was waved off from a sealing vessel which had deposited them offshore in two small boats, and soon disappeared into the labyrinth of ice floes that choked the fjords of eastern Greenland. As the ship receded from sight, so did all contact with the outside world. They were alone, dependent entirely on their own resources against an unknown land and the vagaries of the weather.

An unknown land it certainly was. It was the best part of a month before they were able to properly set foot on it. The extent of the ice floes meant that they were constantly scanning the horizon for a glimpse of the shore, while trying desperately to avoid collisions and damage to the boats. Meanwhile, the prevailing current swept them ever southwards, so that when they finally struggled ashore on a rocky islet they realised that they were too far south to make a valid crossing, and they were forced to row north again, eventually finding landfall near Umivik. They were exhausted, and by now the Arctic summer was well advanced. Some of the men favoured staying there for the winter, and attempting the crossing next year. Nansen was adamant. They would start now, without delay.

> We saw only three things: that was snow, sun, and ourselves. One day was quite like another.[5]

At first their endurance was tested to the limit as they hauled their sledges across a challenging landscape of crevasses, steep slopes and soft snow. Storms from the north confined them to their tent for days at a time, making their progress slow and painful. As the land rose towards a central plateau the cold became excruciating and the ice smooth and polished, ideal for skiing. When the wind was favourable

15

they lashed the sledges together in pairs and hoisted makeshift sails. Nansen recalled their exhilaration as they clung onto the sledges, gliding down the slopes at tremendous speed.

In September, when darkness began to return, the nights brought an unexpected beauty as the aurora danced like a 'terrible fire' across the sky and the moon flooded the ice fields with silver light. It was a wildness that sang to Nansen's soul, even though, by morning, his head in the sleeping bag was often encrusted with rime from his own breath. He did all the cooking himself, partly because the stove was temperamental and partly because he did not want his men to drink the fuel, which was pure alcohol. Nansen admitted the temptation himself; despite his improvements the stove was stubbornly inefficient and struggled to melt enough snow for drinking water.

Thirst was just one of many hardships, which were worse than any of them could have imagined. In particular, the two Lapps, Samuel Balto and Ole Ravna, were convinced that they were going to die. Nansen had only met them a few weeks before departure, and realised too late that their unfamiliarity with discipline would pose additional problems. Wearing their distinctive 'caps of the four winds', the two were venturing out of their homeland for the first time. Although they had lived their lives above the Arctic Circle, and were well used to the climate, they believed they were being led to their deaths by inexperienced strangers. Terrified by the threat of polar bears, they read the Bible with desperate fervour and gave their souls up for lost.

Somehow, Nansen held the party together. On 3rd October, two and a half months after setting out, they arrived in Godthåb (Nuuk) on the west coast. They had missed the last ship home before winter, so their homecoming was delayed until the next spring. Nansen seized the opportunity to learn as much as he could from the Inuit people, who taught him to hunt from a kayak. He was very impressed:

> This small skin-boat... is the best one-man vessel in the world... If
> you are capsized by a sea, and can manage your oar, you can rise
> again and need not be afraid of anything.[6]

16

Overwintering in Greenland proved to be a pleasant experience, and when the Danish steamship *Hvidbjørnen* arrived to collect them in April 1889, the men were sorry to part from their hosts. These happy people, Nansen observed, were like 'children of nature' who did not know real poverty. Samuel Balto's leave-taking was especially hard; he had fallen in love with an Inuit girl who was engaged to another man. As the ship pulled away he was fighting back tears.

On 21st May they arrived in Copenhagen, and a week later Christiania gave a tumultuous welcome to her returning heroes. By that time it seemed as if the whole world knew Nansen's name, and everyone wanted to hear his story at first hand. Marion Sharp, the young woman to whom he had confided his dream, was among the first to write and congratulate him.

That July, Nansen gave a detailed account of his findings to the Royal Scottish Geographical Society. During his 260-mile crossing he had, he said, concluded that the Greenland ice sheet was shaped like a shield, rising rapidly from the east coast to reach a height of between 9,000 and 10,000 feet and falling again gradually towards the west. He gave his opinion that its contours were governed not by the underlying land but by meteorological conditions. The team had experienced snowfalls every day, suggesting that the depth of snow in Greenland's interior was forever increasing. Nansen had an alternative theory: the ice, he said, was constantly moving under pressure. He likened it to an immense layer of pitch that was slowly but inexorably spreading outwards, towards the coast.

This analogy was echoed in an unfortunate supper-time incident which Nansen described:

> I remember one night our cooking apparatus was upset, and all our precious pea-soup was poured out over the canvas floor of our tent; but we did not hesitate: we immediately took hold of each side of the floor, lifted it up, and sucked the pea-soup out of the middle. No drop was lost.[7]

Two months after his appearance in Edinburgh, Nansen was married. His bride was not Marion Sharp, nor any of the other hopeful young

17

women whose paths he had crossed in those early days. His choice was Eva Sars, a dark-haired and enigmatic Norwegian singer whose proficiency on skis nearly matched his own. Eva was single-minded in her own way, and when everything had settled down and Nansen began to look northwards again, she wanted to go with him. In the end she did not, and Nansen had no idea how to comfort her. The story of Fridtjof and Eva is just as stormy and troubled as Nansen's relationship with the Arctic. Eva was jealous of the attention that her handsome husband received from adoring women, while Nansen's restless nature urged him away from the happy home life that Eva craved. Their marriage contained long periods of dark isolation punctuated by moments of joy.

In 1893 Nansen set sail on a voyage like no other. His idea was so mad that no other explorer would have given it a moment's thought. After all, who else but Nansen would dream of allowing his ship to be frozen into the Arctic sea ice, with the intention of drifting over the North Pole? It sounds more like a dark fairy tale, or an extract from one of the Icelandic Sagas. When he departed on his specially designed ship, the *Fram*, he expected to be away for at least five years; although he was absent for only three, his departure still racked Eva with fresh agonies.

In February 1897, when Nansen was welcomed back by the Royal Scottish Geographical Society as their guest of honour at a glittering banquet, he was recognised as one of the greatest heroes of polar exploration. In presenting him with the second Gold Medal in the Society's history (the first was awarded to H. M. Stanley), Professor James Geikie, Vice-President of the Society, paid tribute to a man whose story 'would live to stir the blood and quicken the pulse of all good-hearted men in all time coming.'

Nansen's response was typically modest. 'I really do not deserve so much praise,' he said, 'as I have only done what I thought was my duty. It is an old saying in Norway – I do not think you have it in Scotland – that a man's will is his own heaven... I think when I am praised that my comrades are much more to be praised. My comrades believed in me and they went where most men would say there was nothing to find except death.'[8]

1. *The Scotsman*, 23rd May 1889, reporting on telegram received by RSGS from Fridtjof Nansen
2-7. Dr Fridtjof Nansen 'Journey Across the Inland Ice of Greenland from East to West', *Scottish Geographical Magazine* (1889) 5:8, 393-405
8. *The Scotsman*, 15th February 1897, report of RSGS banquet in the Waterloo Rooms, Edinburgh, on 13th February 1897

REAR ADMIRAL ROBERT EDWIN PEARY

Arctic explorer
BORN: 6th May 1856 (Cresson, Pennsylvania)
DIED: 20th February 1920 (Washington DC)
§
RSGS Silver Medal,1897
Livingstone Medal, 1903
Silver ship, 1910

IN DECEMBER 1897, a steamer bound for New York prepared to depart Southampton Dock on a week-long voyage across the Atlantic. Passengers lined the decks, waving in excitement to friends and family as they embarked. Among them was an ambitious explorer named Robert Peary, who was returning to his native America after giving a number of lectures to British institutions about his adventures in the Arctic. Recalling his warm reception by the Royal Scottish Geographical Society in Edinburgh, he put his hand in his pocket to turn over the gleaming silver medal which they had presented to him just a few days before: it was not there.

The loss of Peary's prize was only temporary – it was soon discovered in the auditorium of a London theatre – but it was in a way symbolic. Robert Peary hungered for fame in a way that alarmed his mother and truly tested the patience of his wife. Glory was what he craved, and he meant to achieve it while he was still young. His career in the United States Navy offered good prospects, but to Peary it merely provided a useful training for bigger and better things. He collected clippings and notes on polar exploration, devoured books by Arctic explorers and pictured himself as the 'discoverer' of the North Pole. He imagined life in the frozen wastes to be not only endurable, but enjoyable. He wrote to his mother that he did not wish to live and die without accomplishing anything, or without being known beyond a narrow circle of friends.[1]

Peary's first trip north was in the company of Christian Maigaard, a young Dane who persuaded him that to travel alone would be suicide. In the summer of 1886 they ventured eastwards nearly 100 miles from Godhavn on Disko Bay in Greenland, pulling their own sledges and escaping from the jaws of crevasses within a whisker of their lives. They wore goggles of smoked glass to protect their eyes against the harsh sunlight reflecting from the snow, and as they slept beneath the midnight sun they tied strips of fur over their closed lids to give an illusion of darkness. It was an important test for Peary, and he soon proved his adaptability. He and Maigaard lashed two sledges together and rigged an improvised sail to ease their passage over the ice. This device lightened the load so well that they had to hurry to keep up with it. Obstacles appeared almost without warning, and each man had to rescue the other on several occasions. Peary slipped into a glacial torrent and was hurtling towards imminent death when the spikes on his shoes snagged on the ice walls, giving Maigaard just enough time to pull him out. In turn, Maigaard stumbled while crossing a deep abyss; he snatched at the rear of the sledge and dangled over the precipice. Peary instantly threw his weight onto the sledge to prevent them both from catapulting into oblivion.

This was the second furthest anyone had ever penetrated the interior of Greenland – only Nordenskiöld in 1883 had gone further – and for Peary it confirmed his life's goal. The Arctic became his second home, an obsession. Speaking at the RSGS in Dundee in 1897, he told his audience that 'if he could stay at a fixed place for five years, as he was ready to do if necessary... he believed that some season the door to the Pole would open or could be pushed open.'[2] His mother and his wife begged him to settle down, but they were wasting their breath.

Unfortunately for Peary, a rival was about to sneak into his obsessively controlled world in the guise of a ship's surgeon. Frederick Cook accompanied him on his Greenland expedition of 1891, and treated Peary for a broken leg which he suffered on board ship. Any friendship between the two men, however, was not destined to last very long.

Meanwhile, some more long-term trouble was brewing.

A 'Furthest North' of 87°06', which Peary claimed in 1906, was achieved by dog sled from Ellesmere Island where the ship SS *Roosevelt* awaited his triumphant return. Peary sowed the seeds of doubt that would later damage his credibility; to the north of Elles-mere Island he claimed to have seen new territory, which he called 'Crocker Land' after his sponsor, George Crocker. Eight years later, an expedition led by Donald Baxter MacMillan proved that this land did not exist.

On 21st April 1908, Frederick Cook checked his custom-made French sextant and believed himself to be standing at a spot which was as near as possible to the North Pole. The ship's surgeon had been nurturing ambitions of his own, and had overwintered at Annoatok in northern Greenland. He had travelled across the ice by dog sled, accompanied by nine Inuit men. Incredibly, the party did not arrive back at Annoatok until April 1909, having miraculously survived the dark Arctic winter.

Around the same time, on 6th April 1909, Robert Peary raised the American flag over a point which he believed to be the North Pole. Since nature had not honoured the North Pole with any distinguishing features, he and his companions built an igloo and posed in front of it for photographs.

To understand why the North Pole was so difficult to pin down, it is important to remember that Arctic ice is not attached to a solid landmass like the Antarctic but instead forms a cap which is constantly shifting on ocean currents. Explorers who set off in a northerly direction often find themselves being borne southwards at a rate that makes their progress even slower. For this reason, the North Pole is an ever-moving point on the surface of the ice that can only be confirmed by careful calculation. In Peary's time, a sextant would have been used to measure the angle of the sun in the sky; the degree of latitude would then be calculated from the date and precise time of day.

Returning to the *Roosevelt*, Peary set a southward course at a leisurely pace at least until August, when the vessel stopped at Cape York. Here, Peary learned from the skipper of a whaling vessel that

Frederick Cook had laid claim to the North Pole a year earlier, and was – belatedly – on his way to announce it to the world.

Suddenly, a stately triumphal procession had turned into a race – first to the nearest telegraph station, and then back to New York.

> The following cablegram has been received by the Royal Scottish Geographical Society in Edinburgh, relative to the discovery of the North Pole: 'Brooklyn, New York, Royal Scottish Geographical Society, Edinburgh: North Pole discovered April 6th, 1909, by Peary Arctic Club expedition under Commander Peary.' – Bridgman, Secretary.[3]

Cook reached New York first, and was greeted with widespread acclaim – but his glow of glory faded quickly when Peary stepped in front of the sun. Peary had powerful supporters, some of whom had paid good money to see their names on maps in perpetuity. Peary's spectacular announcement appeared in the newspapers just a week after Cook's rival claim, and the obvious discrepancy was a subject of bafflement and intense public scrutiny. Meanwhile, Cook's evidence was examined by government officials and his claim was pronounced to be 'not proven'. Cook, it turned out, had a troubled background of his own. Peary was jubilant.

Speaking to a rapt audience of the RSGS in Edinburgh in 1910, Peary relived every moment of his heroic journey in words and pictures. His narrative was positively bristling with military-style detail as he described his programme of marches and the organisation of the team. He was far from proof against a little lyrical embellishment when it came to his own physical fitness, describing himself as being 'in shape beyond his most sanguine dreams of earliest years.' As they neared the Pole, the air, he said, was 'as keen as frozen steel', with a bitter wind 'burning the face till it cracked.'

> The going was even better than previously, and there was scarcely any snow on the hard, granular, last summer's surface of the old floes, dotted with the sapphire ice of the previous summer's lakes.

A rise in temperature to 15 degs below zero reduced the friction of the sledges, and gave the dogs the appearance of having caught the spirits of the party. When we had covered, as I estimated, a good fifteen miles, we halted, made tea, ate lunch, and rested the dogs. In twelve hours' actual travelling time we made thirty miles... I had now made my five marches, and was in time for a hasty observation (at approximately local noon Columbia meridian) through a temporary break in the clouds, which indicated our position at 89 degs, 57 mins.[4]

It was stirring stuff, and the RSGS, like many other institutions, believed that Peary's achievement merited an exceptional token of honour. He was grandly presented with a solid silver ship, specially commissioned from Messrs Brook & Son of Edinburgh. Standing two feet high and weighing over 100 ounces, it represented the type of vessel used by illustrious Arctic navigators in the olden times. Not surprisingly, Peary confessed himself speechless at such a magnificent and unique trophy.

Unfortunately for Peary, karma, like the Arctic ice, swings in a slow but inexorable circle. It was not long before Peary's own evidence, like Cook's, came under scrutiny. In 1911, representatives of the United States Naval Affairs Sub-Committee expressed surprise at the cleanliness of his diary, which they had expected to exhibit the grimy stains and rough wear of an arduous journey. The pages that recorded his arrival at the Pole seemed to have been added afterwards and, to make things worse, he had taken no one with him who was capable of confirming his sextant readings. Official opinion was divided, but deep-rooted doubts were placed on record. Peary, for reasons which he kept to himself, never again revealed his journals and, after this episode, rarely spoke publicly of his achievement.

Of all the explorers who were drawn to the polar regions, Peary in particular seems to have been a martyr to his own ambitions, sacrificing much in the name of glory. His wife, Josephine, was a staunchly supportive partner, even accompanying him on some of his expeditions, but of their first twenty-three years of marriage only three were spent together. Peary's second daughter died while he was in the Arctic, before he had even seen her. The revelation of an Inuit mistress shook Josephine to the core. His mother died in 1901, while he was presumed missing but was in fact living among the Inuit in Greenland. His stalwart companion on all but one expedition, an African-American called Matthew Henson, lived the rest of his life in poverty.

Robert Edwin Peary certainly carved a name for himself among the great explorers of his country, and of his era. To salve his disappointment on one of his early expeditions, he summoned a work party to haul three huge meteorites, believed by the Inuit to be sacred stones, back to his ship, which transported them to a New York museum. He even brought back six of the Inuit people, naive and ill fated, fully expecting that they would become living studies in ethnology. Perhaps the meteorites exacted their revenge, because Peary suffered a breakdown at the height of the North Pole controversy, and was later diagnosed with pernicious anaemia. He died in 1920, only ten years after his glittering reception in Edinburgh.

During his lifetime, it was never certain whether Peary really had reached the North Pole. In 1989, the British explorer Wally Herbert was commissioned by the National Geographic Society to examine the evidence, and regretfully concluded that Peary's claim was untrue. Without realising it at the time, Cook and Peary did a great deal of damage to their own reputations while each sought to discredit the other's, but the full truth will never be known. As Wally Herbert observed, fame can sometimes appear as tragedy disguised as a reward.

Both Peary and Matthew Henson fathered children with Inuit women while in the Arctic. In 1971 Peary's grandson, Peter, reached the North Pole in the company of his half-brother Talilanguaq. With them on the expedition, which was led by Italian explorer Guido Monzino, were Avatak Henson, the Inuit grandson of Matthew Henson, and ten other Inuits. Peter Peary trekked to the Pole again in 1978, as a guide for a Japanese expedition. On both occasions he retraced the route taken by his grandfather in 1909. Perhaps only now, as if carried there by his descendants, can Robert Peary's yearning heart rejoice in standing at the North Pole.

1. Letter from Peary to his mother, 1880
2. *Dundee Advertiser*, 13th December 1897, report on lecture to RSGS in Dundee
3. Edinburgh *Evening Dispatch*, 7th September 1909, report of a telegram to RSGS
4. *The Scotsman*, report on lecture to RSGS in Edinburgh, 25th May 1910

Captain Robert Falcon Scott

Antarctic explorer
Born: 6th June 1868 (Plymouth)
Died: about 29th March 1912, Antarctica
§
RSGS Livingstone Medal, 1904

I N SOME PHOTOGRAPHS of Robert Falcon Scott, there is a look of such sadness in his eyes it seems possible he had an inkling of his fate. Or are we, sensitive to the harrowing story of his final weeks, just seeing our own sadness reflected?

In 1887, Scott was competing in a sailing race in St Kitts when he caught the eye of Sir Clements Markham, Secretary of the Royal Geographical Society in London. Markham was a former naval officer whose adventurous years were drawing to a close, so he found an outlet for his enthusiasm in planning other people's expeditions. He worshipped the British Empire and the Royal Navy and thought they could be brought together in one great, glorious act: the conquest of Antarctica. He was looking for potential leaders and quietly added Scott to his list, struck by his intelligence and charming manner. The eighteen-year-old midshipman had no way of knowing where such distinguished attention would lead.

Meanwhile, a burden of care and responsibility was about to descend upon Scott's young shoulders. Financial disaster, shortly followed by his father's death, left his family largely dependent on his meagre income. Scott was at an age when grand gestures and sartorial extravagance were expected of ambitious young naval officers but he had to pare his spending down to a minimum so that his mother and sisters could keep a rented roof over their heads. Already self-conscious, he steered clear of expensive parties and withdrew further into himself. Perhaps this was the reason for his air of detachment, misread by others as insecurity and distrust.

One day in June 1899, Scott was walking down Buckingham Palace Road in London when he was hailed by Markham, now President of the RGS and pursuing goals of national glory. Would Scott care to become involved with his beloved brainchild, and command a British expedition to the Antarctic?

What a question! To the Victorians, the Antarctic was almost as remote as the moon. It was against the cautious side of Scott's nature, and he must have felt torn. Perhaps, though, he saw a path to riches, or at least a dependable income for life. Maybe the lure of the unknown appealed to his discontented spirit. He might even have seen it as his duty. Whatever his personal reason, he said yes.

At that time, Antarctica was still an unexplored continent. Whaling ships sometimes skirted the fringes of the pack ice but only a handful of men had ever set foot on the coast. In 1900, intrepid Anglo-Norwegian explorer Carsten Borchgrevink overwintered there and ventured a short distance into the interior, reaching a latitude of 78°50'S. It was a brave beginning which others were bound to follow.

In addition to claiming the South Pole or, at the very least, a 'Furthest South' for king and country, Scott was expected to conduct an extensive programme of scientific experiments and collect natural history specimens ranging from marine crustaceans to birds' eggs.

Markham selected crew members without emphasis on previous experience of polar travel; if he had a motto, it was probably 'youth and eagerness will prevail'. One of the most eager was the Third Lieutenant, an irreverent and ambitious Anglo-Irishman named Ernest Shackleton who would soon lose his own heart to the Antarctic.

The RRS *Discovery*, a three-masted sailing ship with auxiliary engines, built in Dundee specifically for scientific research, was the natural choice for this expedition. She set sail for the Antarctic in August 1901 and arrived at Cape Adare in January 1902. From there the expedition sailed south then east, following the Great Ice Barrier (now the Ross Ice Shelf), and discovering new territory which they named King Edward VII Land. Shortly afterwards, they landed on the Barrier where Scott and Shackleton took turns to ascend in a tethered observational balloon, reaching a height of 600 feet.

Finding safe winter quarters was essential. Scott chose the comparatively sheltered waters of McMurdo Sound, where it was hoped that the pressure of the sea ice on the ship would be reduced. With the *Discovery* frozen in for winter, the men began constructing a land base on a promontory they called Hut Point.

In this alien and unforgiving environment the ship and her crew survived for two years locked in the Antarctic ice. They were far from idle, following a strict daily routine in their programme of scientific research. Thousands of geological and biological specimens were collected, and hundreds of miles of coastline were mapped for the first time. At Cape Crozier the crew were the first people to observe and photograph an emperor penguin rookery. Their combined zoological, meteorological and geographical findings would eventually fill ten volumes.

On 2nd November 1902 a three-man team consisting of Scott, Shackleton, and Chief Scientist Edward Wilson set off on a bid for the Pole. They took a team of dogs and five sledges but encountered appalling weather conditions and were forced to turn back at latitude 82°17'. Growing tension between Scott and Shackleton was alleviated in a brief but delightful way on Christmas morning:

> For ninety-two nights the three of them slept in a small tent until they knew almost every stitch of it. The rations were cut down to the lowest possible limit, and 'only a certain amount of conscience' prevented an inroad being made on the small bag which contained the allowance for the following week. On Christmas Day, however, Mr Shackleton unexpectedly produced a plum pudding about the size of a cricket ball. 'It was,' said Captain Scott, 'a day to remember all your life.'[1]

After the first winter, a relief ship sent by the British government arrived with fresh supplies to find the *Discovery* still icebound. Scott opted to remain in the Antarctic for another twelve months. He had an opportunity, however, to send some of his men home, so when the relief ship returned to New Zealand she carried a very reluctant Ernest Shackleton, who was suffering from scurvy.

Throughout the expedition, the *Discovery* remained fast in the ice. When a pair of relief ships appeared in January 1904 to escort her home, a team of men optimistically set about sawing through the two miles of frozen sea towards open water. She was finally freed with the help of explosives, and her captain was spared the ignominy of having to abandon his ship.

Scott arrived home to a shower of honours and probably more attention than he wanted, but he had fulfilled his duty and was now assured of a good income. He must have been glad of the success, for the sake of his family at least. Within a few years he was promoted to the position of Naval Assistant to Sir Francis Bridgeman, Second Sea Lord at the Admiralty. In September 1908 he married sculptor and socialite Kathleen Bruce at Hampton Court Palace. Everything seemed to have come together: comfortable home, lovely wife, successful career. Despite all this, a darkness haunted his soul, personified by Lieutenant Ernest Shackleton.

With a roving eye and a wickedly persuasive tongue, Shackleton was jovial, expansive, spontaneous – everything, in fact, that Scott was not. Shackleton had his eyes set on the ultimate prize of the South Pole and, in 1907, organised his own expedition, sailing south on the *Nimrod*. Although he did not attain the Pole, the expedition made him the proud bearer of a new record for the 'Furthest South'. Scott's sense of pride was inflamed. He had to go back to Antarctica himself.

The *Terra Nova* sailed south in the summer of 1910, stopping in Australia for last-minute fundraising and taking on extra supplies in New Zealand. On board were some old hands from the *Discovery*, including William Lashly, Irishman Tom Crean, and Edward Wilson. They were joined by Henry 'Birdie' Bowers, Lawrence 'Titus' Oates, Edgar Evans, Apsley Cherry-Garrard, and the photographer Herbert Ponting. Scott's second-in-command was an officer of Welsh descent called Teddy Evans. The cost of the expedition was met largely by government support, public donations and loans, and was sponsored by food producers and manufacturers eager to link their names with the glorious endeavour. Edward Wilson stressed that the scientific work was of great importance but Scott knew beyond doubt that this time, the Pole must be his. Other countries had begun to show interest.

In Melbourne he received a telegram from the Norwegian explorer Roald Amundsen: 'Beg leave to inform you *Fram* proceeding Antarctic.'[2] The *Fram* had been Fridtjof Nansen's ship, which survived three years in the Arctic but failed to gain the Pole; now she had a new captain with ice in his blood. Amundsen had originally been heading north, but with Peary and Cook both laying claim to the North Pole he had turned his attention south, keeping his plans secret even from his crew until the *Fram* was beyond recall. Amundsen was skilled, determined, experienced, proficient with skis and with sledge dogs, and was sailing south even as Scott was bidding farewell to his wife in New Zealand. The *Fram*, according to Sir Clements Markham, had 'no more sailing qualities than a haystack'[3], and if Scott could have heard him he might have laughed. Deep down, however, he must have known that it was all or nothing.

On 18th February 1912, Kathleen Scott's thoughts kept returning to her absent husband. That evening she noted in her diary that something strange had happened to the clocks and watches in the house. She wondered whether he had reached a crucial moment.

The day before, on their way back to their base camp, Edgar Evans had been the first of Scott's party to die. The remaining four – Oates, Bowers, Wilson and Scott himself – pushed onwards, hauling their sledges through snowstorms that were savage even by Antarctic standards. Frostbitten, exhausted and malnourished, they were also demoralised. They had reached the Pole on 17th January only to find an empty tent already pitched there: Roald Amundsen, travelling swiftly with a team of sledge dogs, had beaten them to it by thirty-three days. Scott's decision earlier in the journey to send the dog teams back and rely entirely on manpower had cost him dearly; his love of animals had always made him reluctant to use dogs for hauling and in consequence he never fully refined the skill. In contrast, Amundsen, though he trained his animals hard and fed them well, had also steeled himself to kill them for food.

The Norwegians' black marker flag was like a portent of doom for the British party. 'Great God!' wrote Scott in his journal, 'this is an awful place and terrible enough for us to have laboured to it without the reward of priority... Now for the run home and a desperate struggle. I wonder if we can do it.'[4]

Without speaking it outright, each man could sense how it would end. Around 17th March, Lawrence Oates, who knew that he would probably lose both his feet even if he survived the trek, muttered something about being gone for 'some time' and crawled out of the tent into the blizzard. The temperature at that point was -41°C. Just how these men managed to survive for as long as they did in an environment most humans cannot even imagine is beyond comprehension.

Nearly two weeks later, as he lay beside his dying comrades, Scott composed letters to his wife, his friends, the wives of his companions, and to the nation as a whole. He still managed, as Ranulph Fiennes has observed, to write excellent English in the most appalling conditions. His dearest hope, one which he expressed several times, was that some provision would be made for the widows and mothers left behind. For himself, he wanted no outpouring of sympathy:

> We took risks, we knew we took them; things have come out against us, and therefore we have no cause for complaint, but bow to the will of Providence, determined still to do our best to the last... Had we lived, I should have had a tale to tell of the hardihood, endurance, and courage of my companions which would have stirred the heart of every Englishman. These rough notes and our dead bodies must tell the tale...[5]

Memories of Scott linger at the Royal Scottish Geographical Society. In 1904, during a lecture entitled 'Furthest South' given at their meeting rooms in Edinburgh, he had been awarded the Society's Livingstone Medal. In the presence of Sir Clements Markham and Ernest Shackleton, at that time Secretary of the RSGS, Scott gave a two-hour presentation which focused on the more light-hearted aspects of the experience. Afterwards he was the guest of honour at a banquet held in the North British Station Hotel. The newspapers remarked that 'uncomfortable' and 'unpleasant'[6] were his strongest adjectives for danger and suffering. Drama and heroism never sat well with his temperament and, a true naval officer, he made no complaint.

---

1. *The Scotsman*, 12th November 1904, report of Scott's address to RSGS at Synod Hall, Edinburgh

2. Telegram from Amundsen to Scott, sent from Madeira, September 1910

3. *Scott of the Antarctic* by Elspeth Huxley (1977)

4. *Scott's Last Expedition* (Scott's Last Expedition, being the Journals of Captain R. F. Scott, R.N., C.V.O., arranged by Leonard Huxley, 1914)

5. Scott's 'Message to the Public', 29th March 1912, from *Scott's Last Expedition* (Journals of Captain R F Scott, arr. Leonard Huxley, 1914)

6. *The Scotsman*, 12th November 1904

Admiral Edward ('Teddy') Ratcliffe Garth Russell Evans
1st Baron Mountevans

Antarctic explorer
Born: 28th October 1880 (Marylebone)
Died: 20th August 1957 (Norway)
§
RSGS Livingstone Medal, 1913

We shook hands, and said good-bye; as they moved off we gave them three ringing cheers. We little thought that those cheers were the last appreciation those brave men would ever know. We then turned and marched homeward, constantly looking round and watching the other party until they became a little black speck on the great white horizon.

A HANDFUL OF NAMES are held in honour from the days when polar exploration meant sacrificing years of your life, if not that life itself. Perhaps the best known are Nansen, Scott, Shackleton and Amundsen, but alongside them, and just as worthy, are men such as Teddy Evans.

Born in London of Welsh and Irish descent, Evans was a rebellious schoolboy who surprised his parents, and possibly himself, by turning into a first-class naval cadet. He was first posted to the Mediterranean, but those tame waters were not exciting enough for a man dreaming of adventure on the high seas. His chance came in 1902 when he embarked on the *Morning*, a relief ship that was being sent to the aid of Robert Falcon Scott's ice-bound *Discovery* in the Antarctic.

Evans had nothing but praise for Captain Scott, saying that to have known him was 'a great thing in my life'. At first, the admiration was not entirely mutual. Scott, cautious and reserved by nature, was suspicious of Evans's 'boyish enthusiasms', and described him as 'well-meaning, but terribly slow to learn'. However, it seems that Scott replaced his initial scepticism with respect. He named Cape Evans in his honour, and after failing to reach the South Pole at his first attempt, Scott appointed Evans second-in-command of his next enterprise – the *Terra Nova* expedition of 1911.

*

The distance from Scott's winter base on Ross Island to the Pole and back was 1,766 miles – more than twice the distance from Land's End to John O'Groats. Temperatures never rose above -18°C. Given the long and harrowing stages of Scott's fateful expedition, the distances the men had to cover and the unbelievable loads they had to pull, who lived and who died seems just a cruel game of chance. When Scott chose his final team of four to make a bid for the South Pole, Evans was not among them. Instead, he was ordered to head back to the base in McMurdo Sound with William Lashly and Tom Crean.

To wish the Southern party Godspeed, Evans, Crean and Lashly continued southwards with them to a latitude of 87°34'S, then shook hands and took their leave. Evans watched them go. Joining his companions in hauling their sledge northwards, he turned occasionally to see the ever-dwindling figures of Scott and his comrades. He could not have known that the 'little black speck on the great white horizon' was the last he would ever see of them.

Having come within 160 miles of the Pole, Evans was secretly disappointed not to be chosen for the final push. There was no time to brood, however, as a 750-mile journey lay ahead and food supplies were dwindling. On 13th January the little party found themselves above the Shackleton Icefalls, gazing on the vast slopes of the Beardmore Glacier hundreds of feet below. They could either march around them as they had done on the southward journey, which would take three days, or they could launch themselves down the treacherous-looking slope using the sledge as a toboggan and hope for the best. The discussion was short. After packing their skis onto the sledge and harnessing themselves to it, they carefully nosed it over the edge.

At first the sledge jumped and jolted over the hummocks of ice, capsizing frequently and colliding painfully with their feet whenever they tried to steer it. After several hours they reached a smoother section of the glacier, wind-polished and terrifyingly steep. Braking or manoeuvring would be impossible, so the party lay face down on the sledge and held on for their lives as it cannoned down the ice at speeds of about 60 miles per hour. At one point it sprang into the air over an unexpected crevasse. In that split second Evans looked at Crean, who raised his eyebrows in mute answer; almost instantly, the sledge crashed heavily but safely on the far side, rolling over and over until it came to a stop. They descended an estimated 2,000 feet in the space of half an hour. Miraculously, no bones were broken, but in their sleeping bags that night they felt like 'three bruised pears'.

Although the party had ridden a knife-edge of death, there was worse to come. As they descended further, the Beardmore Glacier broke up into a causeway of giant crevasses, deep fissures of blue-black darkness that yawned terrifyingly at their feet. The sledge could bridge narrow gaps, but when the men arrived at a stupendous gulf they realised nothing they possessed would get them across. Their only hope lay in a spur of ice which ran across the abyss from one side to the other. A natural splinter, it was so thin the runners of the sledge only just fitted on it, while beneath it lurked the bowels of the glacier. They would be going, said Crean, 'along the crossbar to the "H" of Hell.'

Lashly went first, shuffling his way across and refusing to look down. As the other two paid out the length of Alpine rope to which he was attached, he prayed that it would be long enough to allow him to reach the other side as he was too terrified to turn back. It was just sufficient, and he scrambled to safety up the opposite ridge. Then it was the turn of Evans and Crean, who had to haul the 400lb sledge. Standing upright, facing each other and locking eyes to prevent each other from glancing down, they pulled rhythmically on the rope. Focusing intently on his friend's face, Evans noticed the deep clefts in his grimy skin and his wind-cracked lips. Neither spoke, apart from Evans's repeated 'One, two, three – heave!' After a few long minutes it was over; they were across, Lashly was reaching down to them, and they were safe.

The worst of the terrain was now behind them. The next threat was different. With many miles still to cover, Evans's knee joints stiffened, then he could not straighten his legs; his gums began to ulcerate, and his teeth became loose. He soon realised he was suffering from scurvy. The effort of marching turned to agony. Then the haemorrhaging began.

Having fainted three times in one day, and assuming death was not far off, Evans told his companions to leave him and send out relief when they got back to base. Crean and Lashly refused to abandon him.

> They said 'No, sir, you have stuck to us,' and said that if he went out they 'would all go out together.' They put him in his sleeping bag and hauled him along with them ...

Evans later remarked dryly that this was 'the one act of disobedience in the expedition'. Lashly and Crean were later awarded the Albert Medal for saving his life.

Only thirty-five miles from the base at Hut Point, blizzard conditions descended on the little party. Lashly and Crean held a hurried council; Crean opted to continue and fetch help, while Lashly would pitch the tent and give Evans whatever care he could. Neither could know whether Crean would be successful. It was Evans's darkest hour.

The next day, the sound of barking dogs heralded their rescue.

Still gravely ill, on 28th February Evans was taken on board the *Terra Nova*, which had just arrived back in the Antarctic with fresh supplies. The expedition's medical officer, Edward Atkinson, remained by his side for a week and nursed him through the most critical stages of his condition. When the gathering pack ice forced the ship to head north to New Zealand, Evans travelled with it. Over the next few months he slowly regained his health.

A year later, Evans was well enough to command the *Terra Nova* as she sailed south again into the long Antarctic summer. The crew were hoping to find Scott and his four companions safe and well, having rejoined the other team members to spend the winter in purpose-built huts on Ross Island. At that time, no communication was possible between any polar base and the rest of the world. The *Terra Nova* broke through the ice in McMurdo Sound in January 1913, almost a year to the day after Scott's arrival at the Pole. She was ready for a celebration, her decks scrubbed, and Jacks and Ensigns hoisted in gala fashion to meet Scott and his comrades.

Evans spied Victor Campbell, Scott's First Officer, among the welcoming party on the beach. He shouted a greeting and asked if everyone was well. After a moment's hesitation, Campbell replied that the Southern Party reached the South Pole on 17th January but that all five were lost as they were returning. At his words, Evans said a great stillness ran through the ship's company and the party on shore.

On 18th November 1913, Evans delivered a lecture to the Royal Scottish Geographical Society at the Kinnaird Hall in Dundee. The typical polar explorer, he said, was no fanatic with a passion for patriotic conquest, but a hero with the heart of a boy, a quick sense of humour and boundless reserves of optimism: 'So far from being grim, he is quicker to see the funny side of things than any other type of man on this earth.' He described some lighter moments of Scott's expedition and revealed that some of the sledge dogs had been brought to Britain and were being idolised as celebrities. Evans impressed his audience with his modesty and complete lack of melodrama, and seems to have won the heart of at least one of the journalists present.

> Commander Evans is himself a perfect example of the modern Viking. Of medium height, square-shouldered, clean of feature and limb, he conveys at once an impression of both resolution and nonchalance. His blue eyes, with long dark lashes, flash with a boyish love of adventure. His smile is warm enough to melt the heart of an iceberg. His dark head is flung back a little, and he walks the platform as though it were the deck of a battleship he was proud to command.

The next evening Evans was once more a guest of the RSGS, this time in Edinburgh where he was presented with the Society's Livingstone Medal. With touching sincerity, Evans revealed that the award was of priceless value to him because nine years earlier, in 1904, it had been conferred on his late leader, Captain Robert Falcon Scott.

Unlike some of men who returned miraculously from the Antarctic only to die in the Great War, Evans not only survived the years of conflict but distinguished himself as an exceptional leader. He commanded HMS *Broke* during the war and received commendation for his actions in the engagement of six German destroyers in the

Battle of Dover Strait, ramming one warship and sinking it, driving the others into retreat. In 1921, as Commander of HMS *Carlisle* in the waters around Hong Kong, he rescued 200 people from a sinking passenger ship and even swam to the stricken vessel to help survivors into the lifeboats.

A portrait painted in 1937 by Sydney 'Sam' Morse-Brown shows Admiral Evans in full naval uniform at the age of fifty-seven. A strong brow and jaw are balanced by the expression of wisdom and gentleness in his eyes. He appears a true gentleman in the old-fashioned sense, honourable and modest, someone who has seen much but prefers to talk little. He outlived both Crean and Lashly, and wrote several books about polar exploration. Beneath his impressive garland of medals the Antarctic still haunted his heart. Writing of his experiences in his book *South with Scott*, he recalled the distinctive sound of pack ice hissing around a wooden ship. It was one of the memories that called him back to the sea.

All references in this chapter from *Dundee Advertiser*, 19th November 1913, report on Commander Evans's lecture to RSGS in Dundee on 18th November 1913

SIR ERNEST HENRY SHACKLETON

Antarctic explorer
BORN: 15th February 1874 (Kilkea, County Kildare)
DIED: 5th January 1922 (on board the *Quest*, South Georgia)
§
Secretary of RSGS, 1904-05
RSGS Council Member, 1905-1907
RSGS Livingstone Medal, 1909
Fellow of RSGS, 1911

O N 25TH MARCH 1909 the Edinburgh *Evening Dispatch* published a short news item which read:

> London, 1 pm. Lloyd's agent at Christchurch, New Zealand, cables that the Antarctic expedition vessel *Nimrod* arrived to-day, all well, in good condition.

Underneath was copied the prompt reply from the Royal Scottish Geographical Society:

> Heartiest congratulations, magnificent result, safe return; hope to welcome you Edinburgh. – Geographical.[1]

On board the *Nimrod* was Ernest Shackleton, Anglo-Irishman, compulsive explorer, swashbuckling hero, hopeless businessman and inveterate dreamer. He was coming home to the rapturous welcome he had yearned for, and the peaceful life his mind wanted but his soul ensured he would never have.

The warmth and depth of regard between Shackleton and the Royal Scottish Geographical Society was entirely mutual, though their connection had got off to a rather shaky start.

In 1903 Shackleton had been sent home early from Robert Falcon

Scott's *Discovery* expedition, officially on medical grounds. Mortified by the slur this cast on his capabilities, he was desperate for a fresh project. The post of Secretary to the Royal Scottish Geographical Society was conveniently vacant, and a little judicious nudging secured him the job. Shackleton moved to Edinburgh with his bride, Emily, and together they stepped into the city's erudite and fashionable society.

With an irrepressible love of life and no regard for convention, Shackleton was not cut out for courtesy and compromise. For many years, the dark musty corners of the RSGS offices in Queen Street had watched time pass like the solemn ticking of a grandfather clock. This quiet dignity was rudely shattered with the horrific installation of a telephone. Shackleton had blown in like a force nine gale, Irish eyes twinkling. 'You should have seen the faces of some of the old chaps when it started to ring today,'[2] he wrote to one of his friends.

It did not end there. In a society whose dress code called for formal tailoring in sombre hues, Shackleton's appearance in a light tweed suit, smoking and lounging in his office or tapping away cheerfully on his new-fangled typewriter, must have given rise to a few mutterings. One morning he walked in on an assistant who, in his spare time, was practising his golf swing by driving the ball into some heavy curtains. Shackleton was delighted. Seizing the club himself, he tried a few shots and promptly smashed the ball through the window and into the street.

Did Shackleton actually do any work? He must have. When the Society held its annual meeting in November 1905, it was revealed – probably in clipped tones – that over the last twelve months its membership had risen by nearly 23 per cent, and that the total number of people attending lectures was 36,000, an increase of 21,000 over the previous session.

> Mr James Currie, the treasurer, reported that largely owing to Lieut. Shackleton's efforts, the finances had considerably improved...[3]

Unfortunately, Shackleton was not there to hear about his success because he had resigned his post to pursue a new ambition. His restless nature was always moving him on to new things and by then he was trying to get into Parliament.

Although he had undoubtedly kissed the Blarney stone, Shackleton was too much of a wild child to succeed in government office. As a businessman, he had one brilliant idea after another but seemed unable to focus on a project long enough for it to succeed. He was torn apart by two conflicting desires: to return to the Antarctic, and to settle down into a life of comfortable domesticity.

The Antarctic won.

The *British Antarctic Expedition* of 1907–1909 was a success for Shackleton in all but one respect. To his enduring disappointment, the Southern Party (Jameson Adams, Eric Marshall, Frank Wild and himself) had been forced to turn back when they were still 97 miles from the South Pole. Allowing wisdom to overrule his thirst for glory, he had realised that to travel any further would have meant loss of life. With a 'Furthest South' of 88°23', Shackleton had come closer to the Pole than anyone else on Earth – but in his heart he still saw it as a failure.

The British public viewed it differently. With the return of the *Nimrod*, Shackleton became a household name, lauded by the media and decorated with a constellation of awards and medals. Everywhere he went he was surrounded by cheering crowds who would bear him aloft on willing shoulders and deposit him reverently onto the platform from which he would deliver his speech.

It is unlikely that the patriarchs of the RSGS, with Shackleton's insouciance still burning in their memories, would have abandoned themselves to quite such transports of delight. Nevertheless, only eight months after the Society had sent its cable of congratulations to New Zealand, the man himself was pacing the floorboards of the Synod Hall in Edinburgh as an honoured guest of the Society. The RSGS had been overwhelmed by the demand for tickets and over two thousand men and women had packed themselves into the lecture theatre on a bitterly cold night in November.

> His sentences fell with a slow, deliberate drawl, ending often in abrupt incompleteness for lack of an accessible vocabulary; but

there was something which gripped in the simple, unvarnished narrative of Antarctic horrors and hardships which might have been lost in a closely studied oration.[4]

Shackleton knew how to command an audience. He told his story simply and with humour, describing the hazards, hardships and heroics of the expedition. As some impressive views of Mount Erebus were thrown onto the screen, he revealed that one member of the party had lost a toe to frostbite in the ascent. 'At least,' he observed dryly, 'he has not lost it. It had to be amputated, but he keeps it somewhere in a bottle.'[5]

He described the discovery and ascent of the Beardmore Glacier, which he had named after his generous sponsor – or perhaps, it was whispered, after his sponsor's wife, with whom Shackleton had been conducting a rather risky dalliance.

Photographs of a group of emperor penguins were shown, the birds apparently listening with enjoyment to a gramophone emitting the strains of a popular dance tune called 'Waltz Me Around Again, Willie'. These were the kind of tales guaranteed to delight an audience of any era: entertaining, thrilling, moving. Underlying them all was a foundation of comradeship and respect, for Shackleton had nothing but the deepest praise for his companions.

> He more than any one realised his debt to those men who were with him both on ship and on shore. Whatever success the expedition had achieved was due to each individual from the lowest in rating to the highest, who worked for the good of their country regardless of themselves. This he said not only for those in command, but for all, from the youngest to the oldest.[6]

After a rapturous reception, Sir Ernest was presented with the Livingstone Medal of the RSGS, which he added to his clutch of prizes as he beat a glorious path to more Society events in Aberdeen and Dundee. Real wealth still eluded him and meanwhile the polar regions were tugging at his soul. When he wrote about his exploits in his lavishly produced book *The Heart of the Antarctic*, Shackleton knew that the story was unfinished; a 'Furthest South' would never be good enough. Ignoring his burgeoning debt, he began planning again.

For Shackleton at least, the lure of the Antarctic was not science or hardship or discovery or even glory; it was about seeking and not finding, the eternal heart-rending quest for something just over the horizon. His wife Emily understood, and when he wrote yearning letters to her from the deck of a heaving ship, promising never to go away again, she read between the lines and forgave him out of love.

The story of Shackleton's third and penultimate foray into the Antarctic has gone down in the annals of history as one of the most extraordinary feats of human endurance. After all, *Endurance* was the name of his ship, inspired by his family motto *Fortitudine Vincimus*: 'By endurance we conquer'. Although Amundsen had already reached the South Pole in 1911, Shackleton planned a daring sequel in crossing the frozen continent from shore to shore, taking a route that passed through the Pole.

Shackleton knew that it would be an epic adventure but could not have foreseen the monstrous challenges he and his men would be called upon to face. In December 1915, his ship crumpled like a matchstick toy in the pack ice. After several months' drifting on floating ice, the crew were forced to act when the floes they were camping on began to break up. They took to the sea in three lifeboats salvaged from the *Endurance*. Six days later they landed on Elephant Island, 150 miles north-east of the Antarctic peninsula. This was the first solid ground that they had seen in months, and their relief was heartfelt:

> The men picked up the sand and ran it through their fingers like men who would do gold... For the first time in six months they did not fear the ice opening, and the very pebbles beneath our backs were just the special promise of our safety.[7]

Somehow they had evaded death – but another danger loomed. Elephant Island was so remote that no one would ever find them there. Unless they sought help, they would starve.

Choosing five men to accompany him, Shackleton embarked on

one of the boldest journeys in the history of exploration: an 800-mile open sea voyage to the islands of South Georgia in a lifeboat named the *James Caird*. After two weeks of tempestuous seas, it was nothing less than a miracle when they made landfall on South Georgia. The three strongest – Shackleton, Tom Crean and Frank Worsley – then had to trek for thirty-six hours across snowfields and glaciers to reach the whaling station on the opposite shore, leaving the others to await rescue. Shackleton later spoke of an unseen guiding hand, a 'fourth man' whose presence was also felt by Worsley and Crean as they struggled to finish a journey that never seemed to end.

At first the captain of the whaling station at Grytviken failed to recognise Shackleton, although he knew him well. All the men looked wild and emaciated, their faces blackened with grime and their clothes in tatters. They were plied with nourishing food and given hot baths and comfortable beds, but Shackleton's mind could not rest while lives still hung in the balance. Not only must he save the men he had left on the other side of South Georgia, but he must collect the crew who had stayed on Elephant Island. He then had to organise the rescue of an entirely separate party which had sailed from Australia and was waiting – in vain – by the Ross Sea, still believing that Shackleton was making the first crossing of Antarctica. Of this last party, three lives were lost before the men were rescued.

Whether or not Shackleton believed in guardian angels, it seems that he had a long-standing conviction about his destiny. According to one acquaintance, he remembered an Irish nurse telling him in childhood that he would die at the age of forty-eight, and he believed her absolutely. In 1921, as he finalised his plans for a fourth expedition to the Antarctic sponsored by his old school friend John Quiller Rowett, he might have wondered if his time was nearly up.

The Shackleton-Rowett expedition was heralded as a scientific venture, with emphasis on oceanography. A small aeroplane would be collected in Cape Town, in which crew member Hubert Wilkins hoped to make a record-breaking flight in the Antarctic. Unfortunately, the *Quest* was a comparatively small ship and poorly fitted; she soon proved to be no match for the tempestuous Southern Ocean. The stop in South Africa was abandoned and engine problems forced a detour to South Georgia. Shackleton, whose big dreams were already going awry, was beginning to feel the strain. He went ashore at Grytviken for a reunion with some of the whalers who had helped to rescue him five years before, but when he returned to the boat he was unable to sleep. In the early hours of 5th January 1922, to the shock and dismay of his crew, he suffered a massive heart attack and died. It was just five weeks before his forty-eighth birthday.

Emily Shackleton chose the little church next to the whaling station in South Georgia as her husband's final resting place. As the nation mourned a hero, Scottish geographer Hugh Robert Mill paid tribute to his friend's 'vivid and dominating personality' and recalled his gift of inspiring the confidence and affection of his companions. Indeed, those who had survived the *Endurance* expedition and the Great War had travelled from far and wide to join him on the *Quest*. Shackleton, said Mill, was 'no vulgar notoriety hunter but a great soul deeply moved by the glory of great deeds grandly done, and his memory will survive as an inspiration to explorers.'[8]

1. *Evening Dispatch*, 25th March 1909

2. Letters to Hugh Robert Mill from Shackleton, 3 & 26 February 1904 (SPRI)

3. *Edinburgh Evening News*, 10th November 1905

4. *Evening Dispatch*, 19th November 1909

5-6. *The Scotsman*, 19th November 1909

7. *The Scotsman*, 14th January 1920

8. Hugh Robert Mill, Obituary of Sir Ernest Shackleton, *Scottish Geographical Magazine* (1922) 38:2, 118-121

WILLIAM SPEIRS BRUCE

Antarctic explorer
BORN: 1st August 1867 (London)
DIED: 28th October 1921 (Edinburgh)
§
RSGS Gold (Scottish Geographical) Medal, 1904

ON THE MORNING of 2nd November 1902, the SY *Scotia* quietly slipped her moorings at Troon and sailed into the Irish Channel. A former Norwegian whaler, 400 tons and barque-rigged, she had been refitted in a Clyde shipyard and was heading south to the bottom of the world. There was no tumultuous farewell, although handkerchiefs fluttered on a handful of tug boats. From her decks, the strains of 'Auld Lang Syne' floated over the water. The *Scottish National Antarctic Expedition* had begun.

The expedition was the brainchild of a thirty-five-year-old Scotsman named William Speirs Bruce, and he was setting forth as best suited his temperament. Not for Bruce the naval splendour of Scott or the showmanship of Shackleton; this soft-spoken scientist had a natural dislike of the limelight. Beneath his gentle exterior lay a fiercely patriotic heart and a will of iron.

Who was William Speirs Bruce, and what had drawn him to the Antarctic? Photographs depict a middle-aged man with pensive eyes and dark hair, slightly greying. Any humour around his mouth is smothered by the obligatory Victorian beard. His face wears a brooding expression, as if sitting for photographs is a nuisance to be politely endured. He does not appear to have the kind of stamina necessary for braving a polar winter, but appearances can be deceptive.

Born in London in 1867, the son of a well-to-do doctor, William Speirs Bruce enjoyed a privileged upbringing and a good education.

He intended to follow his father into the medical profession until a spell at Patrick Geddes's summer school in Edinburgh changed the course of his life. There, Bruce assisted Sir John Murray in studying specimens brought back from the *Challenger* expedition and mingled with brilliant scientists such as P. G. Tait, J. Arthur Thomson and Alexander Buchan. He also met W. G. Burn Murdoch who would become a good friend and with whom he would embark on the *Dundee Whaling Expedition* to the Antarctic in 1892.

Bruce's official title on that expedition was ship's surgeon, though he was not formally qualified as a physician; his main duty was to make scientific discoveries about the wildlife, oceans and climate of the unknown continent. During the voyage he seems to have fallen out with the captain, who tossed some of his specimens overboard in an angry fit. Nonetheless, Bruce must have found the expedition fulfilling; as soon as the ship arrived back in Scottish waters he started to plan another trip.

At this time, only a handful of people had ever been to Antarctica. In his determination to return, Bruce learned to sledge and ski and lived for almost a year at the top of Ben Nevis in the meteorological observatory. Despite a stooping gait he was fit, and Burn Murdoch observed that he could walk sixty miles in a day without turning a hair.

When plans for a British Antarctic expedition were being discussed in London, Bruce must have been one of the most eligible candidates to lead it. It was circumstance and a clash of temperaments which ensured that he did not. The *British National Antarctic Expedition* had the support of the government, the Royal Society and the Royal Geographical Society, and for this reason alone plenty of exposure in the press was guaranteed. Sir Clements Markham, President of the RGS, would permit nothing to cloud his glory. He was as staunch a patriot to England as Bruce was to Scotland. To Markham, the South Pole was a flagstaff upon which the Union Jack would be soon hoisted with full ceremonial splendour.

Bruce had applied to be a member of the expedition and Markham had written a short, non-committal reply, asking him to call when he was next in town; fatefully, Bruce never did. If he had taken himself down to London, and allowed himself to be seen and courted among the clubs, fashionable restaurants and society meeting rooms, he might have found more favour. But all of that was against his nature.

Meanwhile, the vast region of Antarctica lay remote and unexplored and Bruce saw no reason why Scotland should not play a part in the adventure. He announced his intentions quite casually in a second letter to Sir Clements, nearly a year after his initial application. Listing several eminent gentlemen who would be ready to testify for him as a suitable candidate for Markham's expedition, he then dropped a bombshell: he was not, he said, without hope of being able to raise the funds for a second British ship to the Antarctic.

Markham's feelings promptly rocketed from lukewarm tolerance to overheated outrage. Bruce's remaining chances of joining the British expedition were well and truly squashed. In his defence, Bruce did not deliberately send Markham into an apoplexy; rather, it seems his independent nature had been directing him onto a different path all along.

With the backing of the Royal Scottish Geographical Society, and the financial support of several wealthy investors including the Coats brothers of Paisley, he set about acquiring a suitable vessel and adapting her to survive the Antarctic winter. By November 1902, the *Scottish National Antarctic Expedition* was ready to depart on the *Scotia*.

In addition to her crew of twenty-seven, the *Scotia* carried six scientific staff, a taxidermist, an artist, and a handful of sledge dogs. Her captain was Bruce's friend, Thomas Robertson of Peterhead. Below decks were two fully equipped scientific laboratories ready to record and examine a huge range of findings from meteorological observations to ocean depth and Antarctic fauna. In contrast to the expeditions of Scott and Amundsen, Bruce's main priority was scientific research, and he stated quite clearly that no unnecessary sacrifice would be made in attempting to reach the South Pole simply to unfurl a flag. Nevertheless his wife, Jessie, had embroidered a Scottish saltire bearing the initials 'S.N.A.E.' which would undoubtedly have given Sir Clements Markham recurring nightmares.

On 6th January 1903 the ship reached the Falkland Islands and by the end of March she was stuck fast in the ice around the South Orkneys, about 375 miles from Antarctica, in a place they named Scotia Bay. The *Scotia* was well prepared to survive the crushing impact of the ice. Her sides had been strengthened with timbers twenty-five inches thick, and her stores of food had been supplemented by gifts of alcohol and tobacco from the Coats brothers – not that Bruce intended to sit back in an armchair and smoke a pipe. As the season turned towards perpetual darkness, he had a busy programme of work to do. His only disappointment was that the ocean had frozen so far north that he would be unable to reach the continent itself and make an attempt on the Pole.

The men were first tasked with building a hut and a magnetic observatory on the shore of Laurie Island. For materials, they quarried stone from the island and used timber from the ship's supplies. It was a long, cold job.

> Only those who have worked themselves in frozen ground can realise what the quarrying meant. By the end of the time we had broken our picks, so as to render them perfectly useless, handles of heavy hammers lasted only a short time, and ice drills were blunted and twisted out of all reasonable shape.

The hut, in the style of a Highland bothy, offered compact but comfortable accommodation for the hardy few who would stay there when the *Scotia* departed, and housed the scientific equipment for recording the continent's climate, geology, flora and fauna. It was named Omond House after Robert Traill Omond, the first superintendent of the weather station on Ben Nevis, who was a keen supporter of Bruce's venture, and had supplied the plans for the building.

Bruce and his men endured the long, dark winter on board the *Scotia*. Their programme of scientific work consisted of collecting natural history samples, making hourly meteorological and tidal observations, and drilling through thick ice in order to take depth soundings. The night watch was divided into shifts, with Bruce on duty between four and eight o'clock every morning. Leisure time was spent playing games, reading books from the library and listening to Scottish tunes performed by the ship's piper, Gilbert Kerr. To celebrate Midwinter Day they opened a barrel of porter bestowed on them by the Guinness brewery in Ireland, only to find the freezing conditions had separated it into ice and alcohol. The remaining liquid was therefore extremely potent, and they enjoyed an evening of such merriment that it went down in history as 'the night of the porter supper'.

As the light started to return, Bruce saw six of his men safely ensconced in Omond House before setting sail for Buenos Aires, where the *Scotia* stocked up on fuel and supplies. While there, he sought out the British Consul and telegraphed the British Government to ask if they wished to lay a claim to the meteorological station he had established. Eager to see his work continued, he must have been disappointed when the reply came back as negative. He therefore handed it over to a team of Argentinian scientists who accompanied him back to the South Orkneys to relieve the team of six original staff; two of these chose to remain at Omond House for another year.

In March 1904, when the *Scotia* finally set sail for home, she did so without her First Engineer, Allan Ramsay, who had died of heart failure. He was buried on the beach of Laurie Island. Fiercely loyal to his men, Bruce felt Ramsay's loss keenly, but his expedition was still a resounding success. He had explored over 4,000 miles of uncharted ocean and recorded over 1,100 species of fauna and flora; he had discovered new territory, which he named Coats Land after his sponsors; he had set up a Post Office in the South Orkneys and was carrying the first letters from the Antarctic; and he had established the continent's first meteorological station, whose recordings have continued unbroken up to the present day. Remarkably, apart from the one loss, all his men had survived in good health.

The *Scotia* sailed back into the Clyde on 21st July 1904 and was greeted with a hearty welcome. Before a celebratory lunch, Sir John Murray, President of the Royal Scottish Geographical Society, presented Bruce with the Society's Gold Medal and read a telegram of congratulations from Edward VII. Scotland's Antarctic hero, modest and humble to the last, must have permitted himself a contented smile.

All references in this chapter from 'First Antarctic Voyage of the Scotia' by William Speirs Bruce, *Scottish Geographical Magazine* (1904) 20:2, 56-66

ROALD ENGELBREGT GRAVNING AMUNDSEN

Polar explorer
BORN: 16th July 1872 (Borge, Norway)
DIED: around 18th June 1928 (Barents Sea)

§

RSGS Gold (Scottish Geographical) Medal, 1912
RSGS Livingstone Medal, 1925

Around 5 PM on 21st May 1925, six men squeezed themselves into the cockpits of two small aircraft waiting on the frozen expanse of King's Bay, Spitsbergen. The aircraft had open cockpits so the aviators wore thick clothes beneath their flying gear. One after another, the planes taxied across the ice.

Equipped with Rolls-Royce engines fore and aft, the Italian-built Dornier flying boats had been shipped in pieces to Spitsbergen and assembled on the ice. Practice take-offs had been considered too risky in case of damage, but none of the men seemed concerned about the odds. In the first aircraft, which was numbered N24, were Leif Dietrichson, the pilot; Oskar Omdal, the mechanic; and Lincoln Ellsworth, an American millionaire. The second, N25, was piloted by Hjalmar Riiser-Larsen and with him were Ludwig Feucht, a mechanic, and Roald Amundsen.

Both aircraft were heavily loaded. Once airborne, the pilots had to pull back hard to lift them clear of the King's Bay Glacier which lay in their path. Anxious to know if the other plane was airborne, Amundsen turned in his seat to see its wings shining gold in the bright sunlight. Reassured, he could focus on the formidable task that lay before him: his team was heading for the North Pole.

Even as a child, Amundsen had felt an urge to explore. Having soaked up daring tales of Franklin and Nansen, he was drawn towards the polar regions and approached his dreams with no doubt in his mind they would become reality. He even slept with his windows open during the Norwegian winter to prepare his body for the cold climate.

Now aged fifty-two, he was a seasoned explorer with four major expeditions under his belt. He had succeeded in navigating the fabled Northwest Passage, and had been the first to stand at the South Pole. Credit for reaching the North Pole first, claimed by some explorers but disputed by others, was still up for grabs and Amundsen wanted it for himself. He liked to think of himself as 'the last Viking', and he certainly looked the part, standing over six feet in height with an aquiline nose and a haughty stare.

Overflowing with ambition and confidence, what Amundsen lacked was funds – a problem which had plagued him throughout his life. When embarking on his journey through the Northwest Passage in 1903, he had set sail by stealth at midnight to escape pressure from his creditors. This time, although he visualised a successful flight to the North Pole, he had no money to buy the aircraft. It must have been a godsend when Ellsworth stepped in and offered to buy not only the aeroplanes but an airship with which they could make a second attempt should the first one fail. Ellsworth's only condition was that he should be a part of the adventure.

Amundsen's attempt might appear hare-brained but he had a clever strategy. Both planes carried extra fuel but he knew there would only be enough for one of them to return home, and he planned accordingly. Once they landed on the ice, they would simply empty the tank of one plane into the other and return home together in one admittedly cramped aircraft.

Amundsen had gathered equipment and supplies for what he hoped would be a fairly short stay at the Pole. In addition to the fuel, the planes carried a sled, a canvas boat and food rations including salted beef, chocolate, biscuits and dried milk.

Following the successful take-off, the aircraft cruised between 2,000 and 3,000 feet. As the dazzling whiteness of the Arctic ice spread out beneath them, the airmen donned snow goggles and fitted special blinds over their windscreens. Early next morning, with the fuel tank of N25 showing half empty, her crew decided to land and fill up the tank from the fuel reserve. They had travelled 600 miles from Spitsbergen, and had reached a latitude of 87°43'N, 150 miles from the Pole.

As they started to descend, what looked like a smooth ice pack quickly revealed itself to be a field of pressure ridges which had buckled the ice into a mini-mountain range. Worse, a few seconds later the aft engine spluttered and died. Riiser-Larsen made a quick appraisal and chose a landing site: a narrow channel of water, dotted with icebergs and dammed at one end by a wall of ice. He took a careful breath, and guided the stricken aircraft downwards:

> They swept through yards of slush and broken ice, between high walls on either side, stopping just when the plane's nose was up against the end of the opening – a matter of inches saved them from disaster.[1]

Meanwhile Dietrichson began to circle the other plane for landing, bringing it down into a lagoon about four miles away. The aircraft bounced across the slushy surface and crashed into a large floe. As water surged in, the men leapt to safety and landed in a metre of snow. They were unhurt, but it was evident that the plane would not fly again; one engine was mangled, and parts of the structure were rapidly filling with water.

With no means of communication, Dietrichson, Omdal and Ellsworth now had to locate their companions. Despite their close proximity, the terrain was so difficult that it was more than twenty-four hours before they glimpsed the other party, and several days before they were reunited. In the meantime, having no radio contact, their only means of communication was by waving flags.

As they picked their way across a layer of thin ice, all three plunged suddenly into the freezing ocean; Ellsworth hauled himself out first, quickly unstrapping a ski and holding it out to save Dietrichson. Omdal, burdened with a heavy pack, could feel the current dragging him under but Ellsworth caught hold of his coat and pulled him out of the water; he was barely conscious, and five of his teeth had been smashed. All the men were numb with cold and shock, and greeted Amundsen and Riiser-Larsen who had come to escort them to their 'camp' in N25 with profound relief. There, changing quickly into dry clothes and fortified by a warm drink, they took stock of their situation, which was grave to say the least. There was no more talk of attempting to reach the North Pole; their focus was purely on survival.

Knowing that their chances now rested entirely on salvaging N25, the six men were faced with an urgent task. They must remove it from the slushy channel before the water froze around it, then raise it onto the pack ice and create a makeshift runway in order to take off. This was their only means of escape.

> The tools with which they began to launch an attack on the Polar pack consisted chiefly of knives attached to the end of ski poles. 'We had to work and work for our lives,' said Amundsen, 'and we flew at the nearest hummock with tooth and nail.'[2]

Amundsen had a cool head in an emergency, and his leadership qualities stood him in good stead. With superhuman effort, the team turned the plane in the fast-freezing channel, and before the day was over they had manoeuvred it half-out of the ice lane. The mechanics drained fuel from the abandoned N24 and repaired the relatively minor damage to the aft engine of N25. To conserve supplies, the team reduced their rations to three-quarters of a pound of food per day, and slept in the plane at night.

Knowing that the next task would be a long one, Amundsen made a plan of action. According to Riiser-Larsen, the minimum distance required to gather enough speed for take-off was 1,500 feet. The runway would have to be at least 36 feet wide, with an extra 18 feet of snow thrown out either side to allow the wings to pass freely over it. It soon became apparent that shovelling such a huge quantity of snow and ice was beyond the capabilities of the exhausted men. They had removed, by Amundsen's reckoning, around 500 tons in the space of four weeks, but the track was not nearly long enough. Then Omdal had an idea:

It was by accident on the 8th of June that they discovered a way out. One of the party, walking to and fro in thought, tramping down the snow, suddenly said, 'Look here, we can do this.' The next day their great tramping work began. Though it was still snowing, they realised that once the frost had set their tramping would have produced a beautiful track.[3]

On 15th June Amundsen and his party warmed up the engines of N25 in preparation for take-off. They had no food left. All unnecessary equipment had been jettisoned onto the ice, but with six men on board the plane was still dangerously overloaded. By treading down the snow they had created a track 1,500 feet long – but cracks were already developing in its surface. Within hours the summer temperatures, already destabilising the ice, would wreak havoc with their smooth runway. A meltwater pool and a sizeable mound of ice had formed at the end, meaning that they could not afford to overrun. They would have only one chance.

The aircraft rattled and shook as Riiser-Larsen nosed it across the icy plain and accelerated down the runway. Amundsen's stomach churned as the plane bumped and lurched – but it worked! They were in the air. A huge sense of relief swept over Amundsen, but only lasted an instant. Dead ahead, mere yards away, was the mound of ice at the far side of the pool. Five seconds would decide whether they would crash. His normally cool mind watched in horror as the aircraft, seemingly in slow motion, heaved itself clear of the ice with only inches to spare. They were safe.

Eight hours later the seaplane landed in the sea off the coast of Svalbard. Her embattled crew were taken on board a passing ship; the seamen failed to recognise the party at first due to their grimy, half-starved condition, and were only convinced when they saw Amundsen's famous beaked nose.

Although they had fallen short of the Pole, the explorers received a rapturous welcome in Oslo, which Amundsen later described as the happiest memory of his life. During their mission they had also found time to make scientific observations and take soundings that proved there was no land beyond Spitsbergen on the European side of the North Pole.

> The Council of the RSGS desire to assure you of their profound admiration of the magnificent courage and endurance shown by you and your party, and to congratulate you on the valuable scientific results of your work: also to express their sincere gratification at your safe return.[4]

In September 1925 Amundsen delivered a lecture at the Usher Hall, Edinburgh, and was presented with the Livingstone Medal by the Royal Scottish Geographical Society. The following year he led a successful expedition to fly an airship – the *Norge* – over the North Pole from Spitsbergen to Alaska; among his companions were Ellsworth and Riiser-Larsen, and the pilot was the Italian engineer Umberto Nobile. It was a glittering prize to add to his South Pole triumph. The 'last Viking' had earned his place in Valhalla.

Amundsen never married and had no children. By the age of fifty-five he was becoming world-weary; he was too old to travel safely to the places he yearned to visit, and his temperament would not settle for a backstage role. He may well have known, when Nobile crashed an airship in the Arctic in May 1928, that if he joined the rescue mission he might not return, but he still chose to go. His wish that death would overtake him in some high polar region, quickly and without suffering, was fulfilled a few weeks later when his plane was lost in fog in the Barents Sea.

1-3. *The Scotsman*, 1st October 1925, reporting on Amundsen's lecture to RSGS entitled 'Great Polar Flight' at Usher Hall, Edinburgh on 30th September 1925

4. Telegram from the Royal Scottish Geographical Society to Roald Amundsen, 26th June 1925

Sir Walter William ('Wally') Herbert

Polar explorer
Born: 24th October 1934 (York)
Died: 12th June 2007 (Inverness-shire)
§
RSGS Livingstone Medal, 1969

B Y 1960, THE 'HEROIC AGE' of exploration was well and truly over. Gone was the time thousands of people would line a dockside as a ship set sail for the polar regions, her brave crew swallowed by the great unknown for at least a year. In the days of Scott and Shackleton there was no rescue plan, because in the harshest regions on Earth there was no contact whatsoever with the outside world.

On 20th January 1962, when the British explorer Wally Herbert and his team sat poised above the Axel Heiberg Glacier in Antarctica, they must have been grateful for the blessing of radio contact. A few days earlier they had ascended Mount Nansen, a 13,330-foot endurance test of relentlessly stabbing winds and excruciating cold. Now, to complete their return journey, Herbert was confident they could successfully descend the icefalls of this legendary glacier along the exhilarating route taken by Amundsen forty-eight years before. Herbert had even ventured part of the way down and planted flags as markers before radioing the Scott Base for permission to begin the descent; the response came back as negative.

In his frustration, Herbert imagined Amundsen laughing at their inability to move. It took him several days to convince the organisers that he was capable of carrying out his plan. The go-ahead came not a moment too soon, as the men's physical state was deteriorating and they were down to two days' supply of food. By 5th February they had all made it safely down the glacier, complete with sledges and dogs. Those dogs, handpicked and purchased by Herbert from 'delightful old rogues'[1] at Jakobshavn in Greenland, had been on the holiday of a lifetime.

Overall, Herbert was satisfied with the outcome of the expedition; his team had explored an area of 22,000 square miles including the Beardmore Glacier and the Queen Maud Range. Eighteen months later, having completed the maps from his Antarctic survey, he started to look towards the north.

Born in York in 1934, by his early twenties Walter William Herbert was a bored surveyor in Shoreham-by-Sea. An ex-Royal Engineer, he had quickly become disillusioned with military service but was finding it impossible to settle into the daily routine of office work. His heart was pushing him towards the far horizon even as his mind told him he lacked the skills.

On the bus to work one morning, a newspaper fell on his head from the rack above. From the Public Appointments page an advertisement leapt out at him: the Falkland Islands Dependencies Survey, forerunner of the British Antarctic Survey, was looking for young men to work at their isolated land bases in the Antarctic. Prospective candidates were warned that they would be living for thirty months in conditions that would be a test of character and resource. It was the chance Herbert had been waiting for.

Less than a year later, the stark beauty of the polar regions had infected his blood like an incurable fever. He had found his life's calling. Over several years, working first with the Falkland Islands Dependencies Survey and then with the New Zealand Antarctic Programme, he helped to chart huge areas of the ice-bound continent, and became an expert handler of dog teams. The next logical step seemed to be the Arctic. No one had yet made a surface crossing of the frozen Arctic Ocean by dog sledge, so Herbert resolved to be the first. He devoted six years to meticulous planning and in February 1968 he set off from Point Barrow in Alaska with three companions.

Herbert's team consisted of Allan Gill, an experienced polar explorer; Ken Hedges, an SAS medic; and Roy 'Fritz' Koerner, a glaciologist who was in charge of the scientific research. Their journey would take them directly through the North Pole to Svalbard, a journey of 3,620 miles which spanned the Arctic Ocean at its widest. If they were successful, they would achieve a 'first' in the history of exploration.

Because of the long and controversial history of Arctic exploration, however, the identity of the first person to stand at the North Pole may never be known. The reason lies partly in the peculiar difficulties involved in locating the Pole itself, as the ice of the Arctic Ocean is constantly drifting. Early explorers, without the benefit of satellite technology, were unable to verify their stories. Cook and Peary laid claim to it in 1908 and 1909 respectively, but each was discredited. Although overland journeys were still in doubt, other means of transport had succeeded: Amundsen flew over the Pole in an airship in 1926; three pilots from the Soviet Union landed there in 1948; the submarine USS *Nautilus* passed under the Pole in 1958; and in 1968 the American Ralph Plaisted reached the Pole by skidoo. As late as 1969, the same year Armstrong landed on the moon, Herbert was aiming to lead the first confirmed expedition to the North Pole over land, using only sledges pulled by dogs.

Even though modern technology allowed the explorers to keep in regular contact with support teams and emergency services, it was a daring attempt. Unfortunately for Herbert, his love-hate relationship with radio still had a way to run. The summer of 1968 was spent camping on floes and conducting scientific research while waiting for the autumn freeze to set in. Then, in September, Allan Gill stumbled and injured his back while manhandling his sledge. Herbert and Gill agreed that he could safely stay and spend the winter in the Arctic but the expedition's organising committee, speaking to Herbert via radio, insisted that Gill be evacuated, and quickly.

Herbert, never one to hide his feelings, responded by expressing grave and comprehensive doubts about the committee's capabilities. His irate message was picked up by a *Sunday Times* reporter who just happened to have tuned in, and the resulting glare from the world's media was enough to hasten the rate of global warming. Knowing the full story but unable to defend himself, Herbert must have envied the old-fashioned independence of Scott and Shackleton.

Ultimately, any landing by rescue aircraft was made impossible by snowstorms and Herbert's instinct about Gill proved to be sound. Meanwhile the newspapers which had eagerly grasped at the heated exchange between Herbert and his committee gave themselves free rein to speculate about his mental condition. Journalists could not know that Herbert's very heart and soul were bound to the polar regions; he might be impatient of bureaucracy, but he knew the risks and was confident of bringing all his companions home alive and well.

On 5th April 1969, Herbert sent a radio telegram to Her Majesty The Queen with the news that, by dead reckoning*, at 0700 GMT the *British Trans-Arctic Expedition* had reached the North Pole, 407 days after setting out from Point Barrow. Minutes after Herbert had transmitted the message, Allan Gill took some new bearings and discovered that they were, in fact, some seven miles short of their target. The four of them felt the creeping horror of having informed Her Majesty that they had gained the Pole when in fact they had not. Herbert reckoned they still had time to get there that day, but they set off in the wrong direction and after seven miles were still the same distance away. Drifting ice, the bane of so many explorers before them, was playing tricks, making the Pole a constantly moving target. In the end they made a desperate dash, off-loading their sledges to gain speed and cutting their way through ice ridges in order to maintain a precise line. They made it – but overshot the Pole by about a mile in their haste; when they set up camp, the drifting ice took them back over it as they slept. It was, said Herbert, like trying to step on the shadow of a bird that was circling above their heads.

Back home, Herbert's achievement was welcomed by the Duke of Edinburgh, who praised it as one of the greatest triumphs of human skill and endurance, while Prime Minister Harold Wilson described it as a feat of endurance and courage which ranked with any in polar history. No doubt Mr Wilson would also have approved of the 27kg of pipe tobacco that were included in Herbert's regular air drops.

Herbert's success did not end with his arrival at the North Pole; his team returned with the first ever scientific survey of the surface of the Arctic Ocean. The research programme conducted by Fritz Koerner still provides benchmark data for predictions about climate change and fluctuations in the polar ice cap.

In November 1984, Herbert was invited by the National Geographic Society to examine the diary of Robert Peary, whose claim that he had trekked to the North Pole in 1909 had never been fully disproven. From the beginning, the US government had cast doubt on Peary's report, and after his fall from grace Peary had kept his diary to himself. With the permission of Peary's descendants, Herbert would be opening it for the first time in over sixty years. Four years of research followed, drawing Herbert into the mind of the fame-hungry explorer. His task was made even more poignant because on many of his Arctic journeys he had been accompanied by Peary's Inuit grandson, Peter. With sadness, he was forced to conclude that Peary had not stood at the North Pole, although he may have been as little as 60 miles away. He found this research an intensely emotional experience, and developed an almost psychic insight into Peary's mind.

Herbert also scrutinised the reports of Peary's rival, Frederick Cook, and found his evidence to be equally lacking. He described his investigations in a book entitled *The Noose of Laurels* – an apt title, because Herbert knew many critics would be ready to point the finger and accuse him of clearing a path for his own place in history. In truth the verdict was not what he had hoped for, and the responsibility took a serious toll on his health. He seemed to carry a weight of disappointment and grief on behalf of the two explorers. The research he had anticipated as a unique and fascinating challenge had drained his reserves of mental and physical energy, and as his health declined still further he underwent an emergency heart bypass operation.

Despite his considerable achievements, Herbert's name is not one that immediately springs to mind when polar explorers are being discussed. Perhaps this is because his gentle and self-effacing nature left him ill at ease in the spotlight of publicity. Or perhaps it is because he was not focused on 'adventure'; he truly loved the polar lands, and his heart called him back to the ice almost as soon as he returned from an expedition. Throughout history, many explorers knew this kind of yearning, and it was a force that inflicted immense strain on their wives and families.

In this respect, Herbert was extremely lucky. In 1969 he married Marie McGaughey, a member of the public relations team for his *Trans-Arctic Expedition*, and in 1971 he took her and their baby daughter with him to north-west Greenland, where they lived for two years with the Inuit people. Marie overcame her initial reservations about life in such a harsh climate, and ten-month-old Kari was welcomed and loved by the Inuit as one of their own. Marie went on to become a widely respected explorer and writer, learning much about the culture of the Arctic people, including their healing practices and ancient wisdom. Not surprisingly, Kari Herbert has an abiding passion for the polar regions which is evident in her own work as a writer, photographer and TV presenter.

Herbert spent an incredible fifteen years of his life in the Arctic and Antarctic. In that time he travelled well over 25,000 miles, many through landscapes that had seen no human footfall. He was also a talented artist whose paintings reflect his love for the light and landscape of the polar regions. In later years he and Marie lived in a crofter's cottage in the Scottish Highlands, where he continued to indulge his talent for painting; he died there in 2007 at the age of seventy-two.

Described as 'the last of the great pioneers', Sir Wally Herbert received the Polar Medal with Antarctic and Arctic clasps, as well as many other decorations. In 1969 he was awarded the Livingstone Medal by the Royal Scottish Geographical Society 'for his journey from Canada to Spitsbergen via the North Pole'.[2]

*Dead reckoning: a traditional method of navigation, by which a new location can be calculated from a previous fixed position, using the estimated speed, the direction, and time elapsed.

---

1. *Across the Top of the World* by Sir Wally Herbert (1969)
2. Minutes of RSGS Council meeting, 29th May 1969

Sir Ranulph Twisleton-Wykeham-Fiennes

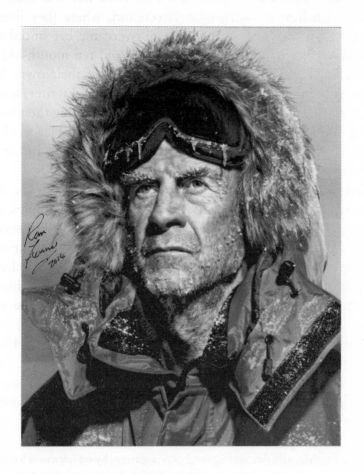

Polar explorer and mountaineer
Born: 7th March 1944 (Windsor)
§
RSGS Livingstone Medal, 1982

IF ANYONE IS A TRUE explorer of the modern age, it is Sir Ranulph Fiennes. His name is synonymous with courage and endurance in the face of our planet's harshest environments and he evokes a real sense of pride and affection in most Britons. For decades his rugged features have appeared regularly in news bulletins, his head cocooned in fur, eyebrows white with frost as he squints against the bright polar sun. Fans have followed his endeavours with admiration and hope, prayed for his safety and even secretly shaken their head a little at his madness. 'Sir Ran' is a unique phenomenon, who should probably come with a health warning.

Extraordinary energy seems to have been with him from an early age. As a child, he was happiest when out of doors. His family moved to South Africa when he was three, and he recalls roaming the valleys below Table Mountain with his gang of friends. He cannot remember his father; Lieutenant Colonel Ranulph Fiennes of the Scots Greys was killed in action in Italy in 1943, just months before his son was born. Fiennes's idyllic 'born free' existence came to an end in 1954, when he returned to England with his mother and three elder sisters. He attended prep school in Wiltshire before being sent to Eton, where bullies made his school years a misery. A rebel to the core, he soon discovered a talent for stegophily – the art of climbing the outside of buildings – and indulged it by night. As the sun rose, students and masters would stare in outrage or amusement at a range of objects

72

– toilet seats, traffic cones, dustbins – inexplicably decorating Eton's noble spires, while Fiennes and his accomplice quietly nursed their bruised and freezing hands in the breakfast queue.

Throughout his young life, Fiennes's driving ambition had been to follow in his father's footsteps and command a regiment of the Scots Greys. He left Eton with four O levels – not quite enough for Sandhurst – so instead entered the Army through the Mons Officer Cadet School. His years in the Scots Greys and then the SAS were punctuated by daredevil escapades that earned him a reputation as a firebrand and ensured his career in the British Army would never be illustrious. He freely admits, 'I realised that my Whitehall file was marked in red for caution.' The end came sooner rather than later; he was arrested after attempting to blow up a controversial film set with 'spare' army explosives he had squirrelled away. His girlfriend's father, already nurturing a deep mistrust, condemned him as 'mad, bad and dangerous to know'. Fiennes paid his fine, dusted himself off and signed up for some more armed service, this time in Oman.

Two years in the Sultan's Armed Forces hardened Fiennes both mentally and physically. He returned to England in 1970 and married his childhood sweetheart, Ginny Pepper, despite the still-bubbling resentment of her protective father. He realised he needed a new career, but was impeded by his lack of qualifications. Together, he and Ginny devised a plan, which turned out to be his true life's path; they would undertake expeditions, and then Fiennes would write books and offer talks about them, using his adventurous spirit as a means of making money. They were young and full of energy; their dreams were fearless.

Drawing on his wide circle of friends and acquaintances from the army, Fiennes began to breathe life into his ambitions. He had already journeyed by hovercraft up the White Nile, and helped to survey the Fabergstolsbre Glacier in Norway. In 1971 he made the first ever north-south traverse of British Columbia by water, a trek requiring him and his team to navigate some of the most dangerous rapids in the world.

Even more daring schemes followed. Ginny imagined a journey around the Earth following the Greenwich meridian through both

Poles; this became Fiennes's *Transglobe* expedition with Oliver Shepard and Charles Burton between 1979 and 1982. Only Fiennes and Burton finished the trek. Their last three months were spent drifting in the Arctic Ocean on an ever-dwindling ice floe, attracting the unwelcome attention of polar bears.

With his friend Mike Stroud, a physician and nutritionist who studied human endurance under extreme conditions, Fiennes made several unsuccessful attempts to reach the North Pole unsupported; the pair then switched their focus to the South Pole, crossing it between 1992 and 1993 and setting the record for the longest unsupported polar journey in history.

The twenty-first century is an era of instant communication and sophisticated technology, rendering the distinction between 'supported' and 'unsupported' journeys increasingly blurred. The generally accepted rules for an unsupported expedition are that there should be no supply depots, killing of animals or assistance in the form of mechanised vehicles or animals. Everyone who starts out on the journey must complete it. There is, however, usually an allowance for radios and GPS equipment as they do not offer any real advantage to the physical effort.

For their Antarctic crossing, Fiennes and Stroud used directional parachute sails, but Fiennes later wrote that he was dubious about their usefulness, unless the expedition happened to strike a particularly 'windy' year. In Antarctica in 1996, Fiennes used modern parasails with much greater success.

Disaster struck in 2000 while Fiennes was attempting to reach the North Pole solo. His sledge slid off a tilting slab of ice into the sea and one of its traces got snagged. In order to rescue his equipment he took off one of his mitts and plunged his left hand into the freezing water. He rescued his sledge, but knew immediately he would have to abandon the expedition. His fingers were so severely frostbitten that it was a gruelling race against time to return to the nearest shelter and radio for help. He was flown to a hospital in Ottawa where surgeons did what they could to rescue his hand; the top parts of his fingers and thumb had, in effect, died. His surgeon advised him to wait five months before assessing the need for amputation but after four months Fiennes was still in so much agony from his 'witch-like talons' that he resolved to do it himself. With characteristic grit, he placed each finger in turn in his Black & Decker vice and gently sawed the useless tips off with a fretsaw. Though his surgeon was not amused, Fiennes was unrepentant, finding fiddly jobs less painful and much less frustrating. He must have been very pleased with himself.

More than Sir Ranulph's fingers were at risk as he faced his next challenge in 2003. He and Mike Stroud planned to run seven marathons in seven days on seven continents, a mere four months after Fiennes had undergone heart bypass surgery. Only someone of his stamina and willpower would even entertain such a dangerous idea. His doctors must have known they were dealing with an unstoppable force. Despite the odds, Fiennes and Stroud succeeded, running consecutive marathons in the Falkland Islands, Chile, Sydney, Singapore, London, Cairo and New York, all within a week.

One of Sir Ranulph's few fears is heights. He explains, as though apologising, that this is why he used to climb buildings at night. Fear did not prevent him from scaling the North Face of the Eiger in 2007, via a route including the Traverse of the Gods, a wall of rock and ice so sheer that a climber glancing down at his feet can see the ground some 3,500 feet below. His mountaineering experience was minimal, so he did some intensive training and relied, as ever, on his exceptional stamina. Fiennes's climbing guide admired his military-style trust and discipline but recalled his alarming habit of leaving gear behind if he was unable to see its purpose.

In 2009 Fiennes climbed Everest, becoming the oldest Briton and the first British pensioner to do so. It seemed there were few goals left to vanquish, but in 2012 he spearheaded a team bound for the Antarctic with the aim of making the 2,000-mile crossing in winter. Not surprisingly, no one had thought of doing this before. The team planned to take core samples from the ice sheet and map the height of the continent using new GPS techniques. Using interactive maps and live scientific data, they would also create an exciting educational resource for schools.

The risks were immense. Once on the ice, a rescue mission would be impossible because aircraft engine fuel would freeze. They would be travelling in constant darkness for six months and braving temperatures as low as -90°C. As they crossed the inhospitable Polar Plateau and the Transantarctic Mountains, the team would be dependent entirely on their own resources. It would be a supreme test of mental as well as physical endurance. The dangers were nothing new to Fiennes, but he was foiled by his hands; during ski training the fingers of his left hand sustained frostbite, which was judged too severe for him to continue. Understandably frustrated, he was evacuated on the last aircraft to leave Antarctica before the start of the winter, leaving his team-mates to carry on. The expedition itself was halted after three months, when the team encountered crevasse fields that posed too high a risk for their vehicles but they still set a record for the longest ever trek during the polar winter.

Fiennes's enduring success has been mingled with personal sadness. When his wife, Ginny, died in 2004, he was left heartbroken. For thirty-two years she had been his soul mate and supporter, often providing the communications back-up for his expeditions. It cost him a great deal of personal courage to continue with his self-imposed challenges. He has since remarried, and has one daughter, Elizabeth.

Through his expeditions, Sir Ranulph Fiennes has raised millions of pounds for charities such as Marie Curie Cancer Care, the Multiple Sclerosis Society, and Seeing is Believing, which tackles avoidable blindness. He is arguably the world's greatest living explorer, however much he might quibble at the title.

Speaking about The Coldest Journey expedition, Fiennes explained, 'I am doing this for many reasons, some of which I don't fully understand. That there is an inner urge is undeniable.'

All references in this chapter from The Coldest Journey website:
   http://www.thecoldestjourney.org

Børge Ousland

Polar explorer
BORN: 31st May 1965 (Oslo)
§
Fellow of RSGS, 2014

THE THING BØRGE OUSLAND most feared was the loneliness. As he gazed out of the helicopter window at the blue-grey landscape, offering nothing but a vast expanse of ice between himself and his goal, he knew that he was physically ready. A seasoned polar explorer, he had done all the practical preparation: his equipment had been carefully researched and tested so that it was as light and as efficient as possible. No outside force could give him the crucial element for success, an impetus that had to come from within. He was going to attempt to reach the North Pole, alone and unsupported. If he succeeded, he would be the first person ever to do so. It remained to be seen whether his mind, as well as his body, was equal to the challenge.

Ousland's childhood home was at Nesodden, a peninsula just south of Oslo. Surrounded on three sides by water, he was naturally drawn to activities like fishing and sailing, and all his family holidays were spent on boats. At the age of twenty he became a professional diver working in the North Sea and in 1989 he joined the Norwegian Special Naval Forces. Nansen was one of his childhood heroes and in 1986, almost 100 years after Nansen's first crossing of Greenland, Ousland and two diving colleagues retraced that journey, taking thirty-seven days to travel from Angmagssalik on the east coast to Umanak in the west.

Four years later, Ousland and two different companions struck out from Ellesmere Island for the North Pole. Although one of them, Geir Randby, had to be evacuated because of injury, Ousland and his second companion Erling Kagge successfully completed the first unsupported ski trek to the North Pole in fifty-eight days, arriving on 4th May 1990. It was a huge achievement, but left something still to do.

No one had yet made the journey to the North Pole alone, without external assistance. An unsupported journey meant that no new supplies would be flown in if food rations ran low and no replacements would be available if equipment malfunctioned. Ousland knew that he would be hundreds of miles away from the nearest human being, in the most inhospitable conditions on Earth. An emergency rescue could take days and would be totally weather dependent. He also knew that, no matter how much training he did in the mountains of Norway, it was impossible to fully prepare his mind for the isolation that would engulf him for several months on the Arctic ice cap.

As his eyes scanned the bleak landscape where he would soon commence his journey, his thoughts lingered on his wife and young son left behind in Norway. Emotions surged to the surface. He hoped that if he broke down, he would be able to wait until the helicopter had departed.

It is impossible to overestimate the challenge Ousland was preparing to face. Beginning on 2nd March, when daylight was confined to just a few hours, he would be man-hauling a sledge over a notoriously difficult terrain where the constant breaking, drifting and colliding of pack ice created ridges and obstacles as far as the eye could see. The Arctic twilight required a hawk-like eye for the opening of new leads – stretches of water which appear when an ice plate breaks up and which are often covered by a deceptively solid-looking layer of snow or slush. Falling into water has always been at the top of a polar explorer's long list of nightmares. If it happens, you must act quickly: haul yourself out, put your tent up and light your stove. Your life depends on it.

Polar bears were an ever-present risk so Ousland carried a .44 Magnum revolver for use in an emergency. He had a system of poles and trip flares erected around his tent each night, upon whose unfailing efficiency he would have to depend in order to sleep. By day, the closely drawn hood of his jacket restricted his peripheral vision, making it difficult to detect a bear approaching from behind. Taking his first steps northwards, he knew that he would have to trust to fate for his protection.

> The demands on equipment on this sort of expedition are... considerably greater than in Greenland or in the Antarctic where the substratum is relatively even. Everything must be extremely solid, particularly skis, ski-sticks and sledges, otherwise they will literally fall to pieces.[1]

His equipment included a 125kg sledge with a double shell that could be converted into a boat. Nesting inside each other, the two separate sledge casings could be taken apart and lashed together with two skis secured over the top. His boots were water-repellent canvas, with plenty of room for movement to help prevent blisters. He had a radio to keep in contact with a manned radio station in Longyearbyen. From the Russian military base of Sredny in the Severnaya Zemlya islands, he would receive information about weather and ice movements based on satellite data.

Then there was the food, designed to provide 6,200 calories per day. Ousland's carefully packed rations of rolled oats, dried milk, sugar, raisins and soya oil could be combined for breakfast and lunch; dinner consisted of freeze-dried salmon or ham with mashed potato and more soya oil. For several months before the expedition he had deliberately been piling on weight so that his body had reserves to draw on in extreme conditions. He drank olive oil by the mouthful. When that made him feel ill he turned to cream. Meanwhile he honed his muscles and strengthened his skeleton by running daily with a heavy pack, often with his two-year-old son as 'ballast' and pulling a car tyre to simulate the sledge. At nursery school, Max Ousland chatted confidently about his dad's fun activities; to him, it was perfectly normal to want to ski to the North Pole.

In those first dark hours on the ice, as the monstrosity of his task struck home, Ousland faced the first phantoms of doubt.

When you are on a trip like that you will meet all sides of yourself
– the bad sides, not just the good sides.[2]

Ousland already knew the Arctic landscape can play tricks with
consciousness. At night, he heard sounds like bears around his tent
– but when he cautiously looked out to check, nothing was there.
Crumpling ice played a constant, random soundtrack ranging from
low grumbling and creaking to sudden sharp cracks like a pistol shot.
It was a landscape with no human memory. Fields of gigantic ice-
boulders dwarfed the figure and disorientated the mind.

Beforehand, Ousland had been curious about how to handle the
psychological challenge of being entirely alone in such a hostile
world. He spoke to a sports psychiatrist, half-expecting to receive a
ready-made solution that he could absorb and practise. The psychiatrist asked him a lot of questions, leading Ousland to realise that the
answers lay inside himself.

During his second night in the tent, he cooked his evening meal and
lay staring at the ceiling. The wind was blowing hard from the south-
west and he already had a problem with his skis: the ski-skins, short
strips on the underneath of each ski which prevent the wearer from
slipping backwards, had both come off. He would have to mend them
if he was to have any chance of continuing. His feet were cold, and the
presence of a wide lead or sea channel to the north-west was gnawing
at his mind. He read a letter that he had brought with him from home,
but it just emphasised his solitude. He took some deep breaths, and to
break the silence he put a cassette into his Walkman and pushed 'play'.
He did not know what was on the tape, so the voice of his friend, Dag
Henrik, came as a complete surprise. He listened to Henrik's stream
of small talk and soothing poetry and felt his spirits lift.

A night or two later, when the storm had passed and he stood
gazing at the glittering vault of the night sky, he remembered why he
loved the Arctic. Here was a pure beauty like no other place on Earth
except the opposite pole. It struck him anew with its deep sense of
peace and timelessness.

Having bound up his ski-skins as best he could, Ousland began to fall into a rhythm of a steady, even pull on the sledge. He developed a daily routine, which was vital for his physical and mental wellbeing. Stretches of relatively smooth ice alternated with expanses of ice-boulders and small leads of open water, just waiting for an unwary footstep. He had to push and pull his sledge over ridges and ice blocks piled shoulder-high, but he was coping well. The better weather encouraged a surge of optimism; as long as he could avoid injury, he knew he could reach the Pole.

A layer of ice inside his sleeping bag a week or so later was a demoralising discovery, especially as his feet were constantly cold. Any sweat on his body froze immediately, forming a solid layer beneath his back; he solved the problem by pushing a waterproof insulation mat inside his sleeping bag to make a barrier between himself and the ice. The sun was now hanging low in the sky, providing cheer but no warmth. Each day he looked forward to the evening meal, when the steam from his cooking pan would warm his frostbitten face.

> I wondered if I'd get nightmares, get frightened out here... but there's nothing here but God's unfettered natural forces, and nature isn't evil, no animal is evil... I think I'm becoming a more rounded person, and am very glad I chose to do this.[3]

One 'essential luxury' Ousland carries on every expedition is an almond cake with custard cream. This is a tradition stemming from an earlier trip, when he and his friends had not packed enough food and fantasised about pastries. From then onwards, he always made sure to take an almond cake. He was a third of the way to the North Pole when he tucked into the first piece. It was more than just an indulgence; regular little treats were an important boost to morale, celebrating minor but important steps on the way to the main goal.

Weeks passed and Ousland neared the Pole. Knowing that the end was in sight made him excited and emotional, but with the ice still breaking up around him, he felt the pressure to stay focused on every footstep. The precise location of the North Pole is notoriously difficult to pin down but Ousland, though alone, had the benefit of GPS. At 2.25 am on 23rd April 1994, in gentle weather with the deepest of blue skies overhead, he reached the end of his journey.

Ousland's achievements since then are a testament to his endurance and passion. Between 1996 and 1997 he made the first unassisted solo crossing of the Antarctic. In 2006, along with Mike Horn, he completed a winter journey to the North Pole, travelling in the perpetual Arctic night. These are just two examples from a long list of ice-bound crossings and ascents.

> It doesn't have to be the first or the longest... one of the most important issues for me is time and the ability to reflect around the issues of man and nature...[4]

On at least two of his polar expeditions, Ousland had no contact with the outside world. He says that he found he was more focused with no one to speak to. Although radio communication can be a lifeline, he believes that personal safety depends largely on behaviour and the precautions taken. Silence is no bad thing if an explorer is in tune with himself and his surroundings.

Ousland recently set up an ongoing project called 'Ice Legacy' in conjunction with French explorer Vincent Colliard. Their aim over the coming years is to ski across twenty of the world's glaciers, collecting scientific data in order to highlight their importance to the Earth's climate and oceans, its ecosystems and human population. The pair also hope to inspire young people to get out and experience the magnificence of the natural world for themselves.

> What you do is not the most important thing; each one of us must find his own narrow path. One is as valid as the other. The main thing is to do it, leave the flock, discover adventure and the glorious feeling of being alive.[5]

---

1. *Alone to the North Pole* by Børge Ousland (1994)
2. Interview at RSGS in Perth, January 2015
3. *Alone to the North Pole* by Børge Ousland (1994)
4. Interview at RSGS in Perth, January 2015
5. *Alone to the North Pole* by Børge Ousland (1994)

VOYAGERS

TIM SEVERIN

Navigator and historian
Born: 25th September 1940 (Assam)
§
RSGS Livingstone Medal, 1988

A ROUND EIGHT O'CLOCK on the evening of June 26th, 1977, a small boat was hauled ashore at Peckford Island on the Newfoundland coast. The arrival of this curious-looking vessel with its shallow, leather-covered hull and battered oilskin sails had been so eagerly anticipated that the narrow roads leading to the island were jammed with cars. As onlookers cheered, four exhausted men came ashore: one of them was Tim Severin, whose fascination with an Irish saint had inspired this epic voyage – by far the furthest he had ever sailed.

St Brendan of Clonfert was born in County Kerry, Ireland, around 484 AD. Facts about his life are impossibly interwoven with folklore and legend, but his various epithets – 'the Voyager', 'the Navigator' and 'the Bold' – depict him as an explorer. Like many other missionaries of that era, he travelled across the Irish Sea to establish Christian monasteries and churches on the west coast of Scotland. Many of his contemporaries settled there, but Brendan's seafaring instincts urged him towards more distant horizons. A medieval manuscript, *Navigatio sancti Brendani abbatis* (The Voyage of St Brendan), tells of how he gathered a party of pilgrims and crossed the Atlantic in a traditional vessel called a curragh. They were looking for the 'blessed isle'; they found excitement beyond their wildest dreams. Their encounters with colossal sea monsters and angry fire-hurling gods are ripe for Hollywood, and a puzzle for historians. Some believe that the story is pure legend, while others suspect that it contains at least an element of truth.

Tim Severin devoted his life to recreating epic journeys. As a student, he made his first expedition by motorcycle, riding across Asia in the footsteps of Marco Polo. When the legend of St Brendan caught his imagination, he had never sailed across oceans but something about the story made him pause. His wife, a student of medieval manuscripts, remarked on something unusual in the early texts describing the saint. She had noticed that, in contrast to many of his contemporaries, Brendan was remembered not for his miracles but for his extraordinary wisdom, revered almost as a gift of clairvoyance. He seemed to know what was going to happen throughout his extraordinary voyage, even when the crew were alarmed, and his abiding calm and belief in divine protection helped to guide them to safety.

Could St Brendan have reached the shore of the New World? It was an intriguing question. As a graduate in geography and history with a knowledge of sailing and a passionate interest in early explorers, Severin decided to try to find out for himself. Using all the academic resources available, he peeled away layer upon layer of legend and found himself with a puzzle that was waiting to be solved. He pored over maps to match imaginative place-names with geographical locations. Meanwhile, a plan was evolving in his mind. He would build a boat, one that matched Brendan's medieval vessel in every possible detail, and he would sail her across the Atlantic.

In Brandon Creek, said to be the original departure point of the saint himself, Severin inspected some curraghs for the first time. These traditional Irish vessels, believed to have changed little since the first Stone Age explorers sailed them around the coast, are still used in western Ireland for fishing to this day. Tarred canvas, now used in preference to leather, was stretched tightly across gracefully curved wooden frames. The craft were propelled by slender oars of a design he had never seen before. Having found what he was looking for, he felt a thrill of excitement – but these boats were small, designed for coastal or inland waters. His own would have to be much bigger if it was to withstand the storms of the Atlantic.

To build a replica of St Brendan's boat, Severin sought out the most knowledgeable and experienced local craftsmen, winkling some of them out of retirement and persuading them, with his gentle charm, into embarking on a labour of love. Colin Mudie, a brilliant designer, provided drawings for the builders to work from while Severin went in search of materials.

The ribs of the hull were cut from pliable Irish ash, while heartwood from an oak tree was used for the gunwales. The masts and oars, which needed to be both strong and light, were hewn from the north-facing side of an ash, where the wood is particularly dense.

Then there was the question of the leather. By examining the relics of leather satchels in which medieval monks carried their sacred texts, Severin was able to ascertain the type and thickness of leather available at that time. What he did not know was how the leather had been made waterproof. Since men's lives would depend on the resilience of the materials, as they had in the time of St Brendan, Severin decided to do some practical investigation with the help of the British Leather Manufacturers' Research Association.

The first step was to obtain samples of leather tanned in different ways and test them. At first, Severin was warned that leather would not last much longer than four days when immersed in water. He knew that a solution must exist, and remembered that St Brendan's boat was said to have been covered with leather tanned in oak bark. By chance – an abiding factor which Severin began to call 'Brendan Luck', because it kept him consistently on the right path – he discovered that a family-owned company producing oak-tanned leather with a centuries-old method of preparation still existed in Cornwall. Experiments proved that oak-tanned leather, when dressed liberally with grease, was two or three times more resistant to water than any other leather.

Severin specified the use of small ox hides, knowing that cattle in St Brendan's time were smaller than their present-day counterparts. Then he phoned a wool grease supplier and ordered three-quarters of a ton.

Binding the leather to the hull was the work of a harness-maker, so Severin placed the task in the magical hands of John O'Connell, who had once stitched harnesses in the Queen's stables. O'Connell taught Severin's team to roll flax for the thread, but his skill in sewing the half-inch-thick leather left them in awe. Two miles had to be stitched, and their fingers were soon sore and bleeding. Forty-nine hides covered the frame, with enough leather to spare for repairs during the voyage. She was named the *Brendan*; for luck, she carried a silver dollar under the mainmast and a phial of holy water in the gunwale.

Tim's initial crew consisted of George Molony and Peter Mullett from England; Irishman Arthur Magan; and Norwegian Rolf Hansen. All were more than willing to endure cramped, cold conditions for the sheer exhilaration of adventure – just as well, as in the spirit of St Brendan their equipment was as simple as possible. Severin believed the medieval voyagers had cooked their meals on a fire that they kept burning in a cauldron, substituted on the *Brendan* for a paraffin stove built into a windproof box. Following the example of early polar explorers, sheepskins would provide insulated sleeping mats. Severin took no chances with personal safety, however: all the crew wore modern sailing suits.

The shore was lined with interested onlookers when the *Brendan* launched from Brandon Creek on 17th May 1976, her hull slathered with wool grease, wind filling her yellow sail.

Most of the spectators were Kerrymen who knew the seas and had sailed them all their lives, though never as far as America! Beneath the excitement, they were fully aware of the risks. Measuring 36 feet in length, the *Brendan* was true to the shape of the traditional curragh. Only 18 inches of her hull lay below the waterline, resulting in a rolling action that made her crew queasy. It was, Severin said, like sailing in a leather banana. No amount of research could tell him how to handle the boat at sea; that knowledge, passed from generation to generation, had been lost for centuries, and it was up to him to rediscover it. He was going to need all the faith of St Brendan, and a few miracles as well.

According to folklore, St Brendan's route took him up the coast of Ireland to the Western Isles of Scotland, north to the Faroes, then west towards Iceland and Greenland. From there, his intrepid party crossed the Atlantic to Labrador in Canada. Old place-names suggest a memory of Brendan's presence in the Faroes, and Norse folk tales recall how Scandinavian settlers in Iceland learned that the 'papas' or 'fathers' had been there before them.

Severin's voyage followed this same route, but had to be accomplished over two successive seasons because of extensive pack ice between Greenland and Labrador, which necessitated some crew changes. The crew's survival was a testament to their endurance, resourcefulness and skill. They soon ditched their rations of high-tech survival food in favour of smoked fish and meat; Tróndur Patursson, who had joined them from the Faroes, caught seabirds to supplement their diet.

The voyage was far from easy. Disaster nearly scuppered their chances of success. One night, as they skirted a fringe of pack ice, they were woken by a sickening crunch and found that the Brendan's hull had been punctured by a small ice floe. In Severin's mind, the best moment of the whole voyage was the discovery that the hole was just below the waterline and therefore repairable; Molony had the longest arms, so was dangled over the side by his feet for three hours while he stitched a makeshift patch onto the hide.

On the night of 25th June 1977, faint pinpricks of light and the scent of pine trees borne on the offshore wind confirmed that they were nearing the Newfoundland coast. After fifty days at sea the Brendan, according to Severin, looked more like a floating bird's nest than an ocean-going vessel, but next morning the crew politely refused an offer from the coastguard to tow her to a safer harbour. Molony leapt ashore onto the rocks of Peckford Island, about 150 miles off St John's. The voyage of the Brendan was complete.

Severin proved St Brendan could have reached North America before the Norsemen or Christopher Columbus using medieval technology and materials. However, in order to prove that the voyage did indeed take place, he would have had to find a relic of the saint himself – not necessarily human remains, but at least a contemporary rock carving or stone dwelling. To strengthen his theory, Severin found many potential parallels along the route: the Faroe Islands could be the 'isle of birds' described in the medieval manuscript; erupting volcanoes in Iceland may have been seen by the terrified monks as violent gods throwing flaming coals down upon their boat. As for St Brendan's famous encounter with a sea monster, when his boat allegedly came to rest on its back, Severin has a convincing explanation. He reported that, day after day, his own boat was visited by whales which swam alongside, seemingly studying it. Perhaps they imagined the whale-shaped vessel was one of their own kind. Severin felt a curious kinship with the medieval navigators and remains convinced this is how the legend of St Brendan's stranding came about.

For many, the voyage in the *Brendan* would have been the achievement of a lifetime. For Severin it was only the first of many expeditions all over the globe, recreating ancient vessels in meticulous detail and sailing in the wake of legendary navigators. He has now turned his hand to writing fiction; his novels draw on ancient fortune hunters setting sail into uncharted oceans. There can be few authors better qualified to write such stories.

Severin speaks about his achievements with modesty and quiet composure. Like many explorers before him, he seems to have known his life's purpose at a young age, and blends an extraordinary sense of adventure with a clear-sighted grasp of how to bring a project to life. His passion for the safety and wellbeing of his crew – he has never lost a single man – has won him a special place in the hearts of his shipmates, many of whom admit they would drop everything to join another voyage.

Tim Severin was presented with the Livingstone Medal of the Royal Scottish Geographical Society in 1988 'for his research in historical geography, for his endeavours in recreating historical and legendary voyages and travels, and for his writings.' Perhaps a similar, backdated honour should go to St Brendan himself for fortitude, endeavour and resilience on the face of a restless ocean.

All references in this chapter from RSGS Newsletter No.4, December 1987

Isobel Wylie Hutchison

Yours ever sincerely Isobel W. Hutchison & "Whitie", an arctic friend

Arctic explorer and plant collector
BORN: 30th May 1889 (Carlowrie Castle, Edinburgh)
DIED: 20th February 1982 (Carlowrie Castle, Edinburgh)
§
RSGS Mungo Park Medal, 1934
Fellow of RSGS, 1932
Vice-President, Council Member, and
Honorary Editor of *Scottish Geographical Magazine* 1946-1953

OFF THE COAST OF ALASKA, a small weather-beaten trading vessel was navigating gingerly around menacing ice floes. Her crew kept a sharp watch on the horizon, eyes straining to glimpse their prize. Few people had ever seen the *Baychimo*, 'ghost ship' of the Beaufort Sea; she was said to appear and disappear without reason. More to the point, she was believed to carry treasure.

Presently, the gaunt black hull of a derelict vessel drifted eerily into sight. Rusting and battered, she was entombed in a pan of ice like a long-dead monarch on a frozen throne. Quickly securing their own vessel alongside, the crew scrambled up a broken ladder and onto the deserted deck. Climbing nimbly after them, spurred by their excitement, was a forty-four-year-old Scotswoman named Isobel Wylie Hutchison.

One of five children, Isobel was born in 1889 at Carlowrie Castle, an elaborate Victorian mansion in West Lothian. As a child she exhibited a talent for poetry, helping to edit a family magazine and keeping regular journals. She enjoyed a privileged upbringing thanks to her family's success in the wine trade, but her father died when she was ten and she lost both brothers before she was twenty. Isobel's diaries fell silent on each occasion. She took her grief deep into her heart, and walking became both an escape and a distraction.

Isobel would sometimes leave home for several days on

cross-country hikes that took her from Blairgowrie to Fort Augustus and from Doune to Oban. Her mother organised dinner parties with eligible naval cadets, but Isobel had seen her older sister's spirit dampened by marriage and was not about to be shackled herself. Instead of curtailing her explorations, she longed to spread her wings even further.

Iceland, in 1925, proved to be a stepping stone and a catalyst for her future life. Travelling there alone, Isobel initially stayed in Reykjavík to visit all the tourist sites, but the wildness of the land-scape demanded further exploration. She explained her wish to a tour agent, who laughed in derision. There was no road map of the island, and most of the 'roads' were rough tracks. Ponies would be needed to cross the many fast-flowing rivers. She would require overnight accommodation. Furthermore, she did not speak Icelandic.

Disheartened, Isobel was on the point of sailing home. The night before her scheduled departure, she attended a lecture by the French explorer Jean Charcot whose ship, *Pourquoi Pas?*, had just arrived from Greenland. Her conversation with Charcot, and the very name of his ship, encouraged her to think again. A few days later, in glorious weather, she set off to walk the 260 miles from Reykjavik to Akureyri in the north. Armed with a phrase book and a sketched-out route supplied by a more helpful guide, she called at farmsteads en route where she enjoyed warm hospitality. She borrowed ponies for fording rivers, and helped with haymaking in return. As she journeyed northwards, a profusion of wild flowers carpeted her path. Safely in Akureyri, she boarded a vessel bound for home, taking with her a new-found confidence and an ambition to see more distant shores.

Charcot had spoken so enthusiastically about Greenland that Isobel resolved to travel there. At the time, however, Greenland was a colony of Denmark and as far as casual tourists were concerned it was a 'closed shore'. Special permits were only granted to those on state business, or scientists pursuing a specific field of research. Fortunately, Isobel's lifelong passion for wild flowers allowed her to list botany as an official purpose when applying via the Danish Consul in Edinburgh. She sailed from Leith to Copenhagen in July 1927 and boarded the *Gertrud Rask* which was taking annual supplies to Danish outposts in Greenland. When she finally walked down the gangplank at Angmagssalik she thought it highly likely she was the first Scottish woman ever to set foot there.

The summer was hot. Isobel had packed a bathing suit in her luggage, but the hordes of biting insects discouraged her from wearing it. Within days her legs were swollen from bites, so she bartered some silk ribbon and woollen fabric for a pair of locally made 'kamiker' – sealskin top-boots – which the Greenlanders habitually wore in defence against mosquitoes. Despite the discomfort, she was delighted at the abundance of flowers, and filled her case with specimens. From Nanortalik, accompanied by a small party of Greenlanders, she embarked on a five-day expedition by umiak (an open skin-covered boat) in search of a sacred grove of birches, believed to be the only trees in Greenland. As they journeyed up the river, Isobel's companions caught and cooked salmon, singing songs around the camp fire so that she was lulled to sleep beneath the stars. The child among the party was so astonished by the sight of the trees that he tried to climb them, and Isobel was enchanted. For a five-pound note, she wrote in her diary, she had purchased one of the loveliest weeks of her life.

By this time the ship which had borne her to Greenland had departed, and Isobel was the guest of Danish officials who were resident there. At a party in Julianehaab she joined in a lively dance to music that was reminiscent of Highland reels, the legacy of Scottish whalers from a century before. She visited Greenlanders in their homes, watching them sew and cook, and wherever possible she supported their local economy through small gifts or purchases. She responded to their curiosity with openness, and was in turn touched by their warmth. During her last few weeks she met polar explorer Knud Rasmussen who was visiting his native Greenland en route to Scotland. Already a legend for his expeditions in the far north, Rasmussen spoke about his recent journey across Alaska and Arctic Canada, perhaps sowing new seeds in Isobel's vagabond heart.

Returning to Carlowrie on Christmas morning 1927, Isobel radiated a joyful new purpose. She started to write about her travels, and before long her articles and poems were earning a respectable income. She read poems aloud on BBC radio, and found herself in great demand as a lecturer. She felt as though she had never been away – but the magic of the 'rime-ringed sun' would not let her rest.

In 1928 she ventured above the Arctic Circle, spending a year in north-west Greenland, and set sail for Alaska in 1933. She was inspired partly by Rasmussen's book *Across Arctic America*, which she described as the greatest treasure in her library, and by her acquaintance with geologists Frank Debenham and James Wordie, who had accompanied expeditions led by Scott and Shackleton respectively. She felt a growing curiosity about northern Alaska and Canada. There was no thought of attempting to reach the North Pole; Isobel had no taste for glory. Indeed, one of her book reviewers remarked that if she complained more about the hardships, she might gain more of a following. Although it was not in Isobel's nature to look for problems, the fact remained that the Arctic was rough and ruthless. A woman willing to tackle such an environment was an unusual, almost scandalous phenomenon.

Supported by Kew Botanic Gardens in her role as a plant collector, and by Cambridge Museum as an ethnographer, Isobel planned a route that would take her from Vancouver via Point Barrow and Herschel Island to Aklavik. From Vancouver she travelled by boat to Skagway, and from there she took a train to Whitehorse, where she boarded a paddle-boat down the Yukon to Dawson. From Fairbanks, she flew to Nome intending to board the *Anyox*, the Hudson's Bay Company's only supply vessel to the western Arctic that year. Bad news greeted her: the *Anyox* would not put into Nome, but would sail past it to Point Barrow. With everything now resting on her timely arrival in Point Barrow, she persuaded Ira Rank, the captain of a 70-foot schooner, to accept her as a passenger. Rank obligingly offered to take her onwards to Herschel Island himself if necessary.

The *Trader* was carrying goods for remote communities in the north: tinned foods and fresh fruit, radios, gramophones, tobacco and silk stockings. According to Rank, the 500-mile journey would take at least five days, stopping at Inuit settlements en route. Isobel cheerfully made the best of it, writing home to her sister that 'The three men on board are awfully decent fellows... I'm getting quite handy at knowing how to make stew out of cans... My one regret is a hot bath.' The bathroom was a bucket in the engine room, and Isobel shared the captain's cramped quarters in the cabin.

Nine days out of Nome, the *Trader* put into the port of Wainwright to be greeted with the exciting news that the *Baychimo*, an elusive 'ghost ship', had been sighted offshore. Tired as the men were, they immediately hoisted anchor and set off to find her. Isobel, who felt herself by now to be a member of the crew, was alert and excited. She knew the *Baychimo*'s history as well as any of them. A former supply vessel of the Hudson's Bay Company, she had been engulfed by ice near Point Barrow in 1931 and abandoned by her crew, mysteriously disappearing during a subsequent blizzard. Now, caught fast in an ice pack, she was sailing the Beaufort Sea with no one at the helm.

It did not take long to locate her. Clambering onto the creaking, ice-bound deck, Isobel took stock of her surroundings. In the deserted saloon, a table was still laid with cups and saucers, with a breakfast menu nearby. Sea charts were scattered around the captain's cabin, while in the hold she saw sacks of furs and rusting typewriters. It was, she observed, as silent as the grave.

While the men salvaged a few things to sell, Isobel picked up some stationery adorned with the emblem of the Hudson's Bay Company, still in good condition. Back on the *Trader*, she wrote to her sister:

> I got a lot of this HBC notepaper on which I am writing you! Also some charts, nugget polish, British flags, and odds and ends including films which still seem quite good, but unluckily don't quite fit my camera! Most of the valuable cargo had already been removed, but Pete and Kari [Palsson] got the ship's compass... it was a most exciting and uncommon adventure...

The *Baychimo* made an exhilarating distraction but winter was approaching and it was essential to reach Point Barrow before the sea began to freeze. Isobel was still hoping to connect with the *Anyox*, but learned with dismay that the ship had struck an iceberg and turned back. There seemed to be no hope of continuing her journey; she would be stranded in Point Barrow for the winter. The solution to her problem came in the shape of a rugged Estonian named Gus Masik.

A fur trader who could turn his hand to anything from mining to boat-building, Masik had accompanied Vilhjalmur Stefansson on the *Canadian Arctic Expedition* of 1913-1916. He was an experienced sailor with a reputation for single-minded independence; if life became too easy, his restless spirit moved him on. When he met Isobel, Masik was making his way homeward to Martin Point. His boat, the *Hazel*, offered no luxuries for a lady, as he carefully pointed out, but Isobel trusted him instinctively and accepted a berth in the cabin. Racing ahead of the weather, they sailed east along Alaska's northern coast while the passage was still open.

Masik lived in a simple one-roomed hut on Sandspit Island, a snow-covered finger of land about a mile long by 100 yards wide. They arrived there on 15th September: the frozen sea prevented further progress by boat, and although Masik promised to take her onwards by dog team, the ice was not yet thick enough for sledging. She was marooned. There was nothing for it but to wait.

Isobel was now faced with a delicate dilemma. With their only neighbours a family of Inuit people, and no contact whatsoever with the outside world, she was acutely aware that all kinds of assumptions could have been made about her relationship with Masik. Setting strong physical boundaries, she made it quite plain that friendship was all that was on offer. Much to his amusement, she walked his dogs every day to the end of the island. At night, Masik regaled her with stories about his adventures; she later collected and published them in a book entitled *Arctic Nights' Entertainment*.

Early on the morning of 31st October, Masik woke Isobel so that she could see the moon, setting blood-red on the horizon. The eastern sky was flushed rose and saffron. An intense blue-green stretched up to the zenith where the last stars still lingered; daylight was receding as the polar winter took hold. Within a few days Masik judged that it was safe to travel.

The sledge journey to Herschel Island took several days and the two stayed in empty Inuit huts wherever possible. On the third night, with no such accommodation on offer, Isobel pitched her own tent and set about cooking their meal of rice and raisins. Masik, meanwhile, built an igloo. There was a short but light-hearted dispute over who was going to sleep where; when she saw the candle-lit igloo glowing like the hood of a daffodil against the indigo sky, Isobel crawled into Masik's snow chamber and gratefully agreed to share it with him. Using Isobel's camera, Masik photographed her at Demarcation Point, which marks the boundary between Alaska and Canada; shortly afterwards they parted, Masik heading home and Isobel continuing east to Aklavik, where a string of plane flights would bring her back to the civilised world. It was a wistful farewell. They would only meet twice more, but maintained contact by letter for the rest of their lives.

Isobel left an incredible legacy of plant specimens for the Royal Botanic Gardens in Kew and Edinburgh, and for the British Museum. A number of the artefacts that she brought back from her travels can be seen in the National Museum of Scotland, while the National Library of Scotland holds many of her papers and drawings. Other treasures are held in Museum of Archaeology and Anthropology at the University of Cambridge and the Scott Polar Research Institute. She was a regular and much-loved lecturer at the RSGS, and the Society holds a collection of her photographs, poetry, paintings, broadcast scripts, notes and books. As for the *Baychimo*, she continued her silent voyage around the Beaufort Sea until at least 1969, which was the last recorded sighting in the Hudson's Bay Company archives.

———————————

All references in this chapter from letter dated 17th August 1933 from
Isobel Wylie Hutchison to her sister, Hilda, RSGS Archives

Isabella Lucy Bird (Bishop)

Explorer and photographer
BORN: 15th October 1831 (Boroughbridge)
DIED: 7th October 1904 (Edinburgh)
§
First woman Fellow of RSGS, 1890

ONE OF THE UNEXPECTED side-effects of being a daring explorer and gifted writer is that your letters home will make your family want to join you; Isabella Bird discovered this while romping around Hawaii in 1873, much to her alarm. She was just beginning to love solitary travel, and her sister Henrietta would severely cramp her style! She sat down to write a hasty reply: although she was having a great time in Hawaii, she would soon be setting sail for Colorado. The key to not being caught, Isabella realised, was to keep moving.

She could not blame her family for being delighted by her letters. She had been a sickly child. A tumour had been removed from her spine when she was nineteen, and she still suffered from recurring bouts of backache, headache and extreme fatigue. Now, aged forty-one, she was bubbling with new energy and her exuberance overflowed into descriptive prose. Her sister must have imagined a miracle cure among the lush rainforests and sparkling blue pools of the Pacific islands. She would have been less keen to learn that Isabella had cast aside her feminine inhibitions and was cantering around Hawaii on horseback, riding astride rather than side-saddle. Neither Henrietta nor polite society as a whole was ready to hear that.

Isabella was born into strait-laced Victorian Britain, where women were expected to dress uncomfortably, act respectably and say very little. Her wanderlust was so strong that she was destined to cause scandal, and her whole life seems to have been a quest for balance between adventure and acceptability. As she followed her wandering star across Colorado, Japan, and vast regions of Central Asia, she refined that balance to perfection.

Her determined nature was apparent from an early age. One Sunday morning when she was just five years old, she felt tired and sickly, so her mother tucked her up in bed and told her to stay there until she got back from church. As soon as she left, Isabella tiptoed out into the rectory garden and danced barefoot on the grass, burying her face in the gold and crimson flowers which were sparkling with droplets after the rain. Then, brimming with happiness, she slipped back indoors and into her warm bed to await her family's return.

Isabella's father, a Yorkshire vicar, believed that children should be taught about the world in a truthful light that didn't mask the less palatable parts in a soft haze of fairy tale and illusion. He took his daughter with him on his rides around the countryside, showing her the wayside plants, crops, animals, farmhouses, cottages and features of the landscape; when they met people he would challenge her to describe them afterwards, encouraging her to explain her impressions with an open mind. What he was doing, in fact, was nurturing a lifelong skill in observation.

Following the death of her father, Isabella moved with her sister and widowed mother to Edinburgh. In 1866, when their mother died, Henrietta found a house in Tobermory on the Isle of Mull but Isabella, for whom the outdoors was a second home, drew the line at the prospect of such a wet and windy climate. Her ill health returned with renewed severity. Perhaps her whole being was rebelling against any further confinement; in the years to come, she would face far worse weather than the gales of a Scottish island. Her doctor advised her to travel and in 1872, with some trepidation, she boarded a ship bound for Australia.

At first she was bored and homesick. In New Zealand she impulsively bought passage to the Sandwich Islands, now known as Hawaii. It was an eventful voyage; the vessel was leaking and dilapidated, the stewards were insulting, and the bread was crawling with ants and weevils. When a hurricane inflicted extreme nausea on most of the passengers, Isabella was unfazed. She helped to nurse one of her fellow passengers, read some Tennyson, got out her sewing and occupied her idle moments by killing cockroaches with a slipper. Life was starting to get interesting.

A few days later, the beleaguered passengers were greeted by the serene blue waters and pounding surf of Honolulu. With time at her disposal, Isabella planned to be more than a passive spectator; she intended to explore. At the top of her wish-list was the volcano of Kilauea, the prospect already filling her with a delicious thrill of fear. The acting British consul, William Green, turned out to be a passionate geologist, but he must have wondered what kind of woman would step off a ship alone and thousands of miles from home, and politely ask for his assistance to explore the islands. She gathered a small exploring party, the ladies armed with umbrellas against the warm tropical rain, and they set off.

The path up to Kilauea's caldera was so hot that rain hissed as it fell upon it. A guide had to walk in front to test the security of the footing. Several times Isabella fell through the cooling crust into holes full of sulphurous steam, burning holes in her gloves as she raised herself out. But the effort was more than repaid by the spectacle that awaited her; gazing into the depths of the lava lake, she marvelled at blood-red fountains and seething whirlpools, crashing and billowing in dazzling grandeur. She was both terrified and delighted. She had found freedom and it was exhilarating.

Hawaii's dynamic landscape helped Isabella to forget her imagined limitations. Having literally experienced a baptism of fire, there would be no stopping her now. Vast regions of the world lay like an unopened book, and her mission was to write the chapters.

After writing to her sister from Hawaii, Isabella sailed to Colorado. Though the Rocky Mountains were known to be dangerous bandit country of pioneers and fur trappers, by this time Isabella was confident she could take care of herself. What she could not anticipate was her heart being stolen by a one-eyed desperado. Jim Nugent was a rugged cattle rancher of Irish descent, with a chivalrous soul and an addiction to alcohol. His disfigurement, Isabella learned, came from being mauled by a bear; but it only served to enhance his appeal. The other side of his face, she thought, could have been modelled in marble.

Travelling with Jim through the snowy wilderness, Isabella slept on a bed of pine needles as wolves howled from the forest and the embers of a camp fire subsided into the night. She helped to drive the cattle, often spending ten hours in the saddle, and in the evenings at his log cabin she cooked supper and listened to his self-penned poetry. Together, they climbed Long's Peak – a challenging 14,259 feet – and left their names in a tin at the summit.

It was never going to last. Jim had a history of violence and crime, and his frank revelations shocked Isabella to the core.

> He goes mad with drink at times, swears fearfully, has an ungovernable temper. He has formerly led a desperate life, and is at times even now undoubtedly a ruffian.[1]

When Jim asked Isabella to be his wife she was faced with a heart-breaking decision. He was, she said, a man whom any woman might love but no sane woman would ever marry. Stifling her tears, she packed her belongings and rode away. Just a few months later, Jim was shot dead in a drunken brawl.

For most women, that might have been enough drama for one lifetime. For Isabella, the adventure was just beginning; the Far East was now calling. In China, Japan and Malaysia, everything was fascinating and everyone was worthy of attention. Isabella's journals glowed with the joy of discovery, discomforts only adding spice to the mix. She rode a yak over a Tibetan mountain summit in the falling snow, and traversed raging rivers in boats made of bamboo with a raised prow and four sails. She hired porters and carrying-chairs but would also take on the most mettlesome of horses.

Henrietta's death from typhoid in 1880 was a grievous blow. Isabella had deeply revered her sister, irrespective of the distance which often separated them. Still in mourning, she agreed to marry John Bishop, an Edinburgh surgeon who had treated Henrietta in her final months and whose compassionate heart offered comfort and support. It seems to have been a marriage of affection rather than passion; Bishop was well aware of Isabella's lust for adventure, joking wistfully that his only rival was the Central Asian plateau. When his health began to decline Isabella nursed him devotedly, but only five years after their marriage he succumbed to anaemia.

Travel, which had long been Isabella's passion, became her salvation. She embarked on a second phase of exploration that led her to India, China, and across the Middle East. Writing about her experiences gave her a purpose, and her books received worldwide acclaim. From her husband's estate she had inherited enough money to be independent, and her income was supplemented by royalties. She was becoming a household name.

Not only did Isabella write vividly and at great length about her experiences, but she photographed them as well. Sir John Scott Keltie, Secretary of the Royal Geographical Society, introduced her to the renowned photographer John Thomson, and at the age of sixty she took lessons with him. She found it an intense pleasure, and was so successful that she was elected to the Royal Photographic Society in 1897. Her travels acquired a new, exciting element; she strapped her camera under her travelling chair, and developed photographic plates under the dark night sky. Her equipment had other uses, too:

> The tripod of my camera served for a candle stand, and on it I hung my clothes and boots at night, out of the way of rats. With these arrangements I successfully defied the legions of vermin which infest Korean and Chinese inns, and have not a solitary tale to tell of broken rest and general misery. With absolute security from vermin, all else can be cheerfully endured.[2]

For Isabella, photography was a passion that rivalled, but never surpassed, the thrill of travel. When she returned to Britain to give lectures, she made good use of her images. In 1891, her talk to the RSGS entitled 'The Upper Karun Region and the Bakhtiari Lurs' may have been the Society's first lecture to be illustrated with limelight views. This technique used the flame of a spirit lamp, brightened by a jet of oxygen and hydrogen, which was directed onto a pellet of lime in a lantern projector; the resulting glow illuminated the slides.

Isabella Bird was made a Fellow of the Royal Scottish Geographical

Society in 1891 and lectured at the Society's London branch in 1892, where she was warmly received. Listeners were spellbound by her tales of adventure, her talks notably attracting many women. Five years later, in November 1897, she returned to Scotland to describe her trek through Western China in an attempt to reach the source of the great Gold River. Travelling by house-boat or open chair with three bearers and four baggage coolies, the party was accompanied by four Yamen runners who inevitably ran away in the face of danger. Isabella's overnight accommodation was less than healthy:

> Many Sze-Chuan inns were good for China, but as she did not keep to the regular stages, she encountered woeful accommodation in dark mud hovels, her servant, after inspecting it, sometimes coming out with a rueful face and the information that she should have to sleep in the 'pig's room'.[3]

Unfortunately, Isabella's curiosity was sometimes returned with violence. No westerner had yet visited some of these remote villages, and a woman travelling alone with no obvious purpose was vulnerable to suspicion and attack. At Liang, her arrival provoked a riot so dangerous that the local Mandarin called out a troop of soldiers to line the streets as she passed through. Further on, outside the village of Lao-Kia Ch'eng, she was pursued by an angry mob throwing stones and threatening murder. A stone struck her on the back of the head, temporarily stunning her. When she recovered consciousness, someone was reasoning with the villagers, explaining to them how risky it would be to kill a foreigner.

Although Isabella's life often hung by a thread, she carried a medicine chest as well as a revolver, and was often besieged by local people hopeful of a cure for a panoply of ailments. She offered as much help as she could, her array of potions and ointments no doubt helping to preserve her life among potentially hostile communities.

The extraordinary landscape more than made up for the discomforts and the danger. Isabella marvelled at mountain corries with exquisitely cultivated terraces, gazed at richly coloured temples perched high on rocky ledges, and saw farmhouses set amid cypress and cedar groves. She photographed tradespeople and craftsmen, distilleries and paper mills; her images capture a way of life that existed before the permeating influence of the western world.

Having crossed the Cheng-tu Plain, Isabella reached Li-fan, where she was told by officials that her journey must come to an end – but a clause in her passport, triumphantly displayed, acted like a letter of safe passage and secured her onward progress. For political reasons, each border crossing required a replacement escort; at the village of Kuri-Keo, as Isabella entered the territory of Somo, she was astonished to see her new guards.

> A Mantzu official escort was at once provided, consisting, not of armed and stalwart tribesmen, but of two handsome laughing girls, distaff in hand, fearless and full of fun, who enlivened the way as far as [the village of] Chute. Before starting each of the girls put on an extra petticoat. Had any molestation been seriously threatened, after protesting and calling on all present to witness the deed, they would have taken off the additional garments, spreading them solemnly on the ground, there to remain till the outrage had been either atoned for or forgiven, the nearest man in authority being bound to punish the offender . . . [4]

Isabella appears to have led two completely different lives. At home in Scotland, she would relapse into fragile ill health and profess herself barely able to get up out of her chair, even as her bags were packed for the next voyage. Whenever she stepped onto a foreign shore she was miraculously filled with an abundance of health, vigour and enthusiasm, laughing at discomforts that would deter many able-bodied men. It is also curious that whenever she needed a guide to reach some far-flung goal, a male companion would present himself, ready and willing to offer the protection of his cavalcade and the authority of his station.

Isabella also learned to revel in the unexpected. On her journey through Malaysia, she arrived at the British Resident's house feeling travel-weary and dishevelled, and was dreading the ritual of dressing for dinner. To her absolute delight, the diplomat was away and she found herself in the company of several house guests, none of whom was human. For three days, her meals were cooked for her by the servants and presented on an immaculate table at which two apes of indeterminate species were also seated, while a friendly Labrador lazed at her feet and tigers roared in the distance. Dullness, she observed, was out of the question.

---

1. *A Lady's Life in the Rocky Mountains* by Isabella Bird (1879)
2. *The Yangtze Valley and Beyond: An account of Journeys in China, chiefly in the Province of Sze Chuan and Among the Man-tze of the Somo Territory* by Mrs J F Bishop (Isabella Bird), 1899.
3-4. *The Scotsman*, 10th November 1897, report of Isabella's opening lecture to RSGS in Edinburgh on 9th November 1897

Sir John Murray

Marine scientist and oceanographer
Born: 3rd March 1841 (Cobourg, Ontario)
Died: 16th March 1914 (Kirkliston, Edinburgh)
§
RSGS Livingstone Medal, 1910
President of RSGS, 1898-1904

S ITTING ON THE SHORE of an inland loch, admiring the glorious Highland scenery, many people witness a curious phenomenon known as a seiche. Pronounced 'saysh', this standing wave is a natural occurrence in all bodies of water, appearing when strong winds and rapid changes in atmospheric pressure cause water to be pushed from one end of a lake to the other and back again. The motion can continue for hours or even days after the wind drops.

The likelihood of experiencing a seiche was not uppermost in the mind of Sir John Murray as he sat in his small boat on Loch Treig in Inverness-shire in 1902. He was engaged in an ambitious project to survey all the freshwater lochs in Scotland and was more concerned about taking depth measurements and looking for plankton. Luckily for Sir John and his companion, James Parsons, the seiche they witnessed was extremely slight, though it would go down in history nevertheless:

> The first seiche in all probability to be recorded in Great Britain was observed by Mr Parsons and myself in Loch Treig in Inverness-shire on the evening of 22nd May last... I noticed that certain stones on the shore were covered and uncovered by the water with great regularity ... Mr Parsons and I found that the amplitude of the seiche was nine-sixteenths of an inch and that the period was nine minutes.[1]

It would have required an extraordinary amount of diligence to record this occurrence; luckily, diligence was one of Murray's greatest strengths. Thirty years previously, in 1872, it had secured him a place on the famous *Challenger* expedition. When the ship returned to Britain after its four-year voyage around the world's oceans, Murray was put in charge of its huge collection of natural history specimens. His report on the findings of the expedition extended to fifty volumes, and took nineteen years to prepare. A talented and devoted scientist, Murray was, like many men of his day, curious about all aspects of the natural world. He was certainly one of the best-travelled; thanks to the *Challenger* voyage, he had sailed through the Strait of Magellan, explored the turquoise lagoons of Fiji and brought back the first ever photographs of Antarctic icebergs. But he believed that an undiscovered world of science lay closer to home, in the depths of Scotland's lochs.

Between 1897 and 1907 he and his small band of assistants surveyed an incredible 562 lochs from Orkney right down to Dumfriesshire. For the depth soundings, they used an ingenious device built by twenty-five-year-old Frederick Pullar, whose father Laurence was a lifelong friend of Murray's and both a director and a principal funder of the survey. Frederick had invented a pulley system by which up to 1,500 feet of galvanised steel wire, weighted at the end, could be wound down into the water; a clamp secured the device to the side of the boat and measurements were taken at regular intervals. By this means a profile of the loch could be built up, enabling its contours to be illustrated on a map.

> The Pullar sounding-machine was used in all the larger lochs, but for small hill-lochs, difficult of access, it was found advisable to construct several small machines... which could be carried in the hand or on a bicycle, and be easily attached to a rowing-boat.[2]

As they travelled the length and breadth of Scotland, Murray and his companions were largely welcomed by the people they encountered, many of whom were understandably curious about what these newcomers were about. In a few places, however, folklore had preceded them by at least a thousand years, meaning that generations of families had grown up in the absolute belief that their local loch was bottomless. On those occasions where Murray found himself with the rather awkward task of having to explain that it was not, the verdict was usually received in offended silence.

Sitting in a boat all day long on a Highland loch at the height of summer may not sound like much of a hardship, but there was work to be done and Murray's team were certainly kept busy. They took water temperatures, collected plankton by dragging silk tow-nets at various depths, and made observations about the colour and transparency of the water. Their exhaustive surveys allowed them to prepare not only a bird's eye view of the loch and the surrounding landscape, but also cross-sections showing the shape and depth of the basin.

By the time Murray had finished, he had taken over 60,000 soundings and described more than 700 species of fauna and flora, including 450 invertebrates and nearly 200 algae. At least twenty-nine of these were new to science, and a further fifty were not previously known to exist in the British Isles. The deepest loch was confirmed to be Loch Morar, at 1,017 feet; Loch Lomond was shown to have the greatest surface area, while Loch Ness had the greatest volume of water (263,162 million cubic feet). Murray had previously done some research into the sea lochs of Scotland, and could now compare these with freshwater lochs; he was startled by the contrasting ways in which depth affected their temperature.

In his detailed analysis of the contours of Loch Ness, which involved 1,700 soundings and the collection of sediments from all depths, Murray makes no mention of the loch's legendary resident so it must be inferred that Nessie was unavailable for interview. Had the monster shown her head, it goes without saying that Sir John and his team would have been poised to take measurements.

At Loch na Bèiste, the 'loch of the beast' in Wester Ross, Murray describes a similar mystery and a local farmer's attempt to solve it. He has a very interesting theory about it himself.

> The loch is reputed to be the abode of a great beast, and Mr Banks, a former owner, attempted to pump out the water for the

purpose of examining the beast, but he failed in drawing off the water. The most probable origin of the rumour about the beast lies in the fact that the moon at a certain time casts the shadow of two stones upon the water, the shadow resembling the outline of an animal.[3]

Tragically, Frederick Pullar, who designed the measuring device, was drowned in 1902 while trying to rescue skaters who had fallen through the ice on Airthrey Loch near Bridge of Allan. Murray was grief-stricken, and was only persuaded to continue with the survey by Pullar's father, who wished to see it completed as a tribute to his son.

Sir John Murray's *Bathymetrical Survey of the Fresh-water Lochs of Scotland* was published in 1910, in six volumes. The 223 beautifully drawn maps, many of them coloured, were prepared by RSGS co-founder John George Bartholomew (see p.317). It was the first comprehensive survey of the depth and nature of Scottish lochs, and represented an important landmark in the science of limnology.

In 1884 Sir John Murray established the Granton Marine Station, the first of its kind in the United Kingdom, to conduct research in the Firth of Forth and the North Sea. In 1894 the station was moved to the Isle of Cumbrae and became the University Marine Biological Station, forerunner of the Scottish Association for Marine Science at Dunstaffnage, near Oban. Throughout his lifetime he made huge contributions to our knowledge of the oceans, discovering the Mid-Atlantic Ridge and noticing sand from the Sahara in deep-sea sediments. During the *Challenger* expedition he was accompanied by a pet parrot called Robert, who enlivened the research with occasional comments of 'What? Two thousand fathoms and no bottom?'

'The Deep Sea' was the title of a lecture by Sir John Murray to the Royal Scottish Geographical Society in Edinburgh on 11th November 1910. He described some of the astonishing forms of life which had been found to exist in the oceans at a depth of three or four geographical miles:

Large and delicate organisms belonging to nearly all marine groups could flourish in these great depths where the pressure was over four or five tons to the square inch, where sunlight never penetrated, and where the temperature approached to the freezing point.[4]

Sir John Murray, one of the founding fathers of modern oceanography, was President of the Royal Scottish Geographical Society from 1898 until 1904. In 1910 he was presented with the Society's Livingstone Medal 'in recognition of his extensive oceanographical work, and more particularly in commemoration of the completion of his great national work, the *Bathymetrical Survey of the Fresh-water Lochs of Scotland.*'[5]

1-4. *Bathymetrical Survey of the Fresh-water Lochs of Scotland* by Sir John Murray and Mr Laurence Pullar (1910)

5. Minutes of RSGS Council meeting, 18th October 1910

MARY HENRIETTA KINGSLEY

African explorer
BORN: 13th October 1862 (Islington)
DIED: 3rd June 1900 (Simon's Town, South Africa)
§
Lecturer at RSGS, 1896

We shot into a narrow channel between a low island and a large sand-bank, and that sand-bank had on it as fine specimens of the West African crocodile as you could wish to see. They also were having their siesta, stretched sprawling on the sand with their mouths wide open; one old lady had a lot of young crocodiles running over her, evidently playing like a lot of kittens, and the heavy musky smell from them was most offensive. We did not, however, complain aloud about this, because we felt hopelessly in the wrong in intruding on these family scenes, and apologetically hurried past. When we were out of earshot, I asked one of my Adjuma crew if there were many gorillas, elephants, leopards, and bush-cow round here? 'Plenty too much,' said he, and I wished myself in England, at the same time regretfully remembering that the last word a scientific friend had said to me before I left home was, 'Always take measurements, Miss Kingsley, and always from the adult male.'[1]

B ORN IN ISLINGTON in 1862, Mary Kingsley was the daughter of a physician, George Kingsley, and the niece of writers Henry and Charles Kingsley. She had a lively intellect, stimulated by reading about natural history in her father's library and listening to his accounts of expeditions to America, Asia and the South Pacific under the patronage of aristocratic employers – but her worldly experience was limited to her own house and garden. Not for Mary the expensive education afforded her brother; she received only a little tutoring in German and that was so she could help her father translate scientific papers.

To make up for the shortfall, Mary took matters into her own hands. She subscribed to *The English Mechanic*, a weekly newspaper describing itself as a 'mirror of science and art', to provide interest and entertainment in her teenage years. Keen to learn about the physics of military mines, she conducted an experiment with a tin of gunpowder which her father had brought back from his travels. When it exploded, she realised it had been placed too close to a tub of liquid manure, which was in turn located next to a line of washing. The results were horrific. Mary probably confined her studies to the library for the next few weeks.

Mrs Kingsley's health deteriorated and when George returned home ill from a voyage abroad, Mary devoted herself to nursing them both. They died in 1892, within a few weeks of each other. Mary, at thirty years old, could probably feel the cold clutch of spinsterhood calling her into a downward spiral of loneliness and poverty. Instead, she chose freedom.

Mary's announcement that she was going to the west coast of Africa sent her friends into varying states of horror. She explained her reasons with cheerfulness and patience. Her father had been especially interested in sacrificial rituals from all over the world and she wanted to continue his work. Africa was the only continent that he had not visited; therefore she would go and live with African tribes and study their customs, while making a separate and equally detailed study of the fish that she found in the rivers. Well-meaning acquaintances regaled her with dire warnings, to which she listened politely and paid no attention.

In the late 1800s West Africa was attracting a lot of attention, predominantly for the wrong reasons. European countries, busy carving themselves a slice of the continent, paid very little respect to the native cultures. As for the wildlife, there was plenty of sport to be had. If asked, the bewhiskered pioneer-statesmen would probably have argued they were only reaping the benefits of extreme personal risk. After all, in the unforgiving glare of the African sun, there were a thousand unpleasant ways to die.

In the light of the twenty-first century it is difficult to appreciate the terrifying risks faced by a woman, alone and inexperienced, setting foot on such a shore. Mary had led a sheltered life but would have had ample time before reaching Freetown in Sierra Leone to hear horror stories of 'lost' explorers and traders in all their lurid detail. She was, however, carrying the ultimate weapon: her attitude. In her books she dwells with dry humour on her naiveté, yet it was her open-mindedness and confident expectation of honesty in return for honesty that disarmed people.

Although the interior of west Africa was largely uncharted territory, a string of busy trading ports lined the coast. Mary forged good relationships with traders and agents of the British and French

119

governments, who shook their heads over her ambitions but allowed her safe passage and did as much as possible to assist her project. Back home she had an ally in London's Natural History Museum waiting eagerly for the contents of her collecting jars: Albert Günther, eminent ichthyologist and herpetologist, whose enthusiastic interest gave Mary the encouragement to persevere.

Clear about the objects of her expeditions and the routes that she planned to take, Mary was not, however, prepared for the labyrinthine meanderings of west African rivers. Her first impressions of mangrove swamps, where the rivers empty lazily into the sea, was the nerve-jangling experience of being marooned in stinking mud at low tide as a forest of white roots rose slowly around her and crocodiles attempted to board her canoe. One particularly persistent visitor she discouraged by dealing him a smart rap on the nose with her paddle. Mary's courage never deserted her, although her heart must have been pounding in her chest.

Enlisting the services of a small band of African helpers, Mary explored the tributaries and rapids of the Ogowé river and trekked many miles on foot through dense rainforest. While she had brought supplies of quinine and a basic medical kit, her practical attitude had not extended to clothing suitable for the hot and humid conditions; she wore exactly the same dress, complete with high-collared black blouse and long voluminous skirts, that she would have worn to a British tea party. Her eccentricity saved her life when she fell into a game trap. This carefully camouflaged pit contained sharp spikes of ebony designed to impale unfortunate animals; Mary's thick skirts snagged on the spears and protected her flesh. She was hauled out, shaken but valiant. Five minutes after she was rescued, one of her bare-legged companions dropped into a second game trap and sustained some nasty injuries. As she bound up his wounds Mary considered herself extremely lucky, and blessed herself for her choice of garments.

Mary took particular care in fulfilling the other purpose of her visit, to study and document the spiritual beliefs of distinct African tribes. Some of these were cannibalistic, but far from regarding them with the abhorrence of her peers, she had a genuine interest in their motives and practices. Winning their trust was, of course, her first priority, or her experience might become all too personal. It is difficult to know how she slept easily at night as their guest; she would always explore her quarters first, and on one occasion she discovered the remnants of an earlier feast still lingering in various stages of decomposition.

Not only did she establish a mutual respect with tribes such as the Fang of Cameroon, carefully recording their particular rituals and beliefs from more than one source to ensure authenticity, but she also negotiated with them to save one of her party who had somehow overstepped the mark and been bound up ready for consumption. This was not the last time that Mary had to plead for her companions' lives, 'for there was not a single crime that my three men were not taxed with having committed, and not only they themselves, but their maternal ancestors (paternal do not count) before them.'[2]

In Old Calabar in Nigeria, Mary met the Dundee-born Mary Slessor, a missionary who had been in Africa for eighteen years and was focusing her attention on dispelling a long-standing superstition among the local people about the birth of twins. It was widely believed that twins were a mark of evil; for that reason both babies and the mother were often killed. Slessor had already helped to save the lives of many women and children, and had set up a makeshift home for them while slowly persuading the people to give up their practice. She was held in high esteem by the villagers and Mary Kingsley greatly admired her.

Trading was a skill Mary learned early in her travels, and she always carried items she could barter. On one occasion, to help herself out of a tight spot, she even parted with several of her own blouses, one of which was soon adorning the shoulders of a proud young warrior. She disliked killing and did not carry a gun, reasoning that it was useless against large mammals and that to brandish such a weapon amongst the Africans would be asking for trouble. Her respect for the beauty of the wildlife she encountered is refreshing and admirable. Far from seeing herself as the mistress of her domain, as colonialists were inclined to do, she often felt like an intruder, catching her breath at the beauty of a leopard seen at close range with an awe that seemed to transcend her fear.

121

Demonstrating a physical resilience that astonished even herself, Mary climbed Mount Cameroon, camping in uncomfortable conditions and dealing briskly with the laziness of her long-suffering companions. She was disappointed, on reaching the 13,200-foot summit, to find that dense mist had robbed her of all the panoramic views she had promised herself.

It is interesting to wonder how the audience of the Royal Scottish Geographical Society reacted to tales of Mary's adventure, when she revealed that wading for two hours up to her chin through a tidal swamp gave her an 'astrachan collar of leeches' and afterwards she felt weak from loss of blood. Fortunately, she and her party had plenty of salt which they hastily applied to the leeches, and Mary was ready to continue after a short rest. The rivers had larger inhabitants, however, from which even a canoe did not offer a great deal of protection:

> We were skirting a long stretch of high hippo grass, my crew cheerily singing their boat song, when an immense hippo rose up on the grass alongside, about six feet from us, stared calmly, and then yawned a yawn a yard wide, and grunted the news of our arrival to his companions, who also rose up, and strolled through the grass with the flowing grace of Pantechnicon vans.[3]

Mary did not speak to the Edinburgh audience herself; she had pleaded indisposition, and at her request Colonel Bailey, Secretary of the RSGS, was reading her paper for her. In Glasgow the next evening she showed the same shyness.

Why did she not wish to speak? There could be several reasons, one of course being genuine indisposition. There are other possibilities: this was Mary's first ever public presentation, and the fear kept firmly bottled amongst the crocodile-infested swamps might finally have got the better of her. She may have been painfully conscious of her educational shortcomings – she parodied her ignorance with great humour in her books but it was a different matter to face an illustrious academic society in person. She may also have felt it was unbecoming for a woman to put herself forward; while exhibiting an extraordinary degree of courage in her travels, at home she took pains to dress and behave with spotless respectability, and vehemently opposed the women's suffrage movement which was gaining momentum at the time.

Mary did, however, have some strong beliefs about the attitudes of Western countries towards indigenous African tribes. She expressed her opinion that they should be allowed to continue in their traditional lifestyles unhindered by most of the 'improvements' of European civilisation. Although she claimed to be an imperialist, it was obvious that she had reservations, and her outspokenness laid her open to criticism from politicians and journalists.

In her address to the RSGS, Mary dwelt at length on the characteristics of the Fang, describing their society and customs as if they were her close friends, a tribute which many of them would have acknowledged to be entirely mutual. As a mark of their regard, they had taken her deep within the rainforest to see a family of gorillas, which she watched in awed silence as they groomed and fed. Mary and her companions remained hidden at a distance of about 30 yards – until, that is, her guide was overcome by a sneezing fit which alarmed the animals so much the young ones fled for cover while the male stood to see where the noise was coming from. After a tense few seconds he followed his family into the forest, leaving Mary to marvel at his 'powerful, graceful, superbly perfect trapeze performance'.[4]

In Cameroon, Gabon, Angola and the Congo, Mary made valuable observations about the courses and ecology of rivers. Of the sixty-five species of freshwater fish she brought back to Scotland, seven were new to science and three now bear her name. Mary's most lasting contribution is, however, harder to quantify. In her books she apologises often and profusely for being an erratic diarist, an incompetent mountaineer, a hopeless geographer. Her achievements tell a different story.

Unfortunately, Mary had only a short time in which to enjoy her acclaim. In 1900, at the age of thirty-seven, she travelled to Simon's Town in South Africa to help nurse soldiers wounded in the Boer War. The hospital was rife with disease and she realised too late that she was in a new kind of danger; within a few months, she had died of typhoid.

With hindsight, it is easy to understand why Mary's contemporaries were at a loss to know what to make of her. She carried no arrogance of power, no superiority of intention. She trod lightly, seeing past the colour of people's skin and leaving respect and appreciation in her wake. When the world was closing in on Africa, she defied the obsessions of acquisitive empires and proved what could be achieved with an open mind.

1-3. Mary Kingsley 'Travels on the Western Coast of Equatorial Africa', *Scottish Geographical Magazine* (1896) 12:3

4. *Travels in West Africa, Congo Français, Corisco and Cameroons* (1897) by Mary Kingsley

Dr Sven Anders Hedin

Explorer of Central Asia
Born: 19th February 1865 (Stockholm)
Died: 26th November 1952 (Stockholm)
§
RSGS Silver Medal, 1897
Livingstone Medal, 1902
Gold (Scottish Geographical) Medal, 1908

The hardships endured by the explorer in travelling through this dreary wilderness were truly appalling. During the first year he travelled for nearly three months through a ghastly country without meeting a single human being apart from his own companions.[1]

THE ROYAL SCOTTISH Geographical Society was preparing to entertain a very distinguished guest on the evening of 16th February 1909. The newspapers were full of his forthcoming address and excitement about his recent geographical achievements; even his personal charm and mannerisms were discussed with enthusiasm. Such was his popularity that the Secretary of the RSGS had been forced to stop selling tickets 'in self-defence'[2]. So who was the red-hot celebrity, the intrepid traveller in the 'ghastly country' of Tibet?

Sven Hedin, whose name has all but disappeared from the annals of exploration.

Three years earlier, amid the ostentatious splendour of Imperial India, the forty-one-year-old Swede was preparing for an expedition. British officials had forbidden him to enter Tibet, and therefore he only had a passport for Eastern Turkestan. He was relying on the fact that no one knew exactly where the Tibetan border was, because it was so bitterly disputed. By the time his absence was noticed he would be long gone.

Over dinner at his hotel in Srinagar that night, there was only one topic of conversation. Everyone was animated by the rumour that a famous explorer had arrived and was about to embark on a dangerous trek. He listened without saying anything. Sven Hedin had an uncanny way of making himself invisible.

Over the coming weeks he gathered mules and supplies. He hired a cook and a meteorological assistant, and was given an escort of four soldiers by the private secretary to the Maharajah of Kashmir. Sir Francis Younghusband had recommended a reliable 'caravan-bashi' or leader who had been with him on his own expeditions, and Hedin hired him without hesitation. He purchased stores of rice, maize, meal and barley, and packed his travelling chests with chronometers, compasses, cameras and sketchbooks. Burroughs, Wellcome & Co. of London had sent him a splendid medicine box which was a work of art, its remedies all beautifully labelled. He carried money-bags with 22,000 silver and 9,000 gold rupees, a revolver and a rifle, and even a small boat with oars and a sail.

Burdened animals struggled over steps cut into the narrow cliffside ledge of the Zoji La Pass. In Leh, the capital of the ancient kingdom of Ladakh, Hedin hired more men and horses. On 17th August the caravan set off up the Chang La Pass and into the rarefied air of the mountains. When they reached the summit, 17,590 feet above sea level, cold wind was ripping at an assortment of coloured streamers, each one representing a prayer. As Hedin's Ladakhi companions cheered and swung their caps in celebration, the party was hit by a passing hail shower which stung the flesh like a whip. Uncharted, uninhabited country lay before them, and they would need all the prayers they could get.

Hedin's expedition, which he recounted to the RSGS, took three years and led him across the western highlands of Tibet to the Trans-Himalaya, which for a short time was called the Hedin Range in his honour.

Once in Tibet, Hedin disguised himself as a Ladakhi, dismissed his old porters to hire new ones, and burned all his European clothes. This was a forbidden land and the penalties for trespassing were severe. He painted his face and hands to disguise his pale skin from the eyes of officials, though on one occasion when his presence was suspected he decided to brazen it out and tell them the truth. They may not have believed him, especially in view of his ragged appearance; in any case, the encounter ended with good humour, and he was allowed to carry on.

Hedin explored Lake Manasarovar and Mount Kailash, and traced the sources of the Indus and Brahmaputra rivers. He described the custom of young Tibetan lamas who chose to live in 'dark grottoes', voluntarily allowing themselves to be walled in, existing in complete darkness until they died. In the monastery of Tashi Lhunpo in Shigatse he had an audience with the ninth Tashi Lama, to whom he gave his cherished medicine box.

> The Tashi-lama, or Panchen Rinpoche... is one of the most remarkable and fascinating men I have met in my life, and I shall never forget the great hospitality and kindness he showed me so long as I was his guest. I arrived just at the time of the Losar, or New Year's festivals, and was invited to every day's play. How very wonderful and picturesque it all was![3]

Central Asia was still a largely unexplored region, full of vast mountain ranges and barren desert, and its wild, mysterious beauty drew Hedin like a moth to a flame. Romance, however, was not his only motivation; he was serious about his geographical work, having studied under the acknowledged European experts of the time. On his expeditions he made careful notes of the landscape and topography, collected rock samples, kept copious journals, took photographs and made beautiful sketches of people and buildings. At the height of his fame he was honoured by royalty and feted all across Europe; his lecture tours often sparked scenes of uncontrolled hysteria. On his arrival at Manchester University, for example, hordes of cheering students extracted him bodily from his car and carried him on their shoulders around the quadrangle before treating him to an impromptu display of chair-juggling and boisterous singing in the Whitworth Hall, where he was due to give an address. To their delight, Hedin displayed his considerable artistic talent by sketching a Tibetan soldier on a blackboard; later this was proudly 'varnished and hung in the Valhalla of fame in the Varsity Union'.[4]

After Hedin's lecture in Glasgow, the newspapers enthused about his youthful-looking figure and his exceptionally modest demeanour, noting that 'he might have been reciting the tale of another man's adventures, so careful was he to avoid the slightest suspicion of egotism or boasting'.[5] He spoke without notes, retaining every detail of the expedition in his remarkable memory, and displayed many of his own photographs, pencil drawings and aquarelles.

Sven Hedin may have been a superstar but he was also an enigma. Personality obviously took a back seat to professionalism, at least on the lecture circuit. In his books, he charts his progress by consecutively numbered camps and records the losses of horses, mules, camels and yaks in terms of steadily increasing figures, suggesting a cold nature that has witnessed death many times and sees it as a mere inconvenience. Yet his descriptive writing is evocative and his response to new lands and new discoveries full of pleasure and reverence. Hedin had the soul of a nomad; where was his heart?

In 1893, a beautiful young Swedish woman called Marie 'Mille' Broman could have given an answer. She had captivated Hedin and her treatment of him, flirtatious and distant by turns, drove him mad. He was leaving to go on a trek through the Pamir Mountains and the Taklamakan Desert, a journey which would take several years, and begged her to wait for him. Mille thought this was too much to ask. With all the passion of an unrequited lover, Hedin sailed away in the vain hope of proving his worth; two years into the trip, he received a message saying that she was engaged to someone else.

The news arrived at a critical moment. Hedin was on the edge of the Taklamakan Desert, bracing himself to attempt a crossing. Difficulties in obtaining enough camels had delayed his departure and with the hot, dry season approaching he knew he should wait. Mille's letter changed everything; as life was no longer worth living, he decided he would rather die of thirst in the desert than kick his heels and suffer in idleness. As the sun rose on 10th April, he gathered his caravan together and set off from Merket.

Hedin paid dearly for his rashness. Not for nothing was the Taklamakan called the 'Sea of Death'. The accuracy of his accounts has been questioned, but it seems he only took half the drinking water necessary for his party's survival. According to another source, it is physically impossible to carry sufficient water for a crossing during that season. In any case, at least one of his escorts died of thirst along with seven of the party's camels. Hedin continued to conduct his research with obsessive fervour but enthusiasm soon turned to desperation. Less than three weeks after setting out, the cravings of thirst took over his mind.

Throats on fire, unable to swallow food, he and a companion named Kasim left the dying camels and continued on foot. Digging for water yielded nothing. After wandering for two days they found to their horror that they had travelled in a circle. Seeing Kasim too weak to walk, Hedin promised to return with water and struggled on alone. Several miles on, as he felt his life force ebbing, he discovered a patch of trees, a dried river bed – and a pool. He quenched his thirst, offered a prayer of thanks, then filled his boots with water and went to Kasim's aid.

By pure chance, Hedin had reached Khotan on the south-western fringe of the desert. Fresh human footprints led him to the huts of nomadic shepherds, who gave him the first food he had eaten for a week. While he slowly recovered, two of his companions, including Kasim, were rescued and reunited with him.

Hedin's ordeal was over, but his adventure was still unfolding. In January 1896 he rediscovered the abandoned oasis town of Dandan Oilik, a sixth century settlement on the Silk Road, where he found evidence of a once-fertile city: the remains of hundreds of wooden houses; a 'temple of Buddha' adorned with wall paintings; and traces of gardens and fruit trees. The site has since yielded rich and fascinating archaeological treasures even though it remains largely unexcavated to this day.

In March the same year he discovered Lake Bosten, one of the largest inland lakes in Central Asia, and noted that it was fed by the Kaidu River. He returned via Khotan, crossing northern Tibet and China to Beijing, where he arrived in March 1897 having travelled 16,000 miles, of which 2,200 were previously uncharted; his maps alone covered 552 sheets.

On his return to Stockholm, Hedin discovered that the rumour of Mille's engagement had been untrue, and sought her out with fresh hope. She told him she would only consent to marry him if he gave up exploring. He angrily refused and instead threw himself into planning his next expedition. Meanwhile Mille accepted another suitor – then, at the last minute, regretted her decision. She wrote a tearful letter to Hedin, declaring her love and begging him to rescue her. Before she could post it she received a note from Hedin offering his formal congratulations on her engagement. Mille never sent her letter and Hedin, who was leaving on another trek, did not hear of her change of heart until eleven years later. By that time, she was already married.

Hiding his grief, Hedin focused his passion on the physical and intellectual demands of his explorations, which became ever more ambitious. Between 1927 and 1935 he mounted an international expedition consisting of specialist scientists from Sweden, Germany and China, with himself as the logistical leader. The party explored Mongolia, the Gobi Desert and Xinjiang, studying the archaeology, wildlife and climate like a travelling university. Hedin solved the puzzle of the 'wandering' lake of Lop Nor, which was caused by the changing course of the Tarim River. He located over 300 important archaeological sites, bringing countless precious relics and manuscripts to light after centuries in the sand and discovered sources of valuable minerals including coal and gold. He also had an unwished-for encounter with Ma Zhongying, the same warlord who had 'entertained' Mildred Cable and her companions against their will (see p.286). Ma Zhongying hijacked Hedin's caravan and detained him for a while, but eventually let him go.

Hedin earned himself a dazzling battery of awards and was regarded as untitled nobility in his home country of Sweden. His lecture tour of Europe in 1935 covered 25,000 miles, equivalent to the length of the Equator. A prolific writer, he produced a stream of books that were devoured by an adoring public. One of his greatest contributions to geography was the *Central Asia Atlas*, published after his death.

Sven Hedin never married and had no children. As he once remarked, Asia had become his 'cold bride'. In photographs from the time he is always smartly top-hatted and great-coated, smiling suavely as he is accompanied into yet another illustrious venue. When he died in 1952, a photograph of Mille Broman was found in his diary by his bedside. He had buried his heartbreak very deep.

1-2. *Evening Dispatch*, 16th February 1909

3. 'Journeys in Tibet, 1906-1908' by Dr Sven Hedin, *Scottish Geographical Magazine* (1909) 25:4, 169-195

4. *Manchester Guardian*, 15th February 1909

5. *Glasgow Herald*, 18th February 1909

Dame Freya Madeleine Stark

Explorer and writer
BORN: 31st January 1893 (Paris)
DIED: 9th May 1993 (Asolo, Italy)
§
RSGS Mungo Park Medal, 1935

D AMASCUS, MARCH 1928: the lemon trees were dusted with
snow and the temperature inside the house was well below
freezing. In a tiny rented room, in a bed alive with fleas,
Freya Stark was shivering with cold and racked by the cramps of
dysentery. It was hardly an auspicious start to her long-anticipated
journey through a land which had haunted her childhood dreams.
For Freya's irrepressible spirit, however, this was just a pothole on
the road to adventure.

Freya Madeleine Stark was born in Paris in 1893, the elder daughter
of two artists who were also first cousins. Her mother, Flora, was a
celebrated beauty but incapable of giving her daughters the love that
they craved, so Freya turned to her father for affection and security.
A lover of nature, in the woods close to their Devon home he would
challenge her to face her fears and walk back to the house alone in
the dark.

Intuitive and intelligent, Freya was a gifted child and avid reader,
devouring the classics and falling under the spell of *One Thousand
and One Nights*. Something about the rich legends of the Middle East
held her imagination captive from an early age, but she would suffer
many emotional blows before she could set foot there.

The first came when her parents separated and Freya and her sister
went to live with their mother in Italy. Flora Stark was impractical
and capricious, and allowed herself to be flattered by a young man

with a persuasive manner and designs on her money and her daughters. Freya devoted most of her young adult years to managing her mother, but when her sister married unhappily and died young, Freya vowed that she would live the rest of her life on her own terms.

Freya served as a nurse in the Great War and suffered heartache when her fiancé rejected her for another woman. Somehow, her joyous spirit survived. Still secretly dreaming of Damascus, she learned Arabic, much to the curiosity of her relatives and friends. She still had a habit of idolising ill-chosen men, who either died or proved themselves entirely unsuitable for her. In an era when marriage was the 'done thing' for respectable women, Freya struggled and refused to be tamed.

Freya's long-overdue arrival in the Middle East filled her with joy. Her first sight of the desert came as a 'shock of beauty'; having driven out of Damascus and past the fringes of human settlement, she watched a camel train several hundred strong pass around her like a rolling wave, reminiscent of the dunes themselves. From the outset, she was determined to be more than a sightseer, more than the kind of traveller who watches from a safe distance.

Shortly after her arrival in Damascus Freya was joined by her good friend Venetia Buddicom, whom she had met six years before on the Italian Riviera. Venetia shared Freya's lively sense of humour and was looking forward to being shown around the places of cultural and historical interest. Freya had written to tell her about a special excursion that she was planning but Venetia had a few doubts. It is easy to understand why.

Several days' ride out of Damascus lay a region called the Jebel Druze, or 'mountain of the Druze'. The Druze are a religious sect whose history stretches back to an ancient and complex rift in the Islamic faith. At the time of Freya's arrival in 1928 they were known to be secretive and deeply suspicious of outsiders, although in the previous 120 years they had received visits from two intrepid lady travellers: Lady Hester Stanhope in 1812, and Gertrude Bell in 1900. Stanhope had described their rituals with horrified fascination and warned that strangers asking questions about religion were likely to be murdered. More recently, the Druze had taken part in the Syrian

Revolt of 1925, an act of uprising rejecting the imposition of French authority at the end of the Great War. Bombed and disarmed, and living under the shadow of a military garrison, the Druze were now licking their wounds and could not be expected to offer visitors the warmest of welcomes.

For Freya, whose curiosity was enlivened by risk, they posed a delicious temptation. Slipping into the Syrian desert amidst a twilight heavy with the perfume of dianthus blossom, Freya and Venetia rode two donkeys and carried the lightest of luggage. Though already in forbidden territory they had hired a local guide, Najm, himself a Druze. This in itself held no guarantee of success; Freya wanted to penetrate into the furthest strongholds of the mountain where the elders or sages of the sect were known to dwell, and they shared their secrets with no one. Just how Freya intended to prise them out is an interesting question.

After five days of travelling, evading the notice of passing French military vehicles and accepting hospitality in desert villages, they arrived at Shabha in the centre of Druze territory. Before they could settle down for the night, they were arrested by French military police.

'Why had they ridden into the Jebel Druze?' Freya had a ready answer for that, and for every other question posed by her interrogators. They had ridden, she said, purely because they were unaware that there were proper roads. If the French garrison could be troubled to make this feature better known, their prospects as a tourist destination would be greatly increased. 'Were the ladies not aware that they were in grave danger?' Perhaps, admitted Freya, but they felt completely safe now. She smiled with devastating charm, which hid a multitude of seething thoughts. Chief among them was the existence of a notebook in which she had scribbled some very unflattering observations about the French; she demanded access to her confiscated luggage and, in the blink of Najm's unsuspecting eye, she snatched it out and stuffed it into his waistcloth, guessing he would not be searched. Najm himself was too horrified to speak.

Back in the privacy of their room, Freya and Venetia giggled like naughty schoolgirls while the French commander pondered the claims of his unexpected guests. Were they really tourists? Or were they, in fact, spies?

Flipping through Freya's copy of Cook's *Tourists' Handbook for Palestine and Syria*, he dismissed the idea. Two such hapless females could know nothing about the art of deception. He underestimated Freya; in her bag was a letter to one of the Druze leaders, given to her by an acquaintance in Brummana whose childhood nurse had once served in the chieftain's camp. Letters, or the promise of them, always had the power to open doors. She was nothing if not prepared, and her network of contacts would have done justice to MI6.

Freya's femininity won the day. By the time she and Venetia were released, their captors had entrusted them with an important message to the supreme spiritual leader of the Druze, whom Freya would not otherwise have dared approach. There was a nasty moment at parting, when the commanding officer chivalrously offered to accompany them all the way to the settlement; Freya deftly turned it into a joke and the two 'distinguished women' waved farewell amid gracious laughter.

A few hours later, as welcome guests of the High Priest of the Druze, Freya and Venetia delivered the letter and did their best to answer his questions. He wanted to know about the religions of Tibet and India – what they worshipped, and what they believed. Freya was dimly aware of a long-held belief among the Druze that a far-off sect, unidentified but sharing a common lineage, would rise up and come to their assistance. Everywhere among the scattered villages, the men's pride was stained with sadness. Sheikh Mut'ib el Atrash, once a powerful war leader, apologised for living in a nomad's tent, and showed them his cloak riddled with bullet holes. They had, he said, no choice but to wait, but they were a strong and resilient people.

Freya looked and listened; later, through her writing, she voiced her disgust at their treatment under a scheme which allowed them no self-respect and no cultural freedom.

Eight years later, in 1936, Freya Stark was a guest lecturer at the Royal Scottish Geographical Society. By this time she was an experienced traveller and her knowledge of the Silk Routes, the merchants who used them and the goods that they carried, made for a fascinating narrative.

A number of commodities recall this traffic by their names: gauze from Gaza, damascene blades from Damascus, fustian from Fustát – the first Islamic capital near Cairo – and muslins from Mosul. These muslins had an interesting history: they were taken overland from Mosul to the Mediterranean, where Italian merchants shipped them to Europe. Such merchants were called from their wares mussolinis, or carriers of muslins from Mosul.

In particular, Freya discussed the ancient origin of the word 'assassin', which was introduced into Europe during the Crusades. Explaining its derivation from the Arabic *hashishin*, 'users of hashish', she took her listeners back to the eleventh century when a passionate young nationalist named Hassan-i-Sabbah rebelled against the Turks. Exiled, he wandered as an outcast in the Elburz mountains of northern Iran, finding ready support among the people of the remote villages; Freya compared them to the Highland clans who rallied around Bonnie Prince Charlie in 1745.

Hassan gathered a band of devoted followers and established a capital for his new sect in the valley of Alamut, building a string of castles from the eastern borders of Iran across to the south-west corner of Arabia. According to tradition, Hassan was known as the 'Old Man of the Mountain', and had an original way of inspiring a sense of fanatical duty in his warriors: he invited young men into a lush green garden where delicious fruits and fragrant plants were growing, and beautiful girls were ready to entertain them. The men were offered hashish to enhance their experience, and when its effects wore off they were utterly convinced that Hassan 'held the gates of Paradise ready for them at their death'. As a result, they could be bidden to carry out any number of premeditated murders without fear. Their success rate soon meant that the word 'Assassin' struck terror into rulers all across the Middle East and Europe.

One of the first known versions of this story comes from Marco Polo, who heard it from two men of Alamut. In 1272, while in Acre on a Crusade, King Edward I was stabbed by an Assassin carrying a poisoned dagger, and only just survived.

Freya, with her love of romance, was lured by these tales into northern Iran to seek the fragments of Hassan's ancient stronghold, nearly 680 years after its downfall at the hands of Mongol armies. There had been a handful of other visitors to the valley of Alamut before, but she intended to make new discoveries.

> I decided to climb into it from Kazvin and then to make over the watershed to the Caspian, in more or less new country whose blankness on the map made it look very alluring.

By the time she was ready to set off, Freya's unusual quest had attracted so much support from the inhabitants of Kazvin that she was receiving daily visits from townspeople offering 'gossip, advice, and quotations from the poets.' On 15th May 1930, having hired a couple of local men as guides, she travelled into the Elburz mountains by mule.

The fleeting season of wild flowers was at its best: scabious, periwinkles, poppies and forget-me-nots mingled with lilies and delphiniums to weave a brilliant carpet of colour. From the heights of the Chala Pass she looked across at a mountain known as the Throne of Solomon and noticed mulberry and walnut trees along the streams, with juniper hugging the wind-scoured slopes. On the third evening she reached the magnificent pinnacle of rock on which the citadel of Alamut stood, its gaunt ruins bathed in the glow of sunset. Scrambling up to the fortress, Freya saw it had been shaped to occupy its natural clifftop platform. Although red and yellow tulips were blossoming in the crevices, she concluded that Hassan's garden of paradise could never have existed there. Re-reading Marco Polo's description, she realised that the whole valley was 'the place called Alamut', and the fertile oases by the castle were the original sites of rich palaces and gardens. Further exploration revealed more fortresses, one of them thousands of feet above the village of Garmarud; Freya believed that she was the only European at that time to have reached it.

Passing out of the valley, Freya made her way through dense forest where bridges spanned the foaming Seh Hizar River and herds of small black cattle were tended by isolated woodland dwellers. By the time she reached Resht on the shore of the Caspian Sea she had only ninepence in her pocket, but received a warm welcome from the British Consul. With characteristic good fortune she managed to secure a free lift back to Kazvin where she arrived at midnight, tired and hungry. She was already planning to go back.

On subsequent visits she explored the valleys of Talaghan to the south and Shahrud to the west:

> During the following year I visited these two also, and found in the latter the city of Shahristan, probably the ancient capital of the Daylamites, and the ruins of Lamiasar, one of the most important of the Assassin castles, which held out for over a year against the Mongol armies and whose location had never been ascertained.

After her address to the RSGS, Freya Stark was presented with the Society's Mungo Park Medal for her explorations in northern Persia. Accepting her prize gracefully, Freya thanked the Society for the honour, which she preferred to look upon as encouragement rather than recognition. It was one of many accolades gathered during her lifetime, all of which she greatly prized. Part of her was seeking to 'fit in' to starched British society when all the time her spirit was lifting her above the boundaries of race and class and station.

Although her enduring legacy is the excellent descriptive writing in her books, Freya was also a gifted diplomat. During the Second World War she placed her knowledge at the service of the British Ministry of Information and helped establish the Brotherhood of Freedom, which urged communities in Arab countries to support the Allied forces.

A passionate and impulsive explorer, she travelled for the joy of it, and perhaps because the little girl in her was still proving to her father that she could find her way alone through a strange and frightening country. She was still going on expeditions when she was in her eighties. A smile should never be underestimated, she said: it can take you a long way.

All references in this chapter from Freya Stark 'The Valleys of the Assassins to the Caspian Sea', *Scottish Geographical Magazine* (1937) 53:3, 155-166

BERTRAM SIDNEY THOMAS

Desert explorer
Born: 13th June 1892 (Pill, Somerset)
Died: 27th December 1950 (Cairo)
§
RSGS Livingstone Medal, 1932

Arabia was, from the point of view of the European explorer, the forbidden country... The blank map itself was a provocation.

A T MIDNIGHT ON 4th October 1930, HMS *Cyclamen* rested at anchor in the port of Muscat. While the town slept, some hushed activity was taking place on the shore. Presently, a rowing boat nosed gently alongside the naval vessel and, after a few minutes, the boatmen pulled out into the open sea with a quiet dipping of oars. Under cover of darkness, Bertram Thomas was about to embark on his long-anticipated journey across the desert of southern Arabia.

So great was the risk of Thomas's proposed undertaking that he only admitted a handful of people into his confidence. By morning, he knew that countless horrible fates would have been invented for him by fertile imaginations but he would be long gone, having secretly transferred himself from HMS *Cyclamen* to the SS *British Grenadier*, which would bear him towards his chosen starting point. To all intents and purposes he was going to disappear for several months; fate would decide whether he returned to the known world or died in one of the most hostile environments on Earth.

Stretching across the southern end of the Arabian Peninsula, the Rub' al Khali or 'Empty Quarter' encompasses about 250,000 square miles and, in terms of volume, is the largest sand desert in the world (although the Sahara covers an area fifteen times greater). Waterholes are few and yield only bitter-tasting water; waves of sand dunes rise to over 800 feet. Daytime temperatures can rise above 50°C, and scattered archaeological remains lie baking in the relentless sun.

Bertram Thomas was no stranger to the Rub' al Khali. After the Great War, during which he had served in Belgium and in Mesopotamia, he was appointed Assistant British Representative in Transjordan. By 1924 he had risen to become the 'Wazir' or Prime Minister of Muscat, and was an honoured companion of the Sultan himself. The Sultan knew of Thomas's love affair with the desert and teased him about it, but would certainly have forbidden any attempted crossing. Thomas knew better than to seek his consent. He kept his own counsel, making several excursions by camel into the desert to plan his route.

In addition to its climate, the Rub' al Khali held another danger, even more deadly: the territories Thomas proposed to cross were jealously guarded by warring Bedouin tribes, for whom the presence of a stranger was an open invitation to murder. Feuding was rife, and revenge killings were carried out according to a complex moral code that had existed for generations. Travelling alone would mean certain death, so he needed to gather a band of reliable companions who were willing to share his adventure. Such was the danger that he would have to travel in several relays, leaving his old escort behind when he crossed a border between one tribe and the next, and relying on the goodwill of new companions to continue his journey. Negotiating skills were going to be at a premium. Fortunately, Thomas spoke the languages of the desert dwellers, understood their faith and knew their customs. Not only was he going to depend on them for his life but he hoped to gain their permission to study their defining tribal characteristics. Some people would have said he was insane.

Only the first few hours of Thomas's expedition went according to plan. From the SS *British Grenadier*, he was taken ashore at Salalah in a dhow. Kicking his heels in the fort of Dhofar, he waited in vain for the appearance of Sahail the Rashidi, who had assisted him on a secret reconnaissance trip the year before and promised to return at the appointed hour. Sahail had taken Thomas's security of two hundred dollars and a dagger, and disappeared into the desert. A year

INAUGURATION OF THE SCOTTISH GEOGRAPHICAL SOCIETY BY MR. STANLEY.

1. Sketch by W A Donnelly depicting the inaugural address by H M Stanley to the newly-formed Scottish Geographical Society at the Music Hall, Edinburgh, on 3rd December 1884.

2. Sir Ernest Shackleton's ship *Endurance* in London docks just before departure in July 1914.

3. Sir Ernest Shackleton, Robert Falcon Scott and Edward Wilson on the *Discovery* Expedition in November 1902, pictured before their attempt to reach the South Pole.

4. Shackleton (far right) showing Queen Alexandra around his ship *Endurance* in South-west India Dock, London, on 16th July 1914.

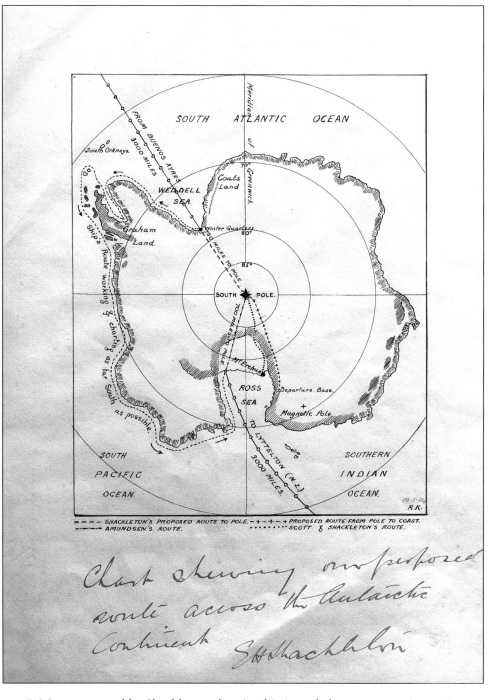

5. Map annotated by Shackleton, showing his intended route across Antarctica on the Imperial Trans-Antarctic (*Endurance*) expedition of 1914-17.

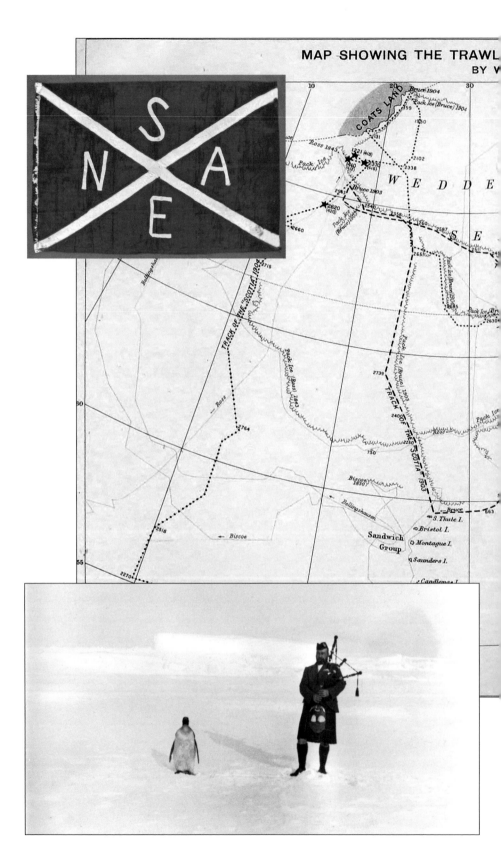

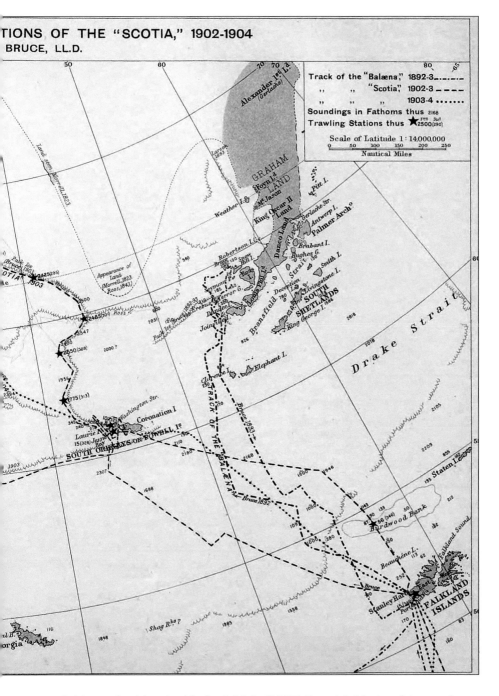

Track of the "Balæna," 1892-3
"   "   "Scotia," 1902-3
"   "   "   "   1903-4
Soundings in Fathoms thus 2168
Trawling Stations thus ★ 2500(290)

Scale of Latitude 1 : 14,000,000
0   50   100   150   200   250
Nautical Miles

6. Saltire embroidered with the initials SNAE (Scottish National Antarctic Expedition) carried by William Speirs Bruce aboard the *Scotia* (1902-1904).

7. Gilbert Kerr, SNAE piper, entertains a bemused Emperor penguin in the Antarctic.

8. Map showing the trawling stations of the *Scotia* during the Scottish National Antarctic Expedition, 1902-1904.

Siems & Hieregaard.   Kristiania.   Toldbodgaden 24.

9. Nansen's Greenland expedition, 1888-1889.
L to R: Ole Ravna, Otto Sverdrup, Fridtjof Nansen, Kristian Kristiansen,
Oluf Christian Dietrichsen, Samuel Balto. Ravna and Balto from Lapland
wear traditional 'caps of the four winds'.

10. 'Carriage by bearers' – a lady's carrying chair, photographed (and probably used) by Isabella Bird in China.

11. 'A traveller arriving at an inn in Manchuria' by Isabella Bird c.1900.

12. A four-sailed boat on the Min River, a tributary of the Upper Yangtze. Isabella Bird travelled on one of these boats.

13. Sven Hedin, photographed at the Pamir Boundary Commission in the Wakhan Corridor, 1895.

ON THE ROOF OF THE WORLD.

DR SVEN HEDIN'S LECTURE—A FASCINATING NARRATIVE.

Reading from left to right—Mrs Smith, wife of Professor George Adam Smith, D.D.; Dr Sven Hedin, Mr Paul Rottenburg, LL.D.; Major Forbes, the Hon. S. T. Von Goes (Swedish Consul), and Sir John Murray, K.C.B., who presided at last night's meeting.

14. Sven Hedin prepares to lecture to the RSGS at St Andrew's Hall in Glasgow on 17th February 1909. Note Sir John Murray on the far right.

15. Fanny Bullock Workman in 1912, posing at 21,000 feet on the Siachen Glacier (Karakoram) with a paper headed 'VOTES FOR WOMEN'.

16. Frederick Marshman Bailey in Tibet, between 1904-09.

USHER HALL, EDINBURGH.

A SPECIAL LECTURE ON

Climbing Mount Everest

1922

Will be given, on behalf of the Mount Everest Committee, by

Mr. G. H. LEIGH-MALLORY

ON

THURSDAY, NOVEMBER 9th,
at 8

Mount Everest (29 00? feet) from the Rongbuk Glacier base camp (16,500 feet).

CHAIRMAN:

John Horne, Esq.,
LL.D., F.R.S.

THE Narrative will be illustrated by many beautiful Lantern Slides from photographs taken on the Expedition.

The profits of the Lecture will be devoted to the funds of the Mount Everest Expedition Committee.

Tickets: Numbered and Reserved, 5/- & 3/-; Unnumbered, 1/- & 1/6

The general management of the Mount Everest Lectures throughout the Kingdom is in the hands of GERALD CHRISTY, The Lecture Agency, Ltd., The Outer Temple, London, W.C. 2.

P.T.O.

17. Leaflet advertising George Mallory's lecture to RSGS in November 1922. The photograph shows Everest from the Rongbuk Glacier base camp.

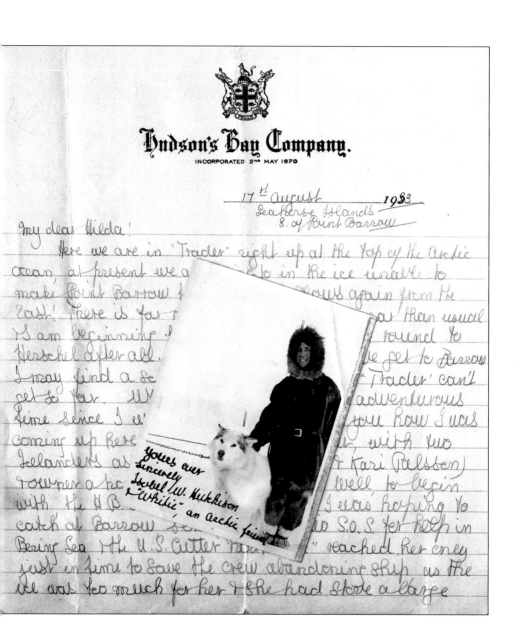

Hudson's Bay Company.
INCORPORATED 2ND MAY 1670

17th August 1933
Seahorse Islands
S. of Point Barrow

My dear Hilda!

Here we are in 'Trader' right up at the top of the Arctic ocean, at present we a[re] ...to in the ice unable to make Point Barrow f... ...ows again from the East! There is far ... ...er than usual I am beginning ... ...round to Herschel after all. ... ...e get to Barrow I may find a ... ...'Trader' can't get to ... ...adventurous time since I ... ...ow I was coming up here ... ...t, with two Islanders a... ...Kari Palsson) ...per a ... Yours ever ...well, to begin with the H.B. sincerely I was hoping to catch at Barrow Isobel W. Hutchison ...e S.O.S. for help in Bering Sea the U.S. Cutter "Whitie" an arctic friend... ...reached her only just in time to save the crew abandoning ship as the ice was too much for her & she had stove a large

18. Isobel Wylie Hutchison in Alaska, resting on the letter Isobel wrote to her sister on notepaper salvaged from the 'ghost ship', *Baychimo*.

19. TOP LEFT: Sir Alan Cobham and Sir Sefton Brancker with the de Havilland DH50 biplane used for the India flight in 1924.

20. Sir Alan Cobham landing his seaplane on the Thames in London on
1st October 1926 after his round trip to Australia.

21. Roald Amundsen by one of the Dornier flying boats used in his bid to fly to the North Pole in 1925.

22. N25 Dornier flying boat, flying up the Oslofjord on Roald Amundsen's return from the Arctic in July 1925.

23. Neil Armstrong receiving the Livingstone Medal (pictured below) from RSGS President, Lord Balerno, in March 1972.

24. First page from the RSGS Visitors' Book dated 4th and 5th December 1884. Among the first signatories are H M Stanley, Joseph Thomson, John George Bartholomew and Agnes Livingstone Bruce, daughter of David Livingstone.

later, much had changed; the Rashid and the Sa'ar tribes were at war, and for all Thomas knew, Sahail could be dead. As he gazed out at the palm-fringed sea, he began to fear his adventure was over before it had begun. He had brought a gun, camel saddles, and boxes for natural history specimens with him, but he still needed provisions, camels and, most importantly, safe passage.

Reluctantly taking two Rashidi tribesmen into his confidence, Thomas despatched a search party into the interior to bring back news. They warned him not to expect their return within forty days, and there was a good chance that they would not come back at all. He spent the next two months in limbo, dining with local merchants, watching the performance of rituals and gossiping with elders and slaves and murderers. Curiosity was growing as to his intentions, steadfastly kept secret. Prepared to abandon his plans and board a British vessel in the harbour, Thomas was delighted when the two Rashidi men arrived back in great excitement. They had not found the elusive Sahail, but brought a group of their own tribesmen, and a train of camels. Thomas's prayers had been answered.

> Twenty-five Bedouins of the desert, none of whom he had seen before, were his companions. They struck northwards over the Qara Mountains, some 3,000 feet high, through frankincense groves and thence into the great unknown Steppe... For 58 days through this wilderness he trekked by means of three relays of camels, and covered in all some 850 miles.

The account Thomas later gave of his expedition makes it sound like a smooth and uneventful passage, which it certainly was not. First, he had to persuade his potential guide, a sixty-year-old Bedouin by the name of Shaikh Salih, to take the risk. Thomas explained that he wanted to cross the desert from sea to sea, coming out at Riyadh, Bahrain or Abu Dhabi.

It was impossible, said Salih. While he could take Thomas into the southern sands, trusting God to deliver them from the Sa'ar, he would not take him into the grazing grounds of another tribe. Also, it would be Ramadan in a month's time. He washed his hands of the idea.

Knowing the pride of the Bedouin, Thomas gave him a day to ponder. On their second meeting, he made his case reasonably, and offered generous payment. The Murra tribe, he reminded Salih, were friends of the Rashid and would not offer violence. This much Salih conceded, but he insisted he could not speak for their treatment of a foreigner and a non-Muslim. Thomas was polite but persistent. With the help of an arbitrator, they came to an agreement.

As he headed into the desert on 10th December, Thomas took care to dress in the same way as his guides in order to arouse the least suspicion. His party included a cook, and their rations consisted of butter, rice and dates, and flour with which to make unleavened bread. Camels provided milk, which was a blessing as Thomas, accustomed though he was to poor water, would not drink from some of the waterholes. The temperatures, which soared during the day, fell to 8°C at night. Hunger and thirst dogged their every step.

Adrift in a vast sea of ridges and dunes, occasionally passing desolate wadi beds with groves of frankincense trees, Thomas mapped his route with a chronometer and a compass. At night he used a sextant to record the positions of the stars, but was careful to conceal his work lest he be accused of practising black magic. As the sun set, his companions told tales of honour and legend. After dark the desert sands shrieked and groaned with inexplicable noises; the starkly beautiful landscape cast a strong spell, and it was easy to be spooked. When a rare thunderstorm slashed the dark skies with lightning, the party split into three excited groups in search of rainwater and drank feverishly at the first pool they found.

Thomas collected hundreds of natural history specimens, of which twenty-one were new to science; he marvelled at towering sand dunes and inspected ancient tracks that the Bedouin assured him led to the lost city of Ubar, the 'Atlantis of the Sands'.

When Salih could go no further, new guides took Thomas through more uncharted territory. On Christmas Eve, the camp was thrown into alarm by an imminent raid; the Bedouin insisted on mounting an all-night vigil, which Thomas, dropping with exhaustion, struggled to maintain. It turned out to be a false alarm after a morning reconnaissance revealed the footprints of wolves.

On 10th January 1931, at Shanna, they turned northwards. They had covered only a third of the distance, and a huge trial of endurance still lay ahead. Through sandstorms, with the camels' milk dwindling as the beasts inevitably lost condition, the party battled bravely from waterhole to waterhole. Such was the honour of the Bedouin that not one of an advance party would quench their thirst until the rest of the caravan had caught up. Water lay at a depth of two fathoms, and Thomas remarked sadly that its brackishness could not be disguised even by desiccated soup. In late January, on reaching the waterhole of Banaiyan, he realised with a great rush of relief that the Gulf of Oman lay only 80 miles ahead.

On 5th February Thomas's party emerged safely in Doha, weary but triumphant. The news made front-page headlines in London and New York, and his achievement is still regarded as one of the finest feats of Arabian exploration.

In the years following his adventure, Thomas published a series of in-depth studies about the cultures of the people who dwelt in the Arabian desert. At that time, he undoubtedly knew more about the Rub' al Khali than anyone else in the western world. He writes candidly but makes no judgement – a tribute to his open-mindedness, as he witnessed many customs which must have shocked him. In a land where violence was commonplace, it speaks volumes about his character that he was treated with kindness and respect. The explorer Wilfred Thesiger, who crossed the Rub' al Khali in 1945, recalled being welcomed by the Bedouin people because he was of the same 'tribe' as Thomas.

At his lecture to the RSGS in December 1932, Bertram Thomas downplayed the significance of his endeavour in typical British fashion. Describing his 850-mile trek, he focused on the geography, the geology, the natural history and the anthropology rather than the hardships; his integrity and calm determination seem to shine out of the photograph that was taken as he accepted his award. He had neither sought nor received any financial help for his expedition, having funded it himself through the need for absolute secrecy. Had his life been lost, no one in the world would have known where to look for him; he loved the desert so dearly that he may have considered even that to be a worthy sacrifice.

All references in this chapter from *The Scotsman*, 16th December 1932, report of Thomas' lecture to RSGS on 15th December 1932

Dr Robert Duane Ballard

Oceanographer and deep-sea explorer
BORN: 30th June 1942 (Wichita, Kansas)
§
RSGS Livingstone Medal, 2001

ADORNED WITH BRONZE cherubs and crowned with a magnificent glass dome, the grand staircase of the *Titanic* cascaded down five decks. Its polished opulence was a source of great pride for the ship's owners, the White Star Line. Thousands of people dreamed of skimming down its graceful curves, including an American scientist named Robert Ballard. The only difference was that Ballard was born thirty years after the luxury liner came to rest on the floor of the Atlantic. To see it, he would have to find a way to get there.

Ballard has always been intrigued by the ocean. As a child, he devoured books such as Jules Verne's *Twenty Thousand Leagues Under the Sea* and studied the sea life of rock pools near his home on the coast of California. He remembers the arrival of the *Trieste*, a bathyscaphe in which Jacques Piccard and Lieutenant Don Walsh of the US Navy plumbed the Challenger Deep in the Mariana Trench. It was January 1960, and Ballard was still at high school; the idea of two men descending more than 35,700 feet to the deepest known part of the Earth's oceans was tremendously exciting. It proved to Ballard that his dream of probing beneath the surface of the sea was entirely feasible.

What Ballard imagined was far greater than the *Titanic*, colossal though the steamship was by the standards of her day. He envisaged a world in which men could live and work under water, studying the

148

ecology and environment of the oceans, and examining the geology of the sea bed. He wanted to travel down to submerged volcanoes and gaze upon the myriad strange species that exist in the perpetual darkness of the abyss. He lived in a time when most of the planet's landmass had been explored; he wanted to step into the vast waters where man had barely dipped a toe.

The problem was that technology was only just beginning to offer such opportunities and the risks were immense. The two daring pioneers on the *Trieste* had been lucky to come back alive. During the descent, which took nearly five hours, one of the windows cracked, so the crew were only able to spend about twenty minutes on the ocean floor. Afterwards, the vessel was pronounced unsafe. The US Navy sent the *Trieste* into honourable retirement, and any plans to revisit the Challenger Deep were shelved for a long time.

In 1977, Ballard gained first-hand experience of how quickly things can go wrong, while in a second-generation bathyscaphe, the *Trieste II*, which was descending into the Cayman Trench in the Caribbean. The vessel crashed into an underwater rock face, rupturing the gasoline tanks which are essential for buoyancy. Hastily dropping every ounce of ballast, the pilots made an emergency ascent, eyes glued to the instruments for a seemingly interminable period until they finally reached the surface.

This narrow escape set Ballard wondering how to avoid such danger in future – an important question because he was never going to stop exploring under water, regardless of the risks. He had spent years preparing, studying chemistry and geology at the University of California and going on to a graduate degree in geophysics at the University of Hawaii. After serving in the intelligence unit of the US Army, he was transferred to the Navy and posted to the Woods Hole Oceanographic Institute in Cape Cod. His formal assignment completed, he continued to study marine geology and ocean engineering there. By the mid-1970s he was considering the use of manned submersibles. He wanted to take one to study the Mid-Atlantic Ridge but his suggestions were met with discouragement; submersibles were risky and expensive.

Ballard decided to prove the doubters wrong. With a PhD in plate tectonics, he longed to bring himself face to face with the physical processes on the ocean floor. His enthusiasm finally paid off when he was appointed head of Project FAMOUS (French-American Mid-Ocean Underseas Study). At last he made several dives in a submersible named *Alvin* to study the rift between the eastern and western Atlantic plates and collect data that could be used to help predict earthquakes.

In the ocean's freezing depths it is difficult to imagine that a submersible could be melted by heat, but that is precisely what happened in 1979 when *Alvin* descended into the East Pacific Rise to look for hydrothermal activity. The crew could see that the temperature probe was malfunctioning, but were at a loss to know why. Meanwhile the two geologists on board marvelled at the landscape of volcanic chimneys from which plumes of black liquid were billowing. The pilot, eager to get closer, guided the vessel right over one of the chimneys to see if they could peer down into the interior. Only on their return to the surface did the designer of the temperature probe examine the device and find that the tip of the holder had melted. Even more alarmingly, he found melted fibreglass on the exterior of the submersible where it had hovered over the chimney. *Alvin* was still intact – but what if a window had melted instead?

Ballard and his colleague, Jean Francheteau, remained undeterred when their turn to descend came the next morning. On the contrary, they were excited at the prospect of glimpsing hydrothermal vents for the first time. They got their wish. In 9,000 feet of water, they stared open-mouthed at the 'black smokers' belching forth a concoction of minerals from deep below the sea bed. *Alvin*'s probe, now carefully modified, recorded temperatures of 350°C, which is hot enough to melt lead. It seemed, said Francheteau, as if these underwater siphons were connected to hell itself.

The pair's findings were revolutionary, allowing scientists an exciting insight into both the physics and the chemistry of hydrothermal vents, and later proving that some forms of marine life – crabs, clams and tube worms – could actually exist in these inhospitable cauldrons.

Ballard's ideas about deep-sea exploration continued to evolve. He had initially been convinced that the future lay in manned submersibles, but the need to protect human life made them bigger and more spacious than they otherwise would be. This increased the cost while limiting their capacity for scientific equipment. Ballard considered that the people on board any submersible were essentially spectators, unable to get out and wander around, their interaction dependent on the vessel's robotic arms. Did they really need to be there at all? Could an unmanned probe be piloted where humans dared not go, an eyeball into the unknown?

Ballard had always dreamed of sharing his passion with a much wider audience, allowing the eyes of the world to see exactly what he was seeing, in real time. He began to build a means of achieving it. His brainwave consisted of three vessels: a research ship at the surface; a large unmanned submersible below it, tethered by a cable; and a smaller capsule, containing cameras and video equipment, which could be piloted remotely into all the dark holes and corners that had previously defied exploration. Developments in fibre-optic cable allowed images to be streamed back to the research vessel, and advances in digital technology meant they could then be beamed around the world. Ballard and his team were not only making major contributions to scientific research, but were also inspiring new generations of young explorers through their direct links with colleges and institutions.

In August 1985, Ballard and a team of scientists were in a vessel in the North Atlantic, patiently towing an unmanned submersible named *Argo* back and forth over a region of sea bed considered by some die-hard optimists to be the last resting place of the *Titanic*. No trace had ever been found of the ill-fated liner, even though she had been the largest movable man-made object on Earth at the time of her sinking. The ocean was vast, and there was a chance she had disappeared altogether; the two sections which broke apart at the surface might have disintegrated on impact, or become lodged in a ravine, or simply settled into layers of sediment.

There were clues to look for, however, and Ballard had already proved how useful they could be. Earlier that year he had been asked by the US Navy to locate the wreck of a lost submarine. During the search he discovered that, although the vessel itself was hard to find, the trail of debris fanning out from the point of impact was much easier to detect. This is what he was looking for as he and his team patiently scanned the continuous stream of images that *Argo* was sending back to base.

Just after midnight on 1st September, the circular plate of a boiler, corroded but recognisable, announced to the bleary-eyed team that they were tiptoeing into the shadow of the *Titanic*.

Could humans be taken down to the wreck, to see it for themselves? Ballard found himself backtracking a little on his dismissal of manned submersibles; in July 1986, he was part of a three-man crew descending in *Alvin* with a little remote-controlled capsule, *Jason Junior*, attached to the exterior. The *Titanic* lies at a depth of about 12,500 feet and *Alvin* took nearly two and a half hours to reach the bottom. In the inky darkness, they piloted cautiously across the sea floor and peered out into the murky water.

Without warning, *Alvin*'s lights fell on an immense black wall which stretched upwards without any apparent end; it was, Ballard said, like gazing up at the walls of Troy in the middle of the night. They rose slowly upwards until the massive prow was there in front of them, looking eerily as if it was still cutting through the water.

A couple of days later, on a subsequent dive, *Alvin* alighted gently on the deck and allowed *Jason Junior* to glide noiselessly down the remains of the grand staircase while Ballard and his crew members held their breath in wonder.

As the world went wild over the news, Ballard made it clear that his team treated the wreck with the greatest respect and removed nothing from the vessel. The *Titanic* is, after all, the last resting place of over 1,500 people, and some of the relics are deeply moving. Alongside his ambitions and curiosity, Ballard has a deep empathy for those lost at sea.

Today, Ballard's lifelong passion is helping to educate and inspire a new generation of scientists. The Inner Space Center at the University of Rhode Island's Graduate School of Oceanography is his research base. In 2008 he founded the Ocean Exploration Trust, whose purpose is to conduct scientific projects using the specially commissioned ship E/V *Nautilus* and the underwater vessels *Hercules* and *Argus*. He describes himself as an explorer first and foremost; his greatest discovery, he has always maintained, is the one he is just about to make.

MICHAEL PALIN

Traveller and writer
Born: 5th May 1943 (Broomhill, Sheffield)
§
RSGS Livingstone Medal, 2008
Fellow of RSGS, 1993

WHAT IS IT LIKE TO cross the International Date Line? To play dhaemon in the sand with camel droppings? To play football with Tibetan monks, or sit on the 'Number One Toilet in Heaven and Earth'? The answers to all these irresistible questions, and many more besides, have been shared with the public by Michael Palin over the last three decades.

In 1989, Palin accepted a challenge to follow in the footsteps of Jules Verne's fictional character Phileas Fogg and travel around the world in eighty days, taking a large number of his fans by surprise. The British public already knew and loved him as a comedian and founder member of Monty Python. Palin was often cast as a rather simple, self-effacing character who felt the sharp end of John Cleese's acerbic wit.

Now, faced with a mind-boggling eighty-day deadline, Palin was contemplating a non-stop trek of 28,000 miles by land and sea. It was a huge commitment and included a fair amount of personal risk. What was he thinking of? As he said himself, he had always been anxious about everything he had done. He felt a burden of pressure, and began to wonder whether he was really up to the job.

The answer turned out to be an emphatic yes. Not only did Palin complete his challenge within the allotted time, but he also created a series for television that was completely unlike anything that had been produced before. Until then, travel presenters had been fairly stiff and formal; their purpose was to educate in a strictly old-fashioned manner. They certainly would not have complained about diarrhoea while they were sailing in a dhow across the Persian Gulf. But it was his honesty that endeared Palin to his audience. After this disclosure to the camera, he felt that he had passed an important turning point; from now on, he could just be himself.

Developing a style that was charmingly his own, Palin took on a succession of challenges that included *Pole to Pole* in 1991 and *Full Circle* in 1995-96, which saw him circumnavigate the lands around the Pacific Ocean. Between February 2001 and February 2002 he crossed the Sahara in a mammoth expedition that saw him bumped and lurched on a variety of uncomfortable vehicles from Tangier all the way down to Mauritania and Senegal; he turned east through Mali and then headed back up across Algeria and Libya, skirting the Mediterranean coast from Tunisia to Morocco. With refreshing openness he shared all the aspects of the trip – not just the exhilaration and the excitement but also the frustration, the anxiety, the danger and the lack of hygiene.

Meanwhile, in sitting rooms across Britain, a quiet revolution was beginning to take place. In a phenomenon nicknamed 'the Palin effect', thousands of armchair travellers were emboldened to pack their bags and head off for the places that they had seen in Palin's programmes, to experience them for themselves. All of a sudden the world seemed closer, more accessible.

As more adventures followed, Palin's TV ratings soared, reaching a peak at 12.5 million, while his accompanying books shot straight into the bestseller lists. No one was more surprised by his success than Palin himself. As a child, one of his hobbies was train spotting, but that was still a world away from the globetrotting adventurer or 'accidental traveller' that he has now become. His mild manners and abiding good nature have earned him the unofficial title of 'Britain's nicest man', an epithet which he downplays with typical modesty. In his own words, he is 'always the pupil, never the professor.'[1]

The 'Number One Toilet in Heaven and Earth', incidentally, is a simple lavatory, half-open to the elements, jutting out over the dizzying chasm of Tiger Leaping Gorge.

Palin is not afraid to do the things aspiring travellers would be most curious about: he describes the dilemma of eating Berber-style, using only three fingers of his right hand; he battles his way into an overcrowded train in Dakar; he laughs at his own clumsiness in dismounting a camel. There are risks, however, as many African countries are far from peaceful and checkpoint crossings are particularly tense. Palin must often wonder, in his darker moments, why on earth he accepts these challenges – but as he watches the full moon rising above Timbuktu, with bats skimming through a lemon and violet sky and hippos burping in the distance, he must surely recall the reason.

The great thing about Palin is that he is interested not just in the landscapes but in the people. He wants to know their names, what they eat, where they live, what they believe and how they make a living. He has a natural curiosity and warmth, and a talent for finding common ground in an emotion or a shared experience. It wins him friends. His books and programmes do much more than scratch the surface – they give a fascinating insight into human life in all the corners of this remarkably diverse and colourful planet. He asks the questions that his viewers would probably love to ask, and he tastes the food that we might not dare to eat.

In 2003, Palin embarked on a journey across 2,000 miles of spectacular terrain in the Himalayas. He travelled to the hidden valleys of the Hindu Kush, exploring ancient cities and remote villages, and trekked along precipitous cliffs where white rivers rage thousands of feet below. He climbed to remote monasteries, rode flimsy-looking boats through whirlpools on the Yangtze, watched a polo match in the Shandur Pass and played cricket with young lads in Rawalpindi. In Dharamsala he met the Dalai Lama, and was somewhat taken aback to find that His Holiness is a fan of his shows. With twinkling humour, the Tibetan spiritual leader confided that he would like to be reincarnated as Palin's travelling companion.

Unfortunately, illness struck while Palin was trekking to Annapurna

Base Camp. He suffered first with altitude sickness and then with an excruciating sore throat that turned to fever. Barely able to swallow or breathe, and with many of his crew similarly afflicted, he struggled heroically to continue filming in an area that is prone to avalanches. From his usual cheerful interest, which saw him chatting with a Sherpa about how best to catch a yeti, he passed through exhaustion to near collapse, and during the night he faced the grim possibility of having to abandon the trip. The cold mountainside that he could see from his window seemed like a sign and a warning: the landscape was beautiful but deadly. It had been a sobering experience, but when the team were finally helicoptered out, Palin still felt extraordinarily fortunate to have experienced it.

Himalaya was an ambitious project, fraught with logistical night-mares, but the resulting TV series and book captured the vibrant spirit, the drama and fragility of this magnificent region. Palin was awed by the cultures that he found there, and said that he felt the series had succeeded in putting the Himalaya into a human perspective. He is always quick to credit the skills of his film crew and back-up team, who laboured under heavy loads in a variety of daunting conditions.

Living in North London with his wife, Helen, whom he married in 1966, Palin continues to publish diaries of his travels. He has also written several novels and children's books. In interviews he comes across as self-critical, admitting that he feels he cannot do something properly without worrying about it. This in itself is quite endearing, in view of the fact that his mantelpiece must be groaning under the weight of awards for his books and programmes.

Palin never makes any extraordinary claims about his own contribution to the planet or our understanding of it, but quietly lends his support to communities under threat. He is an official patron of the charity Freedom From Torture, and of Farm Africa, a charity which helps farmers grow themselves out of poverty. He is a keen supporter of Book Aid International, which sends thousands of books to sub-Saharan Africa. He has also helped to raise money for Survival International, an organisation which defends the lands and lives of tribal people. His work has helped to throw open the doors of the world, not only inspiring people to travel but also sparking an awareness of complex issues for which there is sometimes no easy answer.

Palin's other legacy? Somewhere in the Ténéré desert in Africa, a group of cameleers are probably still toasting each other in splendid British fashion. On his trek through the Sahara, the Touareg taught him a couple of handy words, doubling up with mirth whenever he practised them. One evening, as they sat around a camp fire and raised their glasses of mint tea, Palin proposed his own toast in repayment: a hearty 'Bottoms up', repeated with the greatest of delight. Laughter, as Palin has proved time and again, knows no boundaries.

Michael Palin was awarded the Livingstone Medal for 2008. In March 2009, when the presentation took place, he was a guest lecturer at the RSGS in Edinburgh. He told his audience 'we need more than ever to keep in touch with the rest of the world, to see how others are coping and hopefully to learn something along the way.'[2]

---

1. Interview with Nigel Farndale, November 2013, from www.nigelfarndale.com
2. Michael Palin, lecture to the RSGS, March 2009

HEAVEN
&
EARTH

Sir John Lubbock
1st Baron Avebury

Scientist and polymath
Born: 30th April 1834 (London)
Died: 28th May 1913 (Broadstairs, Kent)
§
RSGS Livingstone Medal, 1908

If we cannot explain the simplest flower, or the smallest insect,
how can we expect to understand the infinite?[1]

WHEN JOHN LUBBOCK was four years old, he started asking his parents questions that made them rack their brains. 'Where do burnt things go?' was an interesting one. He loved nature, and any kind of insect was guaranteed to capture his undivided attention.

His father, a gifted mathematician and amateur astronomer, took great pains to answer John's searching questions as best he could. Even so, he must have breathed a sigh of relief two years later when he heard that a famous scientist was coming to live in a nearby village. He broke the news to his son, who knew that something important was happening and was fully expecting a pony as a gift.

The disappointment must have been severe. Who was Charles Darwin, anyway?

Born in 1834, Sir John Lubbock, later Lord Avebury, was one of the great gentleman scientists of the Victorian era. He has been defined as a polymath, because his interest extended over many scientific fields; he had a genuine love of learning, propelled by a boyish curiosity which never grew old.

Lubbock had a good start in life. His father, Sir John William Lubbock, was a banker in London, and could afford to send all his sons to Eton. Their home was happy, and the Kent countryside offered an endless source of fascination for a young boy. Under

Darwin's influence, his interest in natural history blossomed into a lifelong passion.

> He induced my father to give me a microscope, he let me do drawings for some of his books, and I greatly enjoyed my talks and walks with him.[2]

Lubbock was elected a member of the Royal Institution aged only fifteen; in his early twenties he mixed with the likes of Sir Charles Lyell and Sir Joseph Hooker. It was an exciting time for the advancement of science, but Lubbock had other duties to fulfil. In 1849, at an unusually early age, he had followed his father into the banking business out of necessity when the other partners fell ill. Instead of relinquishing his personal interests, Lubbock simply increased the hours in his day. His diary reveals that his leisure time, even on his days off, was crammed from half-past six in the morning until midnight with lessons in everything ranging from political economy to microscope work. He took only short breaks for lunch, tea and whist.

Lubbock did find time to explore the local countryside, however, and in 1855 he made the important discovery of some musk ox remains in a gravel pit near Taplow station.

Down, 19th July 1855

Dear Lubbock,

> I had a note from Lyell this morning, in which he says you have found the first Ovibos moschatus ever discovered fossil in England... I declare I think it one of the most interesting discoveries in fossils made for some years... I congratulate you, and may this be the first of many interesting geological observations.
> Yours very truly, Charles Darwin.[3]

Three years later, Lubbock's scientific paper on *Daphnia*, a genus of crustaceans, earned him a nomination to the Royal Society. For the young man nicknamed 'Darwin's Apprentice', it signalled the beginning of a long and illustrious career. After being elected to

Parliament in 1870, he balanced the roles of private banker, Liberal MP and ultimately government advisor while delving with his active and energetic mind into a whole panoply of scientific fields. Biology, entomology, geology, anthropology, ethnology – he loved them all and had definite opinions about how they should be taught in schools. He had a gift, which he consciously strove to enhance, of being able to switch his attention instantly and completely from one subject to another – extremely useful in maintaining his vast array of interests. He could apply his mind to almost any subject with outstanding success.

Lubbock was also something of a philanthropist, striving to reduce the statutory hours in a working week. He was responsible for the Bank Holidays Act of 1871, after which, for a short time, all bank holidays were referred to as 'St Lubbock's Days' by grateful workers. Britons have another reason to thank him: his ardent interest in archaeology saved two of our most famous ancient landmarks from destruction.

It began in 1871 with a telegram from the rector of Avebury in Wiltshire. The village of Avebury sits partly within a huge Neolithic and Bronze Age site comprising three stone circles, one of which is the largest of its kind in Britain. Very little was known about it in the late nineteenth century, and some of the land had been sold and divided among local people for new houses. Lubbock received the message just in time; with work about to commence, he learned that the individual landowners were still prepared to part with their holdings for a sovereign apiece, and sent a prompt message back to say that he would buy them all. He subsequently purchased more land including Silbury Hill and West Kennet Farm, thereby saving the entire site from development.

Five years later, Lubbock was asked to chair the Salisbury meeting of the Wiltshire Archaeological Society. Their chosen venue was Stonehenge. As a few impromptu speeches were made, one of the antiquarians suggested that the monument had been erected in Saxon times. Lubbock, standing on one of the recumbent stones to reply, held fast to his theory of the Bronze Age. Meanwhile, the unusual gathering had not gone unnoticed.

The excursion was a large one, conveyed in some twenty-five carriages, and a gentleman farmer who was harvesting, surprised at seeing so large a cavalcade in an out-of-the-way lane, asked his bailiff who they were. 'I reckon, sir,' said the man, to whom the word archaeologists was not as familiar as it might have been, 'it's them Archangels from Salisbury.'[4]

Did Salisbury have its own archangels? Perhaps not, but Lubbock was the nearest thing. In June 1883 he received a plea from another anxious vicar, informing him of 'the threatened invasion of Stonehenge by a Railway Engineer'. The London and South Western Railway was planning to run a line from Graveley to Bristol, passing through Amesbury, Stonehenge, Shrewton, Chitterne, Westbury and Radstock. It would mean devastation for the site and the rector was in despair. 'The engineer proposes to take the line straight through the Cursus!'[5]

Sir John lodged his formal opposition to the bill in Parliament; meanwhile he arranged a meeting with the railway representatives and the MP for Bristol. Somewhat apologetically, the MP asked to be told what a cursus* was, and the engineer had an all-too-ready response: 'They do say it was a British racecourse,' he explained, 'but I assure you it is entirely out of repair, and not the slightest use to anyone now.'[6] Sir John's reaction is not recorded. The railway company agreed to divert the line.

Lubbock inherited a baronetcy on the death of his father, and in January 1900 he was raised to the peerage. His choice of title – 1st Baron Avebury – reflected his love of Wiltshire's ancient landscapes. The new Lord Avebury became a familiar figure in the House of Lords, where he used his authority to support his old friend Charles Darwin's audacious claims about evolution. While Lubbock was active in many academic organisations – the Linnean Society, the Royal Statistical Society and the Royal Anthropological Society, to name just three – once a week he also headed for the golf course, where he amused his opponents by examining the lichen on nearby stones and taking water samples from the pool while waiting for his turn on the green. As he no doubt reminded them, 'If you love one science, you cannot but feel intense interest in them all'.[7]

By now Lord Avebury was a member of so many distinguished societies it is possible that even he, with his phenomenal memory, had lost track. Prestigious invitations were fluttering through his letterbox like confetti, including one from the Royal Scottish Geographical Society, who wished to award him their Livingstone Medal 'for his valuable contributions to geographical science.' Lord Avebury's address to the Society at the Synod Hall in Edinburgh was deceptively entitled 'Scenery of Switzerland' – deceptive, that is, only to the few who were unacquainted with him and might have been expecting to doze away the evening in front of some holiday snaps. What Lord Avebury presented to the RSGS was a discourse on geology based on the latest principles, having applied his enquiring mind to the formation of the Alps:

> In the course of his address, which was illustrated by lime-light views, Lord Avebury dealt exhaustively with the geological aspect of Switzerland, and said geologists had been led irresistibly to the conclusion that the mountains and practically the whole of Switzerland from the Aron to the Reuss was an overthrust, and had come some miles from the south . . .[8]

This was in 1908, several years before the theory of Continental Drift had been conceived. The 'aged veteran of science' was in the twilight of his days, but won the hearts of his audience with 'graceful bearing, courtly courtesy... and distinguished presence'[9]. His good friend, Professor James Geikie, presented him with the Livingstone Medal, which Lord Avebury confessed he was particularly pleased to receive, 'as he had had the honour of Dr Livingstone's friendship'.[10]

Beloved by his family and highly esteemed by his peers, Sir John Lubbock was the embodiment of his own abiding principle that 'happiness and success in life do not depend on our circumstances, but on ourselves.'[11]

Earth and Sky, Woods and Fields, Lakes and Rivers, the Mountains and the Sea, are excellent schoolmasters, and teach some of us more than we can ever learn from books.[12]

*The Stonehenge Cursus is a Neolithic earthwork nearly two miles long. Eighteenth-century antiquarian William Stukeley believed that it was built by the Romans for chariot racing. Its purpose is still unclear, but is thought to be ceremonial.

1. *The Use of Life* by Sir John Lubbock (1894)
2. Notes by Sir John Lubbock, quoted in *The Life of Sir John Lubbock* (1914) by Horace Gordon Hutchinson
3-6. *The Life of Sir John Lubbock* (1914) by Horace Gordon Hutchinson
7. *The Pleasures of Life* by Sir John Lubbock (1894)
8. The *Scotsman*, 20th November 1908: report of address to RSGS by Lord Avebury, Edinburgh, on 19th November 1908
9. *Perthshire Courier*, 24th November 1908
10. The *Scotsman*, 20th November 1908: report of address to RSGS by Lord Avebury, Edinburgh, on 19th November 1908
11-12. *The Use of Life* by Sir John Lubbock (1894)

Sir Archibald Geikie

Geologist
Born: 28th December 1835 (Edinburgh)
Died: 10th November 1924 (Haslemere)
§
RSGS Livingstone Medal, 1905

We can hardly take any country walk ... in which with duly
observant eye we may not detect either some geological operation
in actual progress, or the evidence of one which was completed
long ago.[1]

IN THE LATE SUMMER of 1853 the residents of the parish of Strath
on the Isle of Skye were puzzled by the sight of a young lad slowly
clambering across the hillside, tapping at boulders with a stout
hammer. Day after day they watched him carefully collect the broken
fragments. He seemed pleasant enough, and was perfectly willing to
talk about his strange occupation. To his face they called him *Gille
nan Clach*, the 'lad of the stones'. Privately, they thought he was soft
in the head.

Archibald Geikie had little or no Gaelic, but could tell what the old
women were saying as they eyed him with a mixture of sympathy and
suspicion from the doors of their cottages. He did not care; he was
blissfully happy. Aged seventeen, he had been invited to Skye by the
Reverend John Mackinnon, minister of Kilbride, in order to indulge
his fascination for geology. Geikie's meanderings took him away
from the manse for days at a time, so he slept in tenants' barns on
beds of heather, enjoying the traditional fare of potatoes, oat-cakes,
herrings and eggs.

For Geikie, it was an idyllic few weeks which served to confirm
what his heart had been telling him all along. He had spent two
years in a lawyer's office in Edinburgh, dutifully applying himself
to the preparation of formal letters while in his imagination he was
roaming freely over the undulating hills of his native Midlothian. As

171

a schoolboy, he had found his first fossils at Burdiehouse quarry and the joy of that day was still fresh in his memory.

> As I broke up the blocks of stone and laid open fragment after fragment of plants, delicately preserved, a light seemed to stream into my mind from these buried relics.[2]

The University of Edinburgh was an obvious portal to a career in science but in the 1850s it offered no facility for the reading of geology as an individual academic subject. Although geology and mineralogy were included in the scope of natural history, no practical experience was involved. This in no way discouraged Geikie, a true Renaissance man; he simply went to as many different lectures as he could and soaked up a vast field of knowledge. This approach led him to rediscover his love of Greek and Latin and apply himself enthusiastically to the Classics, while in his spare time he refreshed his grasp of French.

The path was lit for a brilliant academic career until a sudden financial setback left Geikie's father unable to pay for the completion of his study. It would have been a huge blow but for the network of eminent scientists who had befriended the eager young man. The University of Edinburgh was already a centre of excellence and Geikie had come to the notice of figures like Matthew Foster Heddle, George Wilson, Andrew Ramsay and the ageing Hugh Miller. The perfect opportunity presented itself in the newly formed Geological Survey of Scotland, an extension of the existing Geological Survey of Britain, which so far had been limited to England and Wales. At its head was Sir Roderick Murchison, who reassured himself about Geikie's physical fitness at their first meeting; 'To a geologist,' he explained, 'his legs are of as much consequence as his head'.[3]

With Murchison's approval and a warm recommendation from Miller, Geikie was asked to present himself for his first day of work in the field, in a post so perfect it could have been designed specifically for him. During the first few months of his employment, Geikie was often accompanied on his travels around the Lothians by James Young, who was particularly interested in the distribution of black shale in the Carboniferous rocks. Shortly afterwards, Young secured the lucrative right to extract mineral oil over a large region, earning himself the nickname 'Paraffin Young'.

Meanwhile, news of the survey filtered very slowly through the residents of the countryside, and the officers grew accustomed to being variously branded as poachers, sheep-rustlers or even 'nuisance inspectors' tasked with examining the cleanliness of mining villages. There was also the weather to contend with; as Geikie ventured further and further afield he wore out dozens of umbrellas, and was often sent racing after items that had been snatched by the wind.

> I remember an occasion when on a breezy hill-top a map-case, incautiously opened, had its precious contents dispersed far and wide.[4]

In the mid-nineteenth century, geological theories that are now widely accepted, such as erosion by rivers and glaciers, were still new to the minds of even the most forward-thinking scientists. Geikie was blessed in terms of the era he was born into, because he could look at the landscape with observant eyes and ponder its various puzzles with an open mind. He realised that geology was inextricably linked with geography in the way it affected the appearance of the landscape. The shape and contours of hills, the location of gorges and waterfalls, the abundance and type of vegetation; all these features were directly related to the properties of the underlying rocks.

> The mountains and glens, for instance, of Skye, of the Trossachs, and of the Cairn Gorm mountains, have all been carved out by erosion with the same sculpture-tools. Yet the results are in each case very different; because in each of the districts the rocks are distinct.[5]

As for the sculpture-tools themselves, Geikie was fascinated by the ways in which frost, wind and water could reduce solid rock to grains of dust. He realised he could start to explain the past by observing the present because the laws of physics do not change, even over millions of years. He studied the evidence of volcanic activity and concluded that the Earth's surface had been formed and re-formed over a colossal period of time. Though not the first geologist to propose these theories, he expanded on them with intelligent observation and powerful reasoning.

Geikie toured the north-west Highlands in the company of Sir Roderick Murchison, and the two formed a lasting friendship. When the Scottish branch of the Geological Survey became a distinct entity with its own staff, Geikie was appointed its Director. In 1871, Murchison endowed a Chair of Geology and Mineralogy at the University of Edinburgh, and appointed Geikie as its first professor. As the study of geology gathered pace, Geikie produced a number of important books and papers. In 1887 he published *The Scenery of Scotland Viewed in Connection with its Physical Geology*, which contained a geological map of the entire country – a work of beauty and fascinating detail. In the layers of Cretaceous, Carboniferous and Old Red Sandstone, Geikie caught the echoes of a truly ancient world. He described his findings to the Royal Scottish Geographical Society in December 1905.

> By a fortunate series of accidents there had been preserved in the north-west of Scotland a portion of the oldest-known landscape in Europe. So ancient was this fragment that it dated back to a time before the earliest recorded trace of living things which appeared on the surface of the Earth...[6]

Geikie's younger brother, James, was an equally talented and eminent geologist, and both men played important roles in the shaping of the RSGS.

From the directorship of Scotland's Geological Survey, Geikie progressed to become Director of the British Geological Survey, which took him to London. He won many prestigious awards for his research, and was knighted by Queen Victoria in 1891. He even had a mineral named after him: geikielite, which had just been discovered in Sri Lanka. In later life he retired to Haslemere in Surrey where he gave a great deal of support to the town's museum. It still holds many of his collections.

Aside from his rock-gathering propensities, the glimpses which Geikie's journals give of Scotland's cultural landscape are precious and fascinating because he was exploring at a time when many rural traditions were still strong. In the Pentland Hills he found there was still a custom of performing Allan Ramsay's play *The Gentle Shepherd* in the midst of the very landscape which had inspired it, with full justice given to the Doric flavour of the language. As a schoolboy he witnessed the night-time practice of 'burning the water' in the Vale of Gala, described in Walter Scott's *Guy Mannering*, when men with 'liesters' or long spears would hunt for fish in the light of burning torches held aloft over the river. In his memoir he recalled that a train took four hours to travel from Edinburgh to Glasgow and steam ships to the islands, loaded with cattle and sheep, seemed to stop at almost every port on their way to Skye. Geikie documented the Great Exhibition of 1851, and watched soldiers leaving Granton and Leith for the Crimean War.

In addition to his scientific achievements Geikie was a natural artist, and his journals are illustrated with beautiful drawings and watercolours of landforms.

> [The geologist] cannot diminish the romance that hangs like a golden mist over the country; on the contrary, he reveals another kind of romance, different indeed in kind but hardly less attractive, wherein firth and fell, mountain and glen, glow with all the fervour of a poet's dream.[7]

As his reputation grew, Geikie travelled widely in Europe and the US. He was even offered the post of Geologist to the Maharajah of Kashmir, but declined without regret because his heart lay in his homeland. He lived for a while in Ramsay Gardens on Edinburgh's Castle Hill, where he and his wife Alice entertained an eclectic mix of poets, writers, musicians and scientists in the octagonal sitting room of Goose Pie House.

Reading Geikie's reminiscences, in particular his rambling but delightful autobiography *A Long Life's Work*, it is clear how passionate he was, not just about the science of geology but about the natural beauty to which it gave rise. His works are dotted with quotes from Scott, Milton and Wordsworth. He expresses every sympathy with those who prefer to see the drama of human stories in a landscape because he felt the attraction of them himself. Inspired rather than daunted by the scale and mystery of geological time, his curiosity kindled a light for countless other scientists to follow.

   1. *Class-book of Geology* by Sir Archibald Geikie (1890)

2-4. *A Long Life's Work* by Sir Archibald Geikie (1924)

   5. *The Scenery of Scotland Viewed in Connection with its Physical Geology* by Sir Archibald Geikie (1887)

   6. *The Scotsman*, 13th December 1905, report of lecture by Sir Archibald Geikie to RSGS

   7. *The Scenery of Scotland Viewed in Connection with its Physical Geology* by Sir Archibald Geikie (1887)

Sir Francis Edward Younghusband

Himalayan explorer, military officer, British diplomat, mystic
Born: 31st May 1863 (Murree, India)
Died: 31st July 1942 (Lytchett Minster, Dorset)
§
RSGS Gold (Scottish Geographical) Medal, 1905

I T USED TO BE SAID that the sun never set on the British Empire, so widespread were her dominions. The formidable task of managing them all rested largely on a constant stream of eager young men educated at public schools and military academies. Though each was individually talented, they were destined to be moulded by their early twenties into a career and lifestyle that some of them found unnatural, if not completely alien. The life of a British officer posted overseas could be harsh and, if he failed to bond with his peers, lonely. Sensitivity was suppressed, as was an attitude of independence that ran contrary to the commands of superior officers. Francis Younghusband started with an abundance of both.

Born in Murree, India, in 1863, Younghusband's father was a British Army officer while his mother came from an ardent family of evangelists in Somerset. Francis was taken to England for schooling, and when his parents returned to India he stayed with two maiden aunts who fed him on a diet of rigid morality punctuated by regular beatings for disobedience. He soon learned that happiness came a poor second to duty.

When he emerged from Sandhurst he was already a complex mixture of vulnerability and egotism, imbued with patriotic fervour and desperately keen to excel as a military officer. The British Empire provided a splendid stage on which to prove his worth. He was sent to India at the age of nineteen as a Second Lieutenant in the 1st King's

Dragoon Guards. Stationed at Meerut, his sense of propriety was shocked by what he saw as the loose behaviour of his fellow officers. Soon it was noticed that he had a peculiar habit of withdrawing into himself and studying the local wildlife.

When given two months' leave, he decided to trace the footsteps of his maternal uncle, a flamboyant explorer named Robert Shaw who had been the first European to enter Kashgar and whose stories of derring-do had filtered down to Younghusband as a child. Shaw had died five years previously but his nephew found his old house in the hills of Dharamsala, its silent rooms still strewn with dusty books and maps. For a while, Younghusband dwelt on Shaw's colourful but tragically short life. Then he set off on an impromptu trek of his own, over the Rohtang Pass in the Pir Panjal Range of the Himalayas. It was dangerous terrain for a solo traveller but in the ice-cold air, the sight of the snowy summits bathed in moonlight struck him with the power of a transformative vision. To his hungry soul they seemed to symbolise the promise of joy – distant but attainable.

For the next few years, Younghusband managed to weave a promising military career with his new-found passion for exploration. He learned the essential skills of surveying and mapping, and was afforded plenty of opportunities to use them. The reasons were largely political; India was governed by the British Raj, but Russia had long been aware of the country's rich resources and the convenience of her trading ports. The northern fringes of India, folded into natural barriers of inhospitable mountain ranges and deep gorges, became a hotly disputed border country. Beyond, there were rumours that Russia was extending its grip on regions to the east. Much of Central Asia was still uncharted, and new geographical knowledge gave the holder a distinct advantage.

Using rather contorted logic, Younghusband convinced himself – and, more importantly, his senior officers – that it would be a valuable exercise to explore Manchuria, a large region of the Chinese Empire with strategic sea ports opening onto the Yellow Sea. Starting in Newchwang, and taking two officials with him, he travelled through farmland and meadows bright with irises and tiger lilies. He inspected fortifications and slept in roadside inns and ascended the

'Long White Mountain' of Changbai Shan, gazing in wonder at the volcanic lake near its summit. It was a long and sometimes gruelling trek, but at its end he had to admit he saw no immediate threat of Russian encroachment.

Having prepared a detailed geographical report, Younghusband was reluctant to return to the routine of his regiment. When he heard that one of his superiors, Colonel Mark Bell, was to travel to Chinese Turkestan, he asked to join him. Although his plea was refused, he was told that he could take a parallel route across the Gobi Desert, which would be both a valuable mapping exercise and a journey of several thousand miles.

At Kwei-Hwa-Cheng on the edge of the desert, Younghusband hired eight camels, a camel driver and a guide; the latter was an opium addict who would jog along sound asleep on his camel during the daytime and wake only as night fell, whereupon he would navigate unerringly to the nearest waterhole. After seventy days and 1,255 miles the little party reached the town of Hami where Younghusband stocked up on food and hired a mule cart to travel across Turkestan. He passed through the town of Turfan, noting with puzzlement that it lay 300 feet below sea level; he also stayed in Kashgar, where his uncle, Robert Shaw, had once been held prisoner. At Yarkand he received a note from Bell. 'Don't fail to try the Mustagh,' it said.

The Mustagh was a 19,000-foot mountain pass between India and Central Asia, said to have been blocked twenty-five years previously by an avalanche. No European had ever tried to cross it. This rather discouraging prospect spurred Younghusband into action; he hired ponies and handlers, a Balti guide and a caravan leader. In September 1887 they set off up the Mustagh Pass.

The scenery was magnificent and Younghusband stopped many times to appreciate it, feeling as if his dream had been fulfilled. As he admired the pure white peaks gleaming in the sunlight, one in particular caught his attention. He described it as being almost perfectly proportioned; this, although he did not know it, was K2, the second highest mountain in the world.

Though it was nectar for the soul, the physical bodies of Younghusband and his men struggled at such a high altitude. Some gasped for breath, and at night their beards were frozen solid. Younghusband endured it with grim determination but soon optimism turned to dismay; at the crest of the pass, the glacier had fallen away to leave a sheer wall of ice that dropped dizzyingly into the valley below. The stories about the avalanche were true.

Younghusband was beaten. He was not an experienced climber, he had no proper equipment and his leather boots were worn smooth. It was hopeless. As he stared in mute frustration, one of his guides started to cut steps into the ice.

How Younghusband managed to descend the ice wall at the top of the Mustagh Pass awed and entertained his contemporaries for years to come. The men used whatever came to hand – pony ropes, turbans, cummerbunds – and knotted them together to fashion a rope. Younghusband tied handkerchiefs around the soles of his boots to improve their grip. At one stage, the lightest member of the party had to be lowered over the sheer drop, suspended by his waist, so that he could hack footholds for the others to follow. Packs of bedding were thrown down, to be rescued later. The ponies had to be left at the top with Younghusband's servant, who would retrace their steps and lead them to safety. Six hours after beginning the descent, they reached safe ground and were gazing up in disbelief at the route they had taken. All were still alive, although one man had fallen down a crevasse and had to be pulled out. Younghusband was shaking but jubilant. Two days later, limping on bruised and painful feet and desperate for food, they reached a village.

With absolute certainty, Younghusband was able to report that the Russians could not use the Mustagh Pass to gain access to India.

Younghusband deliberately strove to cultivate the image of a dashing British spy. He had an astonishing resilience to physical hardship, and he took pride in his own daring exploits. At times he felt invincible. In 1904 his actions plunged him into one of the most shameful episodes in the history of the British Raj.

Fears about the security of British India were growing, and the Viceroy of India, Lord Curzon, suspected – erroneously, as it turned out – that Russia had signed a secret treaty with Tibet. China had long claimed suzerainty over Tibet, but in practice this was difficult to enforce. Nervous British diplomats fretted over the implications of Russia gaining access to the Tibetan passes. There was also the undeniable lure of the capital, Lhasa; the home of the Dalai Lama had an aura of mysticism that mesmerised curious nations. No one imagined that the Tibetans might be happier as they were, for how could the advantages of capitalism and trade be denied? The very fact that they wanted to be left alone was an offence to the Empire.

In June 1903 a party of British delegates headed by Younghusband ventured a short distance into Tibet from Sikkim and stationed themselves at a settlement called Khamba Dzong. Their intention was to negotiate but it was a fruitless exercise. The Tibetans wished to avoid dialogue altogether, while discouraging any further advance into their territory.

In a report published in *Scottish Geographical Magazine*, Younghusband revealed that the time spent waiting for their response was occupied compiling a detailed study of the geology and flora of this little-known country; several scientists had travelled with him in anticipation of this opportunity. While they worked, Younghusband spent 'every day and every hour enjoying the charming summer climate, and, above all, the unrivalled panorama of the mighty Himalayas at the very culminating point of their grandeur, where all the loftiest peaks in the world were majestically arrayed before us.' The scientists were delighted with their findings, but five months later Britain was no closer to an agreement with Tibet.

Meanwhile, on realising that the British were serious, the Tibetans began to build a five-foot wall – too low to be an effective barrier – across the plain below Guru, south of Gyantse, which lay between Sikkim and Lhasa. In December 1903 Younghusband led about 1,150 British soldiers into Tibet, advancing as far as Tuna, where they halted for nearly three months to allow time for talks. When delegates failed to materialise, they continued their march towards Lhasa. On 31st March 1904 they reached the wall.

It was an extraordinary confrontation. About 3,000 Tibetans had gathered on the other side of the wall, armed with swords and matchlock muskets which were no defence against the British Maxim machine guns and rifles. Most of the Tibetans had never even seen such weapons; it was well known that they did not want to fight any more than they wished to negotiate. Younghusband had vowed not to attack first, and the Tibetan general, Depon Lhading, had promised the same. The problem was that Younghusband was determined to reach Lhasa. A last-minute meeting between the two parties ended in stalemate. Something had to give way.

There are conflicting accounts about what happened next. According to Younghusband, British soldiers had already started disarming the Tibetans but some of them resisted, so the British responded by opening fire. Other sources state that a scuffle broke out which provoked Lhading into firing his pistol at a Sikh guard. In any case, Younghusband's Tibet expedition turned quickly into a massacre.

As the Maxim guns turned on them, the bewildered Tibetans walked slowly away. Most were mown down by the firing, and those who escaped were pursued by mounted infantry. Some lay down with the corpses and pretended to be dead. One of the survivors, whose peaceful world had been shattered by horror, reported that the firing went on for as long as it would take six successive cups of tea to cool. Over 600 Tibetans were killed, including Lhading; of the British soldiers, twelve were injured.

In the weeks that followed, Younghusband's patriotism reached a state of fanatical zeal. When he entered Lhasa on 3rd August he was expecting signs of Russian presence, but he found none. The Dalai Lama had already fled, and the remaining inhabitants greeted the intruders with clapping and chanting, a gesture to drive out evil spirits which the British mistook for enthusiasm. The Treaty of Lhasa, which was the immediate result of Britain's invasion, placed impossible demands on Tibet and was soon revised.

Younghusband's action would haunt him for the rest of his life. A profound change took place within him. As if seeking some kind of solace, he returned to the places he loved most. On his last day in Lhasa a spiritual monastic leader called the Ganden Tripa gave him a small bronze statue of the Buddha. He took it with him on a ride up into the mountains, and as he sat and gazed over the distant summits he was overwhelmed by a sensation of intense joy. Perhaps this was Tibet's answer to hostility: meeting war with peace and fear with love.

That day, Younghusband resolved on a new mission: to spread a message of enlightenment in the world. In his subsequent books he attempted to share his vision for the benefit of mankind, but his attempts to translate it into words elicited a less than favourable response. His readers were baffled by descriptions of the Planet Altair, where highly evolved translucent beings, embodying both man and woman, lived in harmony and communicated through the ether. Such an existence, he claimed, could be compared to Earth-bound relationships such as that of William and Catherine Booth, founders of the Salvation Army. He mixed patriotism with religious fervour, while advocating free love. His kindest critics called him eccentric; the rest said he was delusional.

Alongside this fervent but slightly irregular distraction, Younghusband maintained his lifelong passion for the mountains, and in particular the Himalayas. He campaigned vigorously for British efforts to climb them, and he was Chairman of the Mount Everest Committee throughout the 1921 (*Reconnaissance*), 1922 and 1924 expeditions. George Mallory (see p.194), who met him, described him as a 'grim old apostle of beauty and adventure.'

It could be argued that Francis Younghusband was to Everest what Sir Clements Markham was to Antarctica; he had a dream which he knew he could not accomplish himself, but it was strong and enduring enough for him to plant it in the minds of many daring young men. Just as importantly, both men's contacts and status allowed them to gather influential support.

Writing in his 1936 book *Everest: The Challenge*, Younghusband discusses the attempts on the Himalayan peak, and ponders the philosophical question of whether the mountain's glory would be dimmed by man's eventual ascent of it. He argues it would not; by 1936, thousands of climbers, for example, had already scaled Mont Blanc and its splendour was undiminished. He imagines an exhausted climber standing on the summit of Everest, numb to most sensations until his safe descent, whereupon his joy in the achievement would be enhanced by an even greater respect and admiration for the mountain in its untarnished glory. Living beings, he said, do not just adapt themselves to their environment but strive to rise above it. In essence, that was what he had been trying to do all his life.

> ...towering above all the tumult below, serene and majestic, and looking prouder, loftier, and purer than ever, rose the great peak... and above it lay the calm blue sky, illimitable in its restfulness and light – a sky of bright and liquid azure, through which one seemed able to pierce right into heaven itself. (Describing Chumalhari, sacred mountain known as 'the Bride of Kangchenjunga')

All references in this chapter from Sir Frank Younghusband K.C.I.E. 'The Geographical Results of the Tibet Mission', *Scottish Geographical Magazine* (1905) 21:5, 229-245

FRANK KINGDON WARD

Himalayan explorer and plant collector
BORN: 6th November 1885 (Withington, Lancashire)
DIED: 8th April 1958 (London)
§
RSGS Livingstone Medal, 1936

If you really want some fun in a Tibetan coracle, you must get a native to take you through bad water when he is thoroughly drunk; he fears nothing then, and if you live to tell the story you will have something to boast about all your life.

GETTING EXPELLED FROM primary school is a rare achievement, and for Frank Kingdon Ward it was a source of pride. He and his elder sister were both live wires, but Frank had a touch of the devil in him, which did not sit well with the nuns at the Catholic convent in Bordeaux which the children were attending while they stayed with their grandmother. Frank would bring gifts of caterpillars for the horrified nuns, and his exuberance disturbed the silence of Mass. It was too much. 'They run around like little lizards,' said the Mother Superior despairingly.

Back at his home in Englefield Green in Surrey, eight-year-old Frank would roam around the local countryside and pay unofficial visits to Windsor Castle where he gazed through the windows in the hope of glimpsing Queen Victoria. Boundaries never kept him in or, indeed, out.

Born in Manchester in 1885, Ward was the son of a Professor of Botany at Cambridge University. As a youngster, he overheard his father talking to a colleague who had just returned from the Brahmaputra, a majestic river that rises in the Himalayas and flows through Tibet and Bangladesh before emptying into the Bay of Bengal. According to the traveller, there were places along the banks of the river where no westerner had ever been. Something about that statement struck a deep chord in Frank's mind; from that moment, though unaware of it, he was destined to be among the first explorers to visit those remote sacred mountains and roaring whitewater gorges.

Ward's academic career got off to a reasonably promising start, but his degree in natural sciences at Cambridge had to be cut short when his father died in 1906. Faced with the need to earn money, Ward took a teaching post at a public school in Shanghai. During the holidays he explored Java and Borneo, which only served to confirm what he already knew: he did not want to teach, he wanted to explore. When offered a place on the Duke of Bedford's expedition in western China, looking for new species of mammals, he seized the chance with both hands.

Plunging knee-deep through snowdrifts, chasing herds of takin (a species of goat-antelope) around the rocky slopes, shivering in icy winds at altitudes of 12,000 feet – the mountains could have spelled an early death for someone as reckless and impetuous as Ward. Astonishingly, not only did he thrive, he also managed to contribute two new species of vole and a shrew to the expedition's overall tally. On his safe return he received another offer, even more alluring: on behalf of the Bees Seed Company, he was invited to collect hardy plants and seeds in China's Yunnan Province. This time he would have to beat his own path, because he would be going solo; he would need porters, mules and yaks to carry essential supplies and his equally precious finds, and would have to rely on his own stamina to succeed. Some good social skills and a loaded gun would come in very useful, too.

> 'We climbed great precipices in search of plants, the nicest of which always select the most abominable situations, and one day in a mist I was pursued by a bull yak, and on another occasion in the forest I found myself face to face with a black bear. Then we had a wedding, and the whole village got gloriously drunk; also a funeral, and they got drunker.'

It soon became apparent that Ward's passion knew no limits and he happily embarked on a lifetime of plant collecting in the Far East. His treks resembled a pilgrimage or a quest for the Holy Grail, except he was not searching for just one prize but hundreds, catching the sun in all colours of the rainbow, growing wild in alpine meadows and making jewel-like carpets among the patches of melting snow. To see them, he had to cross rivers raging in flood using a flimsy rope bridge suspended across the gaping chasm, then stumble mile after weary mile along stony mountain passes. He suffered from recurring bouts of malaria, and was often called upon to use his rudimentary medical kit to treat ailing residents in the villages he passed through. He also had a distressing habit of wandering off.

> On the way over the mountains I left the caravan for an hour in order to shoot pheasants, and lost myself for two days and a night in consequence – an unpleasant experience, for the weather was cold and wet, and I had to subsist on what green leaves I could find; they gave me dreadful indigestion.

There was another reason why the Himalayas made a dangerous playground. Sir Francis Younghusband's 'British Expedition' to Tibet in 1904 had ended in a massacre and forced the 13th Dalai Lama to flee to Mongolia; nine years later he returned from exile and re-asserted his country's independence. Tibet was therefore understandably suspicious of foreigners, especially Britons. Ward was taking his life in his hands by crossing disputed borders in the name of botanical science. On one occasion, finding himself lost in the Tibetan mountains without food or shelter, he became crazy with thirst and hunger and resorted to eating rhododendron flowers which he knew held a drop of nectar at the centre. The next morning he stumbled, hallucinating, through bamboo thickets and along the banks of streams. Miraculously arriving at a village, he was taken in by a family who gave him food and saved his life.

Described as a man of energy, endurance and resolution, Ward took a keen interest in the people he met on his travels, and respected their customs and traditions. Accepting their hospitality brought its own risks, however, as he soon found to his cost. Playing drinking games with Chinese merchants was asking for trouble, especially when the alcohol involved was called 'burning spirit'. Then there was the time when he dined with a Tibetan family and somehow became engaged to marry the daughter of the house during the course of the evening.

Ward might have been a botanist first and foremost, but his diplomacy skills must have been remarkable. Nor was he shy of exhibiting his talents where they would be appreciated most. In 1933, on another trip to Tibet, he was invited to dine with the Governor of Zayul. As part of the entertainment, Ward played the ukulele while his companion, botanist Ronald Kaulback, danced the Charleston and the Black Bottom. Ward modestly admitted that this caused a sensation in official circles.

Despite the odds – and he cheated death so many times that he must surely have had nine lives – the beautiful plants that Ward brought back to Britain earned him a place among the legends of his era. He was honoured with numerous with fellowships and awards, and wrote many books about his adventures. He racked up an astonishing twenty-four expeditions in his lifetime, showering eager alpine collectors with gems such as: *Meconopsis speciosa*, which he called the Cambridge Blue Poppy; the lemon-yellow *Rhododendron wardii*, to which he gave his name; and *Primula nivalis*, whose brilliant magenta flowers rise just an inch or so above a tight rosette of leaves. The species *Primula florindae* is named after his first wife, Florinda Norman-Thompson, while the Shirui lily, *Lilium mackliniae*, commemorates his second, Jean Macklin.

> The plateau is already ablaze with crimson rhododendrons and pink camellias... and it is delightful to leave the caravan and wander all day over the wild hills...

Aside from his plant collecting exploits, Ward helped investigate the riddle of the Tsangpo Gorge, a geographical mystery which for fifty years had beguiled the drawing rooms of polite society. In the early 1900s the course of the Yarlung Tsangpo river had yet to be traced, but it was known that it dropped an astonishing 9,000 feet over a distance of just 150 miles. A magnificent cataract was imagined, perhaps 1,000 feet in height, and given the romantic title of 'The Lost Falls'. The gorge itself was said to be a sacred place, a portal to a higher realm promising bliss and rebirth. It was irresistible but also, undeniably, a death trap.

Since the word 'inaccessible' did not register in Ward's vocabulary, he made it his mission to solve the mystery. In 1924, aided by Captain Frederick Marshman Bailey (see p.293), who was employed as a Political Officer in Sikkim, he obtained permission to explore parts of the gorge. His companion was Lord Cawdor, a young Scottish aristocrat who had partly financed the expedition and who kept up a steady stream of mild-mannered complaints. Guided by local porters, they ventured along hunters' tracks, cutting their way through vegetation and slipping over rock faces that were wet with rain. Above them, breathtaking white peaks reared their heads in the clear light of day while way beneath their feet, engulfed in shadow, a monstrous river roared in perpetual fury. The sides of the canyon were so steep that when they pitched their tents for the night they had to dig themselves into the cliff face or lodge themselves against tree trunks for safety. Finally, after a heart-stopping descent, Ward and Cawdor stood on the brink of the thundering water, watching in awe as it hurled itself over a dizzying ledge and disappeared into the depths of the Earth.

Anxious to see the extent of the waterfall, they felled a tree and built a ladder to gain a better perspective. They charted the river as far as they could see, and took altitude measurements; the highest fall that they recorded was a drop of 70 feet, which Ward named the Rainbow Falls. He noted that, according to the Tibetans, between the Rainbow Falls and the river's confluence with another called the Po Tsangpo, there were said to be no fewer than seventy-five individual waterfalls, each with its own guardian spirit. He was captivated by the exquisite plants that grew in the forest: fragrant white trumpets of *Rhododendron nuttallii*, glowing pure yellow at the base; clematis, hydrangea, red-berried skimmia; and giant *Tsuga* trees, in whose mossy branches he was astonished to find the frothy white fronds of *Coelogyne*, an epiphytic orchid that thrives in the cold climate.

Frank could not have known that he was venturing into one of the deepest canyons on Earth. Fed by glaciers in the Himalayas, the river meanders across the high Tibetan Plateau then enters the Tsangpo Gorge where it plunges for about 150 miles on a steep and relentless gradient, thundering over the Hidden Falls and Rainbow Falls and carving a deep channel between the peaks of Namcha Barwa and Gyala Peri. Its course veers dramatically around a bend called the Great Horseshoe, causing an abrupt change of direction that baffled geographers for decades. Only in recent times, with the assistance of satellite images, has its true scale become apparent. The greatest depth of the Tsangpo Gorge is 19,714 feet, over three times that of the Grand Canyon.

> 'The Lutzu are a quiet agricultural people, very friendly, rather good-looking, and nicely dressed; they use the cross-bow with poisoned arrows, and drink vast quantities of a thick soupy liquid made from fermented maize.'

Frank Kingdon Ward was three times a guest of the Royal Scottish Geographical Society, giving talks in 1913, 1920 and 1936. On the last occasion, he was presented with the Livingstone Medal 'in recognition of his expeditions and research work in Tibet and Upper Burma.' He delivered the Society's opening lecture for the season to a packed audience in Edinburgh's Usher Hall, describing his latest expedition from Assam through part of the Tsangpo Gorge and up into the Himalayas. It is a miracle that he survived even one of his adventures, but he seemed to relish the challenges and the hardships that went with them. His achievements would be extraordinary even today.

Ward enjoyed a long-standing connection with the Royal Botanic Gardens in Edinburgh and Kew, and his legacy is one of the most beautiful, bringing joy each year to thousands of gardeners worldwide. In addition, it comes as a delight to know that a species of lizard, *Calotes kingdonwardi*, is named after him; those nuns in the French convent school would certainly have approved of that.

> In 1998 a party that included Kenneth Storm, Ian Baker and Kenneth Cox explored the Tsangpo Gorge in the footsteps of Ward and Cawdor.

They were led by Dungle Phuntsok, grandson of the guide who accompanied Ward in 1924, and learned that oral tradition still preserves the memory of Ward's presence in the gorge with perfect clarity.

All references in this chapter from F Kingdon Ward, 'Wanderings of a Naturalist in Tibet and Western China', *Scottish Geographical Magazine* (1913) 29:7, 341-350.

George Herbert Leigh Mallory

Mountaineer
BORN: 18th June 1886 (Mobberley, Cheshire)
DIED: 8th or 9th June 1924 (Everest)
§
Lecturer at RSGS, 1922

IN THE MIDSUMMER of 1921, a strange procession was winding its way slowly up the mountain pass of Jelep La, through the Chumbi Valley and up onto the high Tibetan Plateau. Nine British men, clad in thick tweeds, rode or walked alongside their heavily laden ponies and mules. With them came a straggling line of porters, cooks and interpreters. All were entering an unfamiliar and hostile world. Icy wind cut through their clothes like a knife, carrying with it particles of dust and sand that irritated their eyes and scoured their skin. Most were already suffering from altitude sickness, and dysentery was rife. The men had been travelling for two months and the route in front of them promised several more weeks of gruelling exertion. They faced the prospect with cheerful stoicism, intent on the object of their expedition.

In 1856 the Survey of India had confirmed the Himalayan peak of Chomolungma to be the highest mountain on the face of the Earth. Renamed Everest after a British surveyor-general, it had bewitched and inspired a generation of young climbers with dreams of a first ascent. Emerging from the darkness of the Great War, the spirit of the nation rose in response to the challenge but no one, including the nine hopeful travellers, knew just how tough it was going to be.

The elder son of a Cheshire vicar, George Mallory was a gifted child. Though only partly aware of his talents, he had a strong grasp of

195

what he did and did not want to do. Climbing was his passion, and at the age of seven the roof of his father's church made a great starting point. He knew no fear, and found it difficult to comprehend in others. As his sister, Avie, once observed, 'impossible' was a word that acted as a challenge to him.

Brilliant at sports, George was also a gifted mathematician, winning a scholarship to Winchester College when he was thirteen. He flourished there, loving it so much that he deliberately failed an entrance exam to the officer training school at Woolwich so he could stay another year. This decision was to have an impact on the rest of his life; shortly afterwards, he and another pupil were taken to the French Alps by one of the college masters for their first taste of real mountaineering.

Attempting to ascend Mont Blanc with two novice schoolboys and no professional guide was the kind of behaviour guaranteed to get a teacher into trouble, even if he was a member of the Alpine Club – on their return the tutor found himself the subject of controversy. But for George, the trip lit a flame that would never go out. He was not discouraged by his first experience of altitude sickness, and relished their early morning starts, climbing beneath the stars until the first rays of sun kissed the peaks with pure gold. There were some terrifying moments, such as his teacher's fall into a crevasse – George hauled him out – and a sudden and prolonged rockfall which could have killed them, but he came home with renewed energy and ready to face his next challenge: the University of Cambridge.

In the first decade of the twentieth century, Cambridge was an oasis for hedonistic young men, for whom the first taste of freedom came like heady summer wine. For four years George immersed himself in a brilliant set that included Rupert Brooke, Duncan Grant, and the brothers Lytton and James Strachey.

At a dinner party in February 1909 he met the mountaineer Geoffrey Winthrop Young, who organised annual climbing parties at Pen-y-Pass in Snowdonia and was the anonymous author of *The Roof-Climber's Guide to Trinity*, which offered an audacious new slant on that venerable Cambridge college. Becoming one of Young's regular house guests in North Wales, George honed his climbing technique on the unforgiving faces of Craig yr Ysfa and Clogwyn y Person. Young observed that his style was uniquely streamlined and elegant; he would set his foot on a ledge in a rock face, fold his shoulder to his knee and flow upwards in one continuous movement. The two forged a lifelong friendship, and for Mallory the summits of Tryfan and the Carneddau, combined with regular expeditions to the Alps, acted as important stepping-stones to an as-yet unseen destiny.

In 1913, as a teacher at Charterhouse School in Surrey, George met Ruth Turner. In photographs their two faces appear remarkably similar, with arching brows and a look of luminous, open-eyed innocence. They married on the eve of the Great War.

When George returned from the unspeakable horrors of the Somme, many of his friends were dead and the world was a darker place. In search of some sign of salvation, he accepted an invitation to join the first *British Everest Expedition* in 1921. The decision was not simple. George and Ruth had settled in a picture-book house near Godalming, and had three young children. The last thing their marriage needed was another agonising separation. But the lure of Everest was gathering strength; it was not a question of whether it would be conquered but when, and by whom. The newly formed Mount Everest Committee, chaired by Sir Francis Younghusband, had already scented triumph and were selecting their team of heroes. George, fit and fearless, with an instinct for seeing his way up any mountain, was high on their list.

Although initially dubious about the shameless flag-waving tone of the project, George was persuaded to think again by his old friend Young. The Mallorys' finances were always in a fragile state, and Young's argument was convincing: the successful ascent of Everest would open doors to a new career, perhaps in writing, with the promise of stability and independence. Young himself was unable to go as he had been hit by a shell in 1917, and was facing the rest of his life with an artificial leg. George must have been struck by the tragic contrast, painfully aware of his own still-untapped potential. Ruth, positive as always, agreed that he should go.

In April 1921 the expedition set sail from England. They arrived in Calcutta five weeks later. It was a reconnaissance party in name

197

at least, with a bid for the summit reserved for later expeditions; all the same, George's nature always pushed against the limits. When he glimpsed Everest for the first time, gleaming and immaculate, jaw-dropping in its height and magnificence, he was daunted but not discouraged. Having made the initial commitment, it was as if his soul had somehow already made the ascent. He just had to make his body follow suit.

The nine-man convoy crossing the Tibetan Plateau was therefore grim-faced but determined. They had taken a roundabout route that curved around from the north, as any approach through Nepalese territory was forbidden. At Kampa Dzong they buried one of their party: Alexander Kellas from Aberdeen, fifty-three years old, who had been impossibly weakened by altitude sickness and dysentery. Shortly afterwards another member, Harold Raeburn, was taken ill and forced to return to Sikkim. These two men were the only members of the expedition with previous experience of the Himalayas, so George became the climbing leader by default. As he observed, they were about to walk off the map.

The party, under the precise military direction of Lieutenant Colonel Charles Howard-Bury, set up camp at Tingri, where they split up into teams with the purposes of surveying, photography and scientific study. Together with Guy Bullock, a former classmate at Winchester and now a dependable climber and trusted companion, George studied the mountain and set his mind to working out an accessible route. The task was simple, yet breathtaking. No explorer had yet come within 50 miles of the mountain they called the 'Goddess Mother of the Earth'. Perhaps nowhere else on the face of the planet did man seem quite so insignificant in terms of physical size. Yet now, with only the experience of climbing European mountains to help him, George was looking at a behemoth nearly twice the height of Mont Blanc and calmly assessing their chances.

Having made Base Camp at the foot of the Rongbuk Glacier, at a height of 16,500 feet, Mallory and Bullock started to explore the possibilities. It was an exercise that demanded time and perseverance as well as immense physical stamina. Glaciers with 50-foot pinnacles blocked their path and at this altitude the mere effort of climbing short distances took a huge toll on the body. Frustrated by clouds that would repeatedly mask their view, and hampered by feverish headaches, the pair slowly and painfully eliminated each possibility in turn. On 18th August, in the company of team member Henry Morshead and a porter called Nyima, they stood at the top of a pass called the Lhakpa La, and realised they were looking at a route to the eastern flank of the North Col. From there, in theory at least, they could reach the North Ridge and ultimately the summit. Persistence had found a way.

With the purpose of the expedition fulfilled, and monsoon winds beginning to unleash their rage on the mountain, the climbing party should have turned back – but George was not one to give up easily. With Bullock, Edward Wheeler and a handful of porters, he struggled to a height of 23,000 feet, halting on a ledge below an ice-cliff with the shoulder of the North Col looming above them. Exhaustion had set in, and only then, with the gale screeching around them, did he concede defeat and turn his steps down to shelter and safety in the company of his stalwart friends.

In February 1922, speaking to a gathering of the Royal Scottish Geographical Society in Edinburgh, George Mallory impressed his listeners with his modesty and boyish appearance. His photographs of the *Reconnaissance Expedition* told their own story.

> Now Everest was seen with its sharp peak, sparkling like a jewel; then with a spindrift of snow whirling to a height of at least 2,000 feet above its summit 'like the hair of an enraged goddess', as the lecturer observed.

Later that year, Mallory announced, he would join a new expedition party to make a fresh bid on Everest. The Dalai Lama had again given his permission for their passage through Tibet, and their proposed route to the summit was now known and planned. Mallory described the landscapes and the customs of the Tibetan people, and evoked images of valleys full of beautiful flowers. The expedition had, he revealed, mapped an area of more than 13,000 square miles of hitherto unknown country.

Strange footprints in the snow were found at a high altitude, and the suggestion was made that there were wild, hairy men about: 'You'll see the only kind we saw,' observed the lecturer; and on the screen appeared a photograph of the party. The zoologist was pointed out as the hero of the mountaineers who had managed to shave every day. The naturalist, it was remarked, returned with many discoveries – including two fleas!

The Society members, alternately awed, entertained and charmed by Mallory's presentation, wished him Godspeed; unfortunately the 1922 expedition was thwarted by disaster. Although it was the first time bottled oxygen was used on Everest, it was also the first occasion on which climbers died; George was grief-stricken when seven porters were swept to their deaths in an avalanche. Again he returned home defeated, and even the knowledge that he had reached a new high altitude – more than 26,000 feet, with Edward Norton and Howard Somervell – could not settle the haunting feeling of guilt that had settled on him.

George, who had quit his job at Charterhouse in 1921, wrote several articles about his experiences and embarked on a none-too-successful lecture tour in the US. He and Ruth never seemed to make ends meet, and were relieved when he was offered an extra-mural teaching post in Cambridge. His first duties, interestingly, were to organise two summer schools: a Foreigners' Vacation Course, and a Teachers' Course in Geography.

Then fate took a hand once again. As Ruth and George were discussing wallpaper for their new house, the letter from the Mount Everest Committee arrived. They were planning a third expedition in 1924, and depending on Mallory to be a part of it. Wryly, George observed that, whatever he decided, it would be a sacrifice. To pursue his dream, he would have to give up many months of precious family life; if he stayed at home, he would see another man become the first to climb Everest. He had been torn in two directions his whole life, as so many explorers were; one part of him craved domestic bliss while the other saw adventure beckoning and was desperate to follow.

In his hours of indecision, one thought kept surfacing. He was still tortured by the loss of life two years before, and if his experience of the snow conditions might help to save others, he felt it was his duty to accept. He obtained a leave of absence from his new job and prepared to leave Ruth once more. This parting, although they could not know it, would be their last.

On 16th May 1924 George sat in the mess tent at 16,500 feet and wrote a letter to his nine-year-old daughter, Clare. It was a warm, sunny day, he said, and he was just about to have tea. If he stepped outside, he could see Everest with a streamer of cloud billowing from the summit; the cloud told him what the weather was doing and how strong the winds were. When it appeared free of cloud in the early mornings, it told him there was a good chance that he might get to the top. Tea arrived as he was writing, accompanied by a warm cake with raisins in it. One day in the summer, he told her, they would all have a tea party with a delicious cake like this one.

Just over three weeks later, together with his climbing partner, twenty-two-year-old Sandy Irvine, he disappeared forever into the swirling mists of the North-east Ridge.

All references in this chapter from *Aberdeen Free Press*, 9th February 1922, report of lecture to RSGS in Aberdeen by George Mallory, 8th February 1922

William ('Bill') Hutchison Murray

Mountaineer and conservationist
BORN: 18th March 1913 (Liverpool)
DIED: 19th March 1996 (Dumbarton)
§
RSGS Mungo Park Medal, 1952

I T WAS THE SUMMER of 1942 and William Hutchison Murray, an officer with the Highland Light Infantry, was somewhere in the north of Egypt. The British Eighth Army was desperately trying to stop Rommel gaining access to the Suez Canal, an important supply route for Allied forces.

As dusk fell in the desert, Murray and his men dug themselves into trenches for the night. Rommel had just captured Tobruk, one of the key ports on the Mediterranean, and Allied hopes of victory were waning. In the near-darkness, a row of ominous black shapes appeared on the edge of an escarpment. Behind them were dozens more. There was no doubt as to what they were: serried lines of Mark IV Panzer tanks, the pride of Erwin Rommel's armoured divisions, now training their formidable weaponry on Murray's brigade.

Destroy all personal items. In the face of imminent capture, that was the drill. Quickly, Murray groped in his pocket for his compass, his identity card... and his notebook. Flicking through it, he glanced at the list of names, all fellow climbers who had shared in his challenges on Scotland's mountains. The memories of those days, fuelled by exhilaration and warmed by friendship, poured through his mind like a shaft of brilliant light. He knew this might be his last thought.

Born in Liverpool but raised in Glasgow, Bill Murray's first taste of mountaineering was on The Cobbler, a peak above Arrochar. He was twenty-one and his curiosity had been piqued by a conversation, overheard by chance, in which a climber had been describing the thrills of An Teallach.

With a naiveté that could have been fatal, Murray decided to go and see what mountaineering was like for himself. Wearing everyday walking shoes, and without either ice-axe or compass, he boarded the train from the city and hopped off by the side of Loch Long. It was April, and the upper slopes of The Cobbler were still glistening with hard-packed snow that was as smooth and treacherous as glass. Undaunted, Murray set off on a solitary climb that would change his life forever. Within a few hours he had learned many lessons, foremost among them the importance of being well prepared and properly equipped. Realising too late that his footwear was hopelessly inadequate, he had to fight for every foothold in the ice. The option of turning back was even more impossible than the challenge of pushing on, so he refused to think of it even as his sense of freedom turned to heart-pounding fear.

Dogged persistence gained him the summit, and then came the revelation: Scotland's landscape lay spread out before him like a map, a breathtaking panoply of peaks rising above shadowy glens where lochs snaked away to the sea. It was wild, vast, overwhelmingly beautiful. Murray, who had never thought much about the brevity of life up to now, felt an urge to know every one of those mountains. In the same instant he realised that it might take him a lifetime to do so – but his heart was set on it.

In the years that followed, all Murray's free time was spent in the mountains. Finding good company in the likes of Bill MacKenzie, Kenneth Dunn and Archie MacAlpine, he paid £30 for an 'oil-eating' Austin Seven and motored up to Glen Coe and Rannoch Moor, camping in high corries on good weekends and in hay barns when the weather turned foul. Winter climbing was still in its infancy; the roads were deserted, the hillsides bare of walkers, and guest houses were few and far between. Undeterred, Murray notched up some admirable 'firsts'.

He also, finally, recognised the need for suitable equipment. Old-fashioned climbing axes were weighty to carry and their long handles made them useless in cramped spaces. With the help of Bill MacKenzie, Murray created a short-handled, lightweight ice-axe by cutting the claw off a slater's hammer.

The Highlands had claimed Murray's heart, but events in the wider world would soon overturn his life. On 3rd September 1939, the day that Neville Chamberlain declared Britain to be at war, he climbed Crowberry Ridge to the top of Buachaille Etive Mòr. He let his mind dwell on the many days and nights he had spent on the mountain, remembering the deep stillness, the ice gleaming in the moonlight and the sense of being at one with creation. He descended slowly, knowing that it might be a final farewell.

Three years later, he was crouching in a trench as shells from British two-pounder guns, launched at short range, bounced off the German tanks in a shower of sparks. The attack lasted only minutes, but Murray's sense of time was lost. Halting in a line, the Panzers raked the trenches with machine gun fire. When they stopped, Murray felt a detached sense of astonishment to find himself still alive. He climbed out shakily and offered himself for surrender.

A young German tank commander approached. After the bone-rattling assault on his vehicle, his hand shuddered wildly on the grip of a pistol. His question came as a surprise. 'Are you not feeling the cold?'

Murray spoke the first words that came into his head. 'It's as cold as a mountain top.'

The officer stared him full in the face. His hostility was gone, astonishment in its place . 'Do you climb mountains?' It turned out he was a keen climber too, looking at a kindred spirit.

From the depths of his tank, the commander fished out a greatcoat, plundered from an earlier assault, which he offered to Murray for warmth. He also brought some chocolate and two bottles of beer. As the iron-clad giants of war rumbled around them, the two men drank a toast to the mountains.

Murray's love of climbing saved his life in the desert, and was his salvation in the years to come. Faced with the prospect of prolonged imprisonment, captured British soldiers resorted to a wide range of activities, some of which were carried out more openly than others. At Chieti in Italy, Murray's first place of confinement, prisoners were allowed to receive parcels from home. His mother, knowing how much he loved reading, sent him the complete works of Shakespeare. As he fingered the fine pages, Murray was struck by a sudden thought. If he swapped this paper for the horribly coarse stuff that masqueraded as tissue in the prison toilets, he would have a plentiful supply of paper on which to write.

So, while his comrades had ample time to reflect on the unexpected appearance of Prospero and Portia in their daily routines, Murray began to delve deeper and deeper into the rich archives of his memory as he compiled a loving tribute to the things he loved best in his life. The abundance of time was a double-edged sword in prison camps, but it allowed Murray to rise above the immediate physical hardships and enter a limitless world of peace and beauty. He learned, he said, to live in the mind rather than in the body. Writing became a form of meditation, and as the weeks went by all his climbs in Scotland's mountains were coming back in vivid detail, down to each step and each hard-won handhold. Full of colour and life, the days flowed through his mind and out of his pen. As his comrades plotted together, making transistor radios and stealthily digging tunnels, Murray enjoyed a different kind of freedom.

Carefully hidden in his army tunic, Murray's manuscript survived a move to Moosburg concentration camp in Bavaria but did not fare so well two months later when he was taken to Oflag VIII F, a former Czech barracks in Bohemia. Each prisoner was thoroughly searched in the presence of Gestapo officers and it was not long before Murray's thick wads of toilet paper were discovered. Deeply suspicious, the guards questioned him and then – mercifully – allowed him to return to his prison cell.

The manuscript was not so lucky. Murray never saw it again.

It would be wrong to say Murray was undaunted. In addition to this loss, news of the worst atrocities of the war were beginning to filter through to the prison camp where he was held. He was a gentle man, for whom peace and freedom were everything, and human suffering filled him with horror to the bottom of his soul. Nonetheless he began writing again. This time, when his draft was finished, he made sure to keep it well concealed.

In 1945, when the liberating trucks of the Allied forces rolled through the prison gates, Murray and his surviving friends must have found their arrival difficult to comprehend. They were emaciated and exhausted, unwilling inhabitants of a dark world no man should ever know. Murray's spirit was dormant, but not dead. Although physically weakened, he knew that the best therapy lay in the mountains.

A few months later, as he swam in the waters of Loch Beinn a' Mheadhoin in Glen Affric, he weighed up the options that were open to him. Life had taught him that happiness lay in the mind. He contemplated entering a monastery, but the mountains which had saved his soul offered another route. Within a month, he received an enthusiastic response from a publisher to whom he had submitted a draft proposal based upon his prison manuscript. The book now bore the title *Mountaineering in Scotland*. Tentatively, Murray began to accept that he might have a talent for writing, and put his monastic ambitions on hold.

Murray went on to become a much-loved writer whose gift for evoking the pure pleasure of climbing and the essence of the landscape won him many admirers all over the world. His ethos was clear and simple: climbers did not 'conquer' mountains, nor did they own them. The joy went far deeper. It was an intense, spiritual response, which he was able to communicate. He inspired thousands of people to experience the mountains, and taught his readers that we have a responsibility to the environment, to preserve its character and its wildness. Once Murray's popularity grew and his books acquired a following, he became keenly aware of the impact of his words and had to tread carefully in order to protect precious landscapes from an overwhelming influx of visitors.

Murray's first experience of the Himalayas came in 1950, when he joined Tom Weir, Tom MacKinnon and Douglas Scott* on the first *Scottish Himalayan Expedition*. All the men had climbed extensively in the Alps but never in the Himalayas. The emphasis was on reconnaissance, but they hoped to tackle some challenging peaks if conditions allowed. At Ranikhet they hired eighteen porters, and they explored the river gorges, glaciers and peaks around Nanda Devi over four months. Most of the wished-for ascents eluded them but their trip was filled with endeavour and enjoyment; Murray remembered the wise words of a friend, who had advised him to measure his success by camps, not summits.

In 1951, a proposal for a reconnaissance expedition to Everest was put before the Joint Himalayan Committee, a body formed by the Alpine Club and the Royal Geographical Society. Murray was named as potential leader. While keen to be part of the expedition, Murray stepped down so that the post could be taken by Eric Shipton, who at that time was acknowledged as the world's most experienced Himalayan climber. The other members of the expedition were Michael Ward, Tom Bourdillon and two New Zealanders, Earle Riddiford and Edmund Hillary.

Murray's difficulty in adjusting to the altitude is thought to be why he was not included in the party chosen for the successful 1953 ascent, but this reconnaissance team played a vital role in helping to define the route taken.

Guided by a wish to share rather than to acquire, Murray gave his services generously to organisations that were close to his heart. As an advisor for the National Trust for Scotland, his survey on the Highland landscape laid the foundation for a programme of landscape protection in the form of National Scenic Areas. He was a founding trustee of the John Muir Trust, and he served as President of the Scottish Mountaineering Club and Chairman of the Scottish Countryside Activities Council.

In *Mountaineering in Scotland*, Murray writes of a metaphorical summit, represented by sunlight, to which every soul aspires. The purpose of life, he believed, is self-fulfilment and, like mountaineers, we are all reaching for beauty and truth. During his darkest hours he glimpsed divine wisdom and his work continues to draw readers to seek it through empathy with the natural world.

* Douglas Scott is a Glasgow-born climber, not to be confused with English mountaineer Doug Scott, who was a member of the *British Everest Expedition* led by Sir Chris Bonington in 1975.

SIR EDMUND PERCIVAL HILLARY

Mountaineer
BORN: 20th July 1919 (Auckland)
DIED: 11th January 2008 (Auckland)
§
RSGS Livingstone Medal, 1953 (with Sir John Hunt)

THERE ARE NO PHOTOGRAPHS of Sir Edmund Hillary on the summit of Everest. When he reached the peak at 11.30 on the morning of 29th May 1953, his first thought was to take a photograph of his climbing companion, Tenzing Norgay, then to record the jaw-dropping panoramic views from the highest point on Earth. He even noted with interest that he could see all the northern slopes of neighbouring Makalu, the world's fifth highest mountain, as yet unclimbed, and took some careful shots to study when he got back down.

Both men took their oxygen masks off and breathed the freezing air for a few precious minutes, letting the wind sting their faces with needles of ice. Beaming with delight, Tenzing hugged Hillary as they stood on the small platform of snow, the first men ever to do so. There was nothing but a yawning, dizzying space beneath their feet in every direction. Legions of lofty blue-white mountains stretched away to the far horizon, plainly showing the curvature of the Earth.

Hillary felt no elation. Rather, he felt a quiet sense of satisfaction at a job well done. As he replaced his mask and prepared for the long trek back, he imagined their achievement would not be of much interest to anyone besides other mountaineers.

How wrong he was. The pair descended to a wildly excited and clamorous world.

The first people to hear about Hillary and Tenzing's victory were, of course, the other members of their climbing team. Equipped with only short-range walkie-talkies, they had to spread the news of their success in person. Their first stop was the South Col, where George Lowe greeted them with hot soup. After a sleepless night they progressed down to Advanced Base Camp where the expedition leader, John Hunt, welcomed them with a huge sense of relief. To Hillary, who had still not come to grips with the scale of his achievement, the look of joy that spread over Hunt's tired face was ample reward in itself.

As the pair sipped mugs of tea they recounted their story to James Morris, a correspondent for *The Times* who had accompanied the expedition. Their triumph could not have come at a better time; Britain was preparing to celebrate the coronation of Queen Elizabeth II on 2nd June. Working quickly, Morris wrote his report and descended as fast as he could to Namche, where he telegraphed the news to the British Embassy in Kathmandu. As a result, the newspapers on the morning of the coronation bore the joyful headlines of Hillary and Tenzing's success, strengthening the hope slowly bearing Britain out of her post-war gloom.

Meanwhile, the climbing party cautiously picked their way over the Khumbu Glacier and continued their descent towards Kathmandu. John Hunt had hurried on ahead to make preparations for their departure, and it was he who sent a messenger speeding back up the trail, carrying the first letters of congratulation. One of the envelopes was addressed to *Sir* Edmund Hillary, and the New Zealander examined it with amusement followed swiftly by disbelief. The letter inside confirmed that he was indeed a newly created Knight of the British Empire. His overwhelming reaction was shock; he was, he felt, far too impoverished to bear such a title. Somehow he could not make this honour correspond with the image he had of himself, strolling around his hometown of Papakura in his dirty old overalls. Life was never going to be quite the same again.

Edmund Hillary was born in Auckland in 1919, the son of a beekeeper who produced honey as a commercial enterprise. He and his younger brother Rex would help their father harvest the produce of 1,600 hives. Bee stings were an occupational hazard, and the labour of handling 90lb boxes of honeycomb was physically exhausting, but Hillary loved the freedom and constant activity, especially when all the hives were swarming.

The Hillary family lived an unpretentious life and followed the Anglican faith, though Hillary found himself uninspired by Sunday school and regular church attendance. He was more attracted to the idea that healthy living and physical fitness promoted wellbeing, and loved to explore the great outdoors. He roamed all over the neighbouring Waitakere mountain ranges, accompanying organised climbing parties, helping to carry loads and beat trails through the dense rainforest. He enrolled at the University of Auckland to study science and maths, and chose to run there from home every day instead of taking public transport. He gave up on his studies after two years, realising that his future lay elsewhere. He had fallen under the spell of the mountains; it was, he said, an act of worship just to sit and look at a distant summit.

Climbing expeditions in the mountains of New Zealand resulted in journals filled with tired but happy reminiscences. During the Second World War he was stationed in Fiji as a navigator on flying boats, and his free time was spent immersed in Frank Smythe's books about the Himalayas. After the war he joined the New Zealand Alpine Club and in 1948, he partnered with Harry Ayres to make the first ascent of the South Ridge of Mount Cook. He was certainly ready for a bigger challenge when in 1951 he was accepted onto Earle Riddiford's New Zealand expedition to the Garhwal Himalayas in north-west India; the principal goals were the peaks of Nilkanta and Mukut Parbat.

The enigmatic British climber Eric Shipton, already a legend in mountaineering circles, was in the Himalayas at the same time as Hillary, leading the *Everest Reconnaissance Expedition*. The New Zealand Alpine Club saw irresistible potential and set some enquiries in motion. The result was a telegram from Shipton to the New Zealand team, who by that time were extracting themselves from the slopes of Mukut Parbat with painful feet and a happy glow of achievement. Shipton had room on his expedition for two more, he wrote. They should bring their own food, and would have to catch up with his team, who were already on the move. After a brief debate, Hillary and Riddiford were chosen and set off on an excited dash across the north of India.

Faced with the prospect of meeting one of his long-standing heroes for the first time, Hillary was suddenly conscious of his own humble beginnings, and became anxious. What if Shipton was a typical 'English gent' who dressed impeccably and shaved every day? He need not have worried. The reconnaissance party turned out to be a reassuringly 'disreputable looking bunch', and Hillary breathed silent thanks he would not have to change for dinner. The apprehension turned out to be mutual; Shipton was silently relieved by the New Zealanders' unshaven faces and scruffy clothes, and when they devoured a rather unpalatable meal with cheerful enthusiasm, it was obvious they were going to fit in.

The findings of the expedition laid the foundations for the successful Everest expedition two years later. Crucially, after many exploratory treks, Hillary and Shipton saw a new route to the summit, approaching from the south and along what George Mallory, in 1921, had called the Western Cwm. British mountaineer Michael Ward, one of Shipton's reconnaissance team, had long believed that such a route existed. It would mean crossing the formidable Khumbu Glacier, a death-trap of giant ice pinnacles and crevasses, but it might be possible – and Shipton believed it was.

Two years later, when Hillary received his invitation to join the *British Everest Expedition* of 1953, it came from Shipton, as the prospective leader. But Shipton's independent nature was ill-suited to large-scale expeditions, and after a period of rather awkward manoeuvring on the part of the Joint Himalayan Committee, British Army colonel John Hunt was appointed instead. Hillary was initially doubtful about the change, but Hunt turned out to be a supremely capable leader, balancing level-headedness with sensitivity.

As the assault on Everest began, a daunting volume of supplies, including cumbersome oxygen equipment, had to be ferried in painful stages from one camp to the next. The logistics of this operation meant ascending to a pre-determined point with a heavy load, depositing it safely, then returning to the camp below. A team of

Nepalese Sherpas had been engaged; their leader (or 'sirdar') was Tenzing Norgay, whose dazzling smile seemed to lighten the most extreme circumstances. Hillary had already forged a bond with Tenzing, who had saved his life when an ice-shelf gave way under his feet; as Hillary fell, Tenzing instantly struck his axe into the ice and secured the rope. After this incident the two climbed together regularly, and Hillary knew that if he was called to make a bid on the summit he would want Tenzing with him. Each had an indomitable spirit; Hillary jokingly called them the 'tigers of the party'.

In the whirlwind of media attention following their ascent, Hillary managed to retain a sense of proportion and balance. To escape the crowds, he would retreat to the wild and beautiful Waitakere Ranges of his homeland, where he had first discovered his passion for climbing.

Despite his initial reaction to the news of his knighthood, Hillary was independent-minded and had a strong sense of equality. For several years after the expedition, he continued to list his occupation as 'beekeeper'. He recalls his joyous reception back in Auckland with fellow New Zealander George Lowe, during which he was given a white chair to sit on, symbolising Everest; this chair was, he said, the only piece of furniture he owned for quite a while. He was a living example of his own philosophy, namely that a person need not be born a hero to achieve the extraordinary; all that is needed is motivation.

Hillary returned to the Himalayas many times, making two unsuccessful attempts on Makalu, before focusing his attention on improving the living conditions of the Nepalese people. He set up The Himalayan Trust which established a number of schools, hospitals and clinics, built bridges over rivers and provided fresh water supplies. It was, he said, an ideal way to repay the Sherpas for the loyalty and support that they had given him. Comradeship was still, in his opinion, the greatest gift of all, and he cherished the shared the thrills and dangers of the mountains in the company of those he loved best.

Sir Edmund Hillary was presented with the Livingstone Medal of the Royal Scottish Geographical Society on 5th October 1953 'for perseverance and will-power in reaching the summit of Everest'. The medal was awarded jointly with the expedition's leader, Sir John Hunt, when both men gave a lecture to the Society in Edinburgh. Acknowledging the honour, Hillary expressed a wish that the medal could have been given to all the members of the expedition: 'After all, it has not been two men who have climbed Everest, and if any of the others had done anything less than they did, we would never have got there.'

All references in this chapter from Presentation of the Livingstone Gold Medal, *Scottish Geographical Magazine* (1953) 69:3, 131-132

Sir Christian ('Chris') John Storey Bonington

Mountaineer
BORN: 6th August 1934 (London)
§
RSGS Livingstone Medal, 1991

CHRIS BONINGTON's name summons first and foremost an image of mountains. As one of Britain's best-known climbers, he has spent much of his life on the roof of the world either leading expeditions in the Himalayas or making a series of astonishing ascents in places as far flung as Antarctica, Chamonix and Patagonia.

Bonington was only sixteen when he was first bitten by the climbing bug. Inspired by W. H. Murray's writing, in his school holidays he hitch-hiked north from his home in London, lured by the vertical walls of Snowdonia and Glen Coe. This passion stayed with him through military training at Sandhurst and three years of army service in Germany. Eventually, he realised it was not just a hobby that could be fitted around a day job; his true path in life led upwards, into the mountains.

Bonington spent several seasons in the Alps and the Dolomites honing his skills, making several first ascents and forging lifelong friendships. For some climbers, this would be enough but for Bonington the most glittering prizes still lay to the east, in the Himalayas.

In 1970 he led an expedition to climb the south face of Annapurna, an almost legendary 9,800-foot wall of rock and ice at a height of nearly 23,000 feet above sea level. Annapurna was guaranteed to push any climber's skill and stamina to the utmost, so Bonington's choice of team members was crucial. The team reached the summit, but Bonington was devastated when Ian Clough, a long-standing friend and climbing partner, was killed by an avalanche during their descent.

With the ultimate goal of the world's highest mountain never far from his mind, Bonington laid claim to several Himalayan peaks before leading the *British Everest Expedition* of 1975.

At that time, no Briton had set foot on the summit of Everest. While the British John Hunt had led the triumphant 1953 expedition, it was Edmund Hillary, a New Zealander, and Tenzing Norgay, a Nepalese Indian Sherpa, who had reached the summit. In addition, no one had ever climbed Everest via one of its faces. Bonington had tried and failed to scale the fearsome South-west Face in 1972. Two of his fellow climbers, Doug Scott and Dougal Haston, persuaded him to change his mind and he now favoured a more accessible route via the South Col.

In the decades leading up to 1975, most of the Himalayan mountains were conquered using siege-style expeditions which involved a large quantity of equipment and supplies. Progress was steady, and a series of base camps was built before the final assault on the summit. The teams were large, often accompanied by native Sherpas, and it was accepted that only a handful of members would be fit enough to make it all the way to the top. This contrasts with the 'Alpine' method of climbing, which could be described as more of an ambush; the ascent is made swiftly in smaller teams who carry a relatively light burden of gear. As mountaineering methods evolved, Bonington's Everest ascent was one of the last major siege-style expeditions.

The provisions, transported from Britain to Kathmandu in two trucks, comprised 1,000 crates of food along with tents, ladders, ropes and breathing apparatus. Assembling enough rations and equipment to support a hundred people in extreme conditions over a period of twelve weeks was a logistical nightmare. To make it even more complicated, the supplies had to be divided into 60lb loads so they could be carried by Sherpas.

After some brilliant climbing and route planning by team members, in particular Nick Estcourt and Paul 'Tut' Braithwaite who negotiated Everest's formidable Rock Band, Bonington was in a position to choose teams for the summit attempt. For the first try he selected Scott and Haston, who on 24th September 1975 were the first Britons to stand on the summit of Everest. It would be another ten years before Bonington would do the same. The team's Herculean efforts, the appalling conditions which they endured, and the losses of Mick Burke and a young porter named Mingma are described in Bonington's book, *Everest the Hard Way*.

Bonington's achievements make impressive reading, but merely listing them does not do them justice; each climb had its own character, often shaped by the spirit of the team, and each brought its own unique set of challenges. Quite often, the thrill of success was followed by immediate concerns about the safest route of descent. Sometimes it was tempered with grief at the loss of a team member. Gifted climbers tread a knife-edge of risk, and no one was ever under any illusions about the stress endured by families and friends.

In addition to the physical risk, there was also a financial one. For mountaineers, the ability to make a career out of their lifelong passion has always been elusive. At first Bonington had no real idea how to achieve it. He is naturally shy, and believes with hindsight that he was too impatient to make a good instructor, preferring to focus on his own goals of climbing 'to the limit'. He realised, however, that he could be a communicator who shared the thrill of the mountains and inspired others to experience it as well. He began to write books about his expeditions, and before long the British public had embraced him affectionately as the godfather of climbing.

Communicating in the digital age brought its own demands, as Bonington soon discovered. After a gruelling climb, instead of curling up in his tent and going to sleep, he would fire up a computer and write a blog post about his day. At the time, his exhausted mind felt that he was better off in the early years, when life was simpler. As a consequence, however, Bonington is one of the few mountaineers who has these precious records of continuous experience from the time when climbing teams had little or no link with the outside world, stretching right through to the twenty-first century with satellite positioning and instant communication.

Bonington once said that, for him, the pleasure of climbing lay not so much in standing on a summit as in seeing what new challenges revealed themselves on the other side. There were, he explained, always other horizons to go beyond. Although Everest is hailed as his greatest triumph, he remembers the pure joy of adventure on the slopes of Shivling, a distinctive twin-peaked mountain in the Indian Himalayas. In 1983 he was invited to speak at a mountaineering conference in Delhi and, in his words, decided to extend his stay with 'a little expedition': a hair-raising first ascent of Shivling's western peak in the company of friend Jim Fotheringham. The pair had just seven days to complete the climb because, as Bonington disarmingly explains, Fotheringham had to get back to his dental practice.

Shivling tested their nerve to the utmost. At one stage they found themselves clinging like spiders to a vertical wall as an ice sheet rained car-sized boulders all around them. Having taken it in turns to stand on the needle-sharp summit they descended in the dark, ropeless and without head torches. Afterwards, Bonington recalled the exhilaration. The challenge, he said, had all the elements that make a great adventure: wild scenery, a magnificent objective, spontaneity and the thrill of risk, and the compatibility of a small team.

In August 2014, as part of another small team consisting of climber Leo Houlding and explorer Andy Torbet, Bonington stood on an Orkney clifftop and surveyed the dizzying spectacle of the Old Man of Hoy. This slim finger of Old Red Sandstone rises 450 feet from the pounding waves, and Bonington was preparing to scale it. It would not be the first time; his earlier climb, the first recorded, was in 1966. But now, mentally steadying himself for the challenge, he confessed he was 'downright apprehensive'. He had, after all, just celebrated his eightieth birthday. He was no longer as lithe or as flexible as he had been in his youth. His fellow climbers believed he could do it – but did he believe in himself?

Later that day, having climbed stubbornly through gusty winds and squally rain, Bonington stood with Leo Houlding on top of the pillar. The surface had been slippery from the outset but after completing the second pitch, Bonington knew he was going to succeed. The triumph was poignant because he had lost his beloved wife, Wendy, to motor neurone disease only a month before. Speaking with emotion shortly after the climb, Bonington said that he had been thinking about her as he made the ascent, remembering that she was his 'rock' during his lifetime of challenges. During his eighties, he said, he wants every day to mean something; he intends to make his later life as rich and exciting as possible, and hopes to encourage others to do the same.

In addition to raising money for research into motor neurone disease, Bonington is actively involved with many other charities, including the British Exploring Society, the British Orienteering Foundation, the Outward Bound Trust, the John Muir Trust, and Community Action Nepal. His eyes still light up with the joy of the mountains and in the hearts of countless young climbers he has helped to inspire, he commands a deep sense of affection and respect.

Sir Alan John Cobham

Pioneering aviator
BORN: 6th May 1894 (London)
DIED: 21st October 1973 (Bournemouth)
§
RSGS Livingstone Medal, 1926 (presented in 1928)

S IR SEFTON BRANCKER, Britain's Director of Civil Aviation, was planning to go to India. In 1924 the journey usually entailed a lengthy sea passage, and he was discussing the prospect with de Havilland test pilot and all-round aviation daredevil, Alan Cobham.

'Nothing could be simpler, my dear chap,' Cobham probably said. 'I'll fly you there.'

The two pored over some maps and worked out a route to India that would allow them plenty of stopovers for refuelling and refreshment. From Cologne they would fly to Berlin, Warsaw, Lemberg, Bucharest and Constantinople; across Turkey to Alexandretta; south-east to Baghdad and Basra, then down the Persian Gulf to Karachi. Knowing it was possible to fly this route in the summer months, Brancker suggested that they should go in the winter instead. If it proved to be viable, it could be added to the schedules of commercial airlines. If it proved impossible, well, they were guaranteed an adventure.

On 20th November 1924, Cobham's DH50 biplane roared into life and taxied down the runway of Stag Lane Aerodrome in Edgware, North London. On board, in addition to Cobham and Brancker, were Arthur Elliott, Cobham's trusted engineer, and a Romanian general whom Brancker had invited at the last minute. Luggage space was almost non-existent; Cobham noticed with cheery good humour that the plane was heavily overloaded. It was a low-key beginning to a flight that would help to change the course of aviation history.

Given that Cobham blazed a trail through the skies at a time when aviation was still a new and risky venture, it comes as a surprise to discover that he died of old age. What saved him and his many passengers was his ability to land any kind of aircraft anywhere, with or without the aid of an engine.

Having enlisted in the Royal Flying Corps during the Great War, Cobham was truly bitten by the aviation bug. When the war was over he became a pilot for de Havilland at Stag Lane Aerodrome. In 1921, a wealthy American called Lucien Sharpe was looking for a pilot to fly him around the historical sites of Europe. Cobham leapt at the opportunity, seeing it as a marvellous means of promoting air travel both to the government and the general public. On their 5,000-mile journey, he and Sharpe landed at seventeen cities in the course of three weeks. Sharpe, good-natured and eccentric, was passionate about good wine, classical music and ancient history. His chosen itinerary was a whistle-stop version of the Grand Tour: Milan, Gerona, Seville, down into Morocco and Algeria, then back up to Florence and Venice, passing through the smoke plume of Vesuvius as they landed in Naples. Since they were flying with the cockpit open, this must have made them cough!

When Cobham learned that Sir Sefton Brancker intended to travel to India by sea, he was dismayed. Surely, he thought, the Director of Civil Aviation should arrive by air! Brancker's mission in India was to investigate the potential for airship stations; at that time, airships were considered a safer and more viable means of transport than aeroplanes, especially for long-haul commercial flights. Cobham held a different view. He had just lifted the trophy in the King's Cup Air Race, and could fly a biplane as if it was an extension of his own body. He was convinced that the future of commercial aviation lay in aeroplanes. Seizing the chance to prove his point, he persuaded Brancker to think again.

The flight to India was a challenge, not a race. Passage from Britain to India on board a P&O liner took about twelve days; Cobham was not competing with that time. On the contrary, Brancker had a network of business contacts throughout Europe and beyond, and he was using this opportunity to visit as many as possible.

In Poland, bad weather kept the aircraft grounded so Brancker and his friend went on by train to Bucharest. They missed a great deal of excitement when a few days later, as the DH50 crossed the Carpathians, Cobham and Elliott found themselves heading for the side of a mountain with cloud above them and a sea of fog below. Spying a snowy field about the size of a postage stamp, Cobham brought their little biplane down to an abrupt landing. The pair staggered down to the nearest village, where Cobham, already a worldwide celebrity, was instantly recognised. The owner of the Post Office welcomed him warmly and placed his switchboard at his disposal. Cobham, unruffled and debonair as always, mustered some soldiers to help dig a makeshift runway, and in a jiffy the aviators were back in the air.

Reunited in Bucharest, Cobham, Elliott and Brancker flew on to Constantinople, where Cobham discovered the aircraft had a cracked cylinder block. Unruffled, he cabled Stag Lane and ordered replacement parts to be sent via the Orient Express while the party enjoyed a welcome spot of sightseeing. Arriving in Karachi on 30th December, they made leisurely progress through Delhi and Calcutta, and reached Rangoon on 6th February 1925.

Brancker's string of business appointments in India left Cobham kicking his heels. In Calcutta he decided to while away the time by giving himself an aerial tour of the Himalayas. Acting on impulse, he flew up to Jalpaiguri, taking with him a British diplomat who was also a keen photographer. Landing there caused a sensation; no one in that region had ever seen an aircraft before, and word spread like wildfire. A guard of Gurkhas failed to deter the huge crowds who threatened to damage the plane out of sheer curiosity, so elephants had to be brought in, forming a defensive circle that no one would dare to cross.

Having deliberately lightened the aircraft, Cobham found that the engine functioned well at a maximum altitude 16,000 feet but the controls responded sluggishly in the thin air. He should perhaps have paid equal attention to the impact on the human body. As he was marvelling at the splendid views of Everest and Kangchenjunga, he became slightly concerned about the welfare of his passenger. Instead of taking photographs, his friend was suffering from oxygen starvation, something which seemed to bypass Cobham entirely. After a brief but tense argument, a prompt landing was in order – and possibly a stiff gin and tonic afterwards.

When Brancker had fulfilled all his commitments in India, he was no doubt looking forward to an uneventful flight back to London. No mountain ranges got in the way this time, and in fact everything went splendidly until they encountered a snowstorm over the Black Forest. The aircraft was overloaded – Cobham's wealthy passengers always had a habit of buying bulky souvenirs – and this time he could find no convenient field. Realising that he would have to land uphill in deep snow, he shouted to Elliott and Brancker to scramble to the back of the cabin and take the luggage with them; the plane needed to be tail-heavy to stop it flipping over on its nose. A few seconds later, the engine practically stalling, Cobham drove the aircraft into a bank of snow and pulled back the joystick. They rolled for about 30 yards and then juddered to a stop. Breathless silence. They were all alive.

This time the plane had to be dismantled and shipped in pieces to Stuttgart, where it was rebuilt. The trio flew home via Paris, and were greeted in Croydon with a grand reception on 17th March 1925. Anyone who complains about the delays of modern long-haul flight might do well to read Alan Cobham's memoirs.

Only months after his safe arrival back in England, Cobham took to the air again for a 94-day journey to Cape Town, South Africa. Naturally, he wanted his itinerary to include some of the continent's spectacular sights, but as he flew low over Victoria Falls, spray from the water got into the engine of his biplane and caused it to cut out. With the plane hurtling downwards, Cobham pulled back on the control stick and forced it into a steep climb; the engine choked, died, caught again, and spluttered its way back to life. His passenger, a professional photographer for whom the phrase 'stiff upper lip' must surely have been invented, just carried on filming.

Honours poured in, but Cobham had still not achieved his dream. In his vision, Britain was 'a nation of airmen', with a landing strip beside every town. In his view, air transport held the key to excellence in communications and travel, and he wanted Britain to lead the world in the skies as it had on the seas. With his daring exploits he did not seek glory for himself; he wanted to convince the government that significant investment should be made in civil aviation.

> 'The aircraft industry at this juncture should receive every assistance possible, so that it might try to capture the markets, not only of the Empire but of the world, and give them a new industry which they needed so badly.'

The government, like the British public, was still slightly wary of these new-fangled flying machines, but Cobham had another card up his sleeve. He was going to deliver a petition to Parliament, calling for a more forward-thinking aviation policy. To do this, he had intended to fly himself from Rochester to London, but the thought struck – as perhaps it would only ever strike Alan Cobham – that his plea would have more impact if it was delivered via Australia.

On 30th June 1926, Cobham set off in his DH50, now converted to a seaplane with the addition of floats; Arthur Elliott was on board once again as his engineer. Cobham should have been in fine spirits, but a dark premonition had been dragging at his mind and a strong instinct was telling him to abandon the flight. He tried to shrug it off, but by the time they reached Baghdad he felt so sick that he had to physically force himself to continue. Their next destination was Bushire in the Persian Gulf, but sandstorms meant that they had to fly low over the swamps around Basra.

As Cobham struggled to see the route ahead, the aircraft was rocked by a sudden explosion. Elliott, from behind, reported that a petrol pipe must have burst – then noticed that he was bleeding. What they had initially thought a technical fault was, in fact, gunfire. Elliott had been shot by a marksman on the ground. Bedouin tribes were taking a defiant stance against recent bombings by the RAF, and in low visibility the plane's identity could have been mistaken.

Whoever the culprit was, Elliott needed urgent medical attention. Landing in Basra in the searing heat, Cobham summoned assistance and a doctor was called, but it was too late; Elliott had died.

For once, Cobham was at a loss. Overcome with grief and guilt, he had no heart to carry on. It took some strong rallying messages from his wife and his close friends, including Sefton Brancker, to persuade him to complete his journey. Steeling himself, he found an RAF engineer who was willing to take Elliott's place, and carried on towards Australia.

Cobham was greeted by rapturous crowds in Melbourne on 15th August, and on 1st October he arrived back in Britain, landing his seaplane on the River Thames outside the Houses of Parliament. An estimated one million people, almost a quarter of the population of Inner London, turned out to watch. This time, both King and Parliament sat up and took notice. Cobham was awarded a knighthood, his ideas about aviation no longer sounding so crazy.

What next, for a man who had paved the way for long-haul commercial flights? The Great British public remained to be convinced, largely because they had no real first-hand experience of aeroplanes. If they could not come to see the planes, Cobham reasoned, then he would take the planes to them, offering joy rides, and an aerial spectacle that they would never forget.

For four years, between 1932 and 1935, Cobham toured almost every major town in Britain, putting on air shows in the summer, often at the rate of two a day. He gathered a fleet of planes and recruited pilots, a parachutist, wing-walkers and a female glider pilot. Over the green fields of Britain, a troupe of biplanes dipped, swooped and soared in crazy mock battles, thrilling the crowds so much that keeping overexcited spectators off the landing strip became a major problem. Nothing of the like had ever been seen before. Cobham's Flying Circus became a barnstorming phenomenon, sweeping the nation quite literally off its feet.

In 1928 the Royal Scottish Geographical Society presented the Livingstone Medal to Sir Alan Cobham, 'for his two flying expeditions from London to Cape Town overland over Africa, and from London to Melbourne and back.' Speaking of his quest to make flying simple, safe and straightforward, Sir Alan reassured his audience that 'any adventures that he might have had by air across the world had been the result of pioneer flights of survey... These adventures would never have occurred on an air route in regular operation. On properly organised air routes there should be no adventure, for adventure invariably meant danger, and whenever flying became dangerous, it ceased to be commercial.'

Sir Alan Cobham had such a far-reaching vision that it is easy to forget he was born over 120 years ago. In 1939, he was told by a Wing Commander in charge of selecting prospective pilots for the Second World War that three-quarters of the candidates had taken their first flight with Cobham's Flying Circus. Without doubt, he helped to inspire a generation. As a founding director of Airspeed, an aircraft manufacturing company, he helped to pioneer a new technique for aerial refuelling which is still in use today. He married the love of his life, a beautiful actress called Gladys Lloyd, who won his heart when she was one of the few clients he failed to impress. Modern-day aviation owes him a great deal, and his energetic attitude to life is just as refreshing today as it was then.

All references in this chapter from *The Scotsman*, 23rd November 1928, report of
  lecture by Sir Alan Cobham to RSGS in Edinburgh, 22nd November 1928

Neil Alden Armstrong

Astronaut and aeronautical engineer
Born: 5th August 1930 (Wapakoneta, Ohio)
Died: 25th August 2012 (Cincinnati, Ohio)
§
RSGS Livingstone Medal, 1971

O N THE SURFACE OF the Moon, Neil Armstrong was having trouble sleeping. He and his companion, Edwin 'Buzz' Aldrin, had covered the windows in the Lunar Module and had tried to make themselves as comfortable as possible in the cramped space. Both had donned their helmets to protect their lungs from the dust that they had carried inside with them on their space suits – minuscule particles which were now floating freely around the cabin and which smelled, said Aldrin, rather like wet ashes. In their carefully monitored schedule they had been allocated seven hours of rest, but the temperature had dropped to a chilly 16°C and the Module's brightly illuminated control panel could not be dimmed, creating an unexpected problem of light pollution. Then, as they settled themselves down for the 'night', they realised that there was another light source, beaming relentlessly into their cabin from outside; an instrument known as the Alignment Optical Telescope was trained on the heavens and streaming light from Earth's blue-and-white sphere straight into the Module. No cover that they rigged up could diminish it. So, watched by the wakeful eye of their home planet, the two men settled down for an uncomfortable and fitful sleep.

Exactly thirty-three years earlier, on 20th July 1936, Armstrong had experienced the thrill of flying for the first time. Aged only five and accompanied by his father, he was taken up in a Ford TriMotor,

231

affectionately known as a 'Tin Goose', for a short flight above his native Ohio. A passion for aviation was ignited, and by the time he was eight or nine he had filled his bedroom with model aircraft that he built himself. From an early age he realised that speed and efficiency depended on good design; he had the mind of a born mathematician and an appetite for solving problems.

In the summer of 1946, Armstrong received flying lessons from veteran army pilots on an airstrip near his hometown of Wapakoneta. He took to the sky in an Aeronca Chief, a light monoplane, and within a week of his sixteenth birthday he made his first solo flight. It was true that he gained his wings before his driver's licence, but with typical modesty Armstrong always dismissed any undue praise. Two other boys from his school year learned to fly at the same time, so in that sense his achievement was not unique, but none of the others would have flown themselves 300 miles from Wapakoneta to West Lafayette in Indiana at the age of sixteen just to pre-register for Purdue University. With his quiet determination, Neil was in a league of his own.

Having embarked on a course in aeronautical engineering, Neil realised with a pang of regret that most of the record-breaking 'firsts' had already fallen to the pioneers of aviation who were his childhood heroes. In one important sense at least, he had been born several decades too late. He was, however, training as a naval cadet at a time of great technological advancement. This was the era of the X-planes, a succession of experimental aircraft developed by the National Advisory Committee for Aeronautics, forerunner of NASA. In 1946 the first of these, the Bell X-1, became the first aircraft to break the sound barrier in level flight. By the late 1950s the series had arrived at the X-15, which was capable of reaching the edge of outer space at a speed of over 4,500 miles per hour.

Armstrong was one of the X-15 test pilots. Now an experienced aviator and a veteran of the Korean War, he found himself on the brink of the most outstanding 'first' in the history of exploration. By the end of the decade, declared President John F Kennedy in 1961, the United States would send a manned mission to the Moon. Of course, this was mostly about beating the Russians, whose space-flight programme was threatening to humiliate the US. The USSR had launched the first satellite, Sputnik 1, in 1957, and had put the first man (Yuri Gagarin) into orbit in 1961. American citizens, aware of the nuclear weapons being brandished by both superpowers and fearful that World War III would burst upon them with cataclysmic suddenness, seized on Kennedy's aspirations and followed NASA's progress with a zeal born of desperation and pride. The men chosen for the Apollo missions would feel a burden of expectation like no one before or since. In addition to being immaculately trained and supremely fit, they were upholders of the American dream. Everything about their lives would be in the public arena, open to infinite scrutiny and comment. Perhaps only someone like Neil Armstrong, famously spartan with words and guarded with his emotions, had a chance of surviving.

On 19th July 1969, as the Apollo 11 spacecraft moved into orbit around the Moon, her crew of three were trying to answer an interesting question. What colour was the lunar surface? Michael Collins, the Command Module Pilot, reckoned that it was Plaster-of-Paris grey. Buzz Aldrin decided that it was brown, while Armstrong saw it as tan. Because their spacecraft repeatedly circled the lunar sphere, they were able to witness it in many different lighting conditions, from the deep charcoal shadows of dawn or dusk to the rosy glow of midday. Their discussions were relaxed but Armstrong, the Mission Commander, was keeping a keen eye on the alien landscape passing beneath them, actively looking for a specific site that had occupied his mind. Very soon he and Aldrin would be asked to enter the Lunar Module, aptly known as the 'Eagle', and undock it from the spacecraft so they could fall into a lower orbit and ultimately descend to the Moon's surface. He wanted to be sure that they were heading for the right place.

A few hours later, as he glimpsed the distant Earth rising from the window of the orbiting Lunar Module, Aldrin caught his breath and gazed in wonder. He pointed it out to Armstrong, whose reaction was non-committal. He had just taken the Module through a roll, during which the radar antenna had been pointed deliberately towards the Moon. This had confirmed their height, and with the Module now upright again he was carefully studying the features below so that he could gauge the timing of their approach into the Sea of Tranquillity.

He suspected that they might be going to overfly the predicted landing spot. If they did, he would have to pilot it manually, choosing a suitable location quickly and by eye. He was alert, but did not anticipate any difficulty until, 3,000 feet above the lunar surface, the first alarm sounded in the Module's computer.

Back in Houston, a ripple of suppressed panic ran around the control centre as the best brains in the US strove to identify two repeated and unprecedented alarm lights. It took only fifteen seconds; the software was being overloaded. It was safe, if slightly unnerving. Confirmation was relayed to Armstrong and Aldrin; the watching public were largely unaware of the tension. Unflinching, Armstrong prepared to land. There was about fifty seconds' worth of fuel left in the tank.

Most of Armstrong's colleagues would have agreed that he was calm under pressure. He could swiftly assess a problem and reach a decision, while offering no hint whatsoever about what was going on in his mind. As a test pilot, he never made any spontaneous remarks that could be quoted and challenged later. People who met him for the first time often came up against a kind of façade that they interpreted variously as composure or remoteness, depending on their expectations. Yet his smile was wide and generous. Those who worked with Armstrong knew him as a great commander. He could, according to his friends, fly an aircraft as if he was wearing it.

Janet Armstrong, watching on live TV in the company of her two young sons, knew her husband better than most. The two had met at Purdue University, married in 1956, and shared their own private joys and tragedies. She held her breath as he made a feather-light touchdown on the Moon. Houston erupted with joy. The entire world was in uproar. As he squeezed himself through the hatch and prepared to walk into the history books, the man with nerves as cool as steel was expected to give an emotional response. The world waited. Janet silently willed him to be descriptive.

That's one small step for man... one giant leap for mankind.

Armstrong, it seemed, was the calmest of all.

After he had delivered the pronouncement, whose syntax would tease historians and reporters for generations to come, Armstrong applied himself to the work in hand, for which there was a daunting checklist. With his first steps on the Moon he discovered that the lunar surface was fine and powdery; he was able to kick it up with his boots but it compacted into distinct footprints beneath his feet. He collected some soil and rock samples. When Aldrin joined him they began to make a number of observations and communicate them to Earth. The Moon's landscape, reported Armstrong, had a stark beauty of its own which reminded him of the high desert of the United States. He saw ridges and craters, some of them 50 feet tall but most about a foot or two in height. He confirmed that the rocks were light grey on the outside but when broken they showed a darker interior, like basalt.

250,000 miles away, in the sitting rooms of the world, Armstrong's clear but impassive voice was strangely at odds with his bouncing gait, which looked irresistibly like effervescence. The Moon's gravity is one-sixth that of the Earth, so an astronaut weighing 360lb (including his cumbersome suit and backpack) is converted to a mere 60lb on the lunar surface. With no real facility for practising prolonged movement in such conditions, Armstrong and Aldrin had to improvise and find the best walking technique during their first minutes on the Moon. Unwittingly, in their slow-motion skipping they captured the jubilation of their audience. 'Like children playing hopscotch' was one verdict. In reality, moonwalking needed every effort of concentration because the terrain was surprisingly varied and their helmets restricted their vision vertically downwards. Only on the steps of the Lunar Module, as he prepared to re-enter the cabin, did Armstrong permit himself anything approaching levity. At ground level he crouched down and then half-leapt, half-floated up to the third step of the ladder. It was a spontaneous action, made out of curiosity, he later admitted, to see what would happen.

Having spent two and a half hours on the Moon's surface, during which they took several photographs, planted an American flag, and answered a call from President Nixon, the two astronauts closed the door of their landing craft. In theory, they were supposed to brush themselves off before they re-entered the cabin, but the dust that clung to their suits was so light that it followed them in.

They had fulfilled their duty. All that remained was to launch their little capsule back into the blackness of space, place it in a precise orbit, dock it safely with the Command Module in which Collins was keeping a lonely vigil, and return to Earth. Though they had been awake for nearly twenty-two hours, Armstrong found it hard to tell if he was tired. His prevailing emotion was one of relief. Sleep was essential.

On US national television two commentators, Eric Sevareid and Walter Cronkite, were discussing the scenes they had just witnessed. They agreed that Armstrong had sounded rather laconic and unemotional, even though his mother, Viola, had been interviewed and declared that her son was 'thrilled'. They confirmed the feeling of joy that came from seeing Armstrong and Aldrin moving with such apparent ease in a landscape that was thought to be cold and desolate and forbidding, and they pondered Armstrong's description of 'pretty', wondering if the Moon had a strange beauty that was known only to the men who walked there. Cronkite thought that this beauty would be something that future astronauts would miss; Sevareid took the idea a step further, saying that from this day everyone else would feel like strangers to these men, that they had disappeared into another life where we could not follow. The Moon, he said, had treated them well; how people on Earth would treat them was a question that filled him with foreboding.

In 1972 Neil Armstrong was a special guest at the Usher Hall in Edinburgh, where he was presented with the Livingstone Medal of the RSGS. Three years after the moon landing, Sevareid's gloomy prophesy had not been fulfilled. Armstrong was, and still is, an icon of the space age, a man without ego or flamboyance, extending our quest for knowledge to the most distant horizon in the history of human exploration.

MISSIONARIES
&
MAVERICKS

Dr David Livingstone

African explorer and missionary
BORN: 19th March 1813 (Blantyre, South Lanarkshire)
DIED: 1st May 1873 (Ilala, Zambia)

§

Daughter, Agnes, was a co-founder of RSGS
and endowed the Livingstone Medal in his honour

'**D**R LIVINGSTONE, I PRESUME?' History has immortalised the words which Henry Morton Stanley claimed to have spoken on meeting the long-lost explorer in Africa in 1871. The two men are often pictured doffing hats in true British style on the shore of Lake Tanganyika while scores of delighted African tribesmen look on. Afterwards they enjoyed a feast of chicken, goat's meat and rice, and drank sweet tea poured from a silver teapot into beautiful china cups.

It is an alluring image, but beneath the heartiness of the celebration lay a stark truth: Livingstone was a weak and dying man. Racked by malaria, emaciated and almost toothless, his mind and body were driven only by willpower. Stanley tried to persuade him to abandon his mission and rejoin his family in England but Livingstone refused. He had a goal, and would not give up while there was still life in his body.

David Livingstone was one of seven children. His father, a Sunday school teacher and tea salesman in South Lanarkshire, was driven by religious zeal, while his mother was said to be a delicate little woman with a cheerful disposition and beautiful eyes. For poor people in the early nineteenth century, education took a back seat to necessity so David worked in the local cotton mill from the age of ten to help support his family. Despite the fourteen-hour working days, he was so eager to learn that he would devote several hours to his school books and began studying medicine and theology at the University of Glasgow in 1836. His ambition was to become a missionary doctor, and to this end he travelled south to join the London Missionary Society.

In March 1841, aged twenty-eight, Livingstone arrived in Cape Town to take up his first post at the Moffat Mission in Kuruman, a small town on the edge of the Kalahari. From there, his task was to explore the land to the north and find a site for a new mission station. This would be no comfortable safari; much of Africa's interior had never been seen by a European, and most of its people had never laid eyes on a white man. A warm welcome was by no means guaranteed.

Like all the explorers of his time, Livingstone was exposing himself to a host of largely unknown tropical diseases and, to compound his difficulties, he was severely mauled by a lion in 1844, resulting in a permanently injured left arm. As he recuperated at the Moffat Mission, he fell in love.

Livingstone's bride was Mary Moffat, a Scotswoman whose father, Robert, had founded the Moffat Mission at Kuruman. Mary had lived in Africa for much of her life; she had absorbed the Christian teaching of her parents and was quiet, dutiful, and courageous. Livingstone adored her. Mary accompanied her husband on many of his journeys; accustomed as she was to the unforgiving climate, pregnancy and childbirth brought fresh risks. With their young family, the Livingstones crossed the Kalahari twice, enduring stifling heat and mosquito bites which caused malaria in two of the children. The loss of their fourth child only six weeks after she was born left Mary weakened and ill. Forced to conclude that his family would fare better at home, Livingstone sent them back to Scotland.

Meanwhile, in 1852, he began to contemplate an expedition on a much bigger scale. Alongside his mission to spread the word of gospels, he was infused with a new zeal.

> My business is to publish what I see, to rouse up those who have the power to stop it, once and for all.[1]

241

Shortly after his arrival in Africa, Livingstone had witnessed a fourteen-year-old African boy being sold to a slave merchant in exchange for a gun. The British Empire had abolished slavery in 1833, but other European countries were still engaged in the trade. People were being captured in their thousands by African and Arab merchants, chained together and forced on a merciless march to the east coast, where they were placed on board ships bound for the Middle East and America. Livingstone was appalled, and vowed to dedicate every last breath to stopping the atrocity. He believed that he could see a way to save the African people, calling his plan 'the three Cs': Christianity, commerce, and civilisation. If he could prove that the great Zambezi River was navigable, he could bring in not only missionaries but legitimate sources of trade such as cotton and coffee. Instead of slaves, Africa would have alternative commodities for sale. Livingstone saw the river as an artery into the heart of Africa, carrying the light of freedom and peace. This was the vision that drove him forward.

With the help of a Chief of the Kololo, and supported by many Africans as interpreters, Livingstone followed the Zambezi westwards through many hundreds of miles of uncharted territory. Travelling by canoe and sometimes on foot, he packed biscuits, coffee and tea, and spare clothes for use when he reached 'civilised life'. Other chests contained his books and almanacs, medicines, compasses and a sextant. He carried a rifle, and his companions had several muskets between them; with these, they hoped to obtain enough meat to live on. As a back-up, Livingstone had packed a tin of beads which he intended to barter with tribes he encountered in exchange for food. He would sleep in a simple tent, covered by a sheepskin blanket.

Alligators and hippos were not the only danger; tsetse flies and mosquitoes were a constant menace. Already suffering from malaria, Livingstone experimentally dosed himself with his own concoction of quinine and purgatives which gave some relief from the fever. The remedy was so effective that it was later marketed by Burroughs, Wellcome & Co. as 'Livingstone's Rousers'.

As he travelled down the Zambezi, Livingstone noticed white columns of vapour rising from the horizon and mingling with the clouds. He was approaching one of Africa's most magnificent spectacles: Mosi-oa-Tunya, the 'smoke that thunders'. Edging his canoe onto a small island, Livingstone peered down over the mesmerising 350-foot waterfall that he renamed Victoria Falls in honour of his queen. He was the first European to see the falls, which he described as the most wonderful sight he had witnessed in Africa. Angels, he mused, must have gazed on it in their flight.

Continuing westwards, Livingstone's party emerged at Loanda in Angola in May 1854. Although it was a magnificent achievement, he was dissatisfied, believing that the route was too difficult and an easier alternative must be available. He turned around and ploughed back towards the east, crossing the entire continent once more and reaching the coast of Mozambique two years later. Livingstone had become the first European to cross Africa, and had seen a huge potential for trade. Vast regions could be dedicated to cotton growing, which could be shipped down the rivers and exported, providing a much-needed raw material for British mills. Just as importantly, the cotton would be grown by free Africans instead of slaves on American plantations. Livingstone just had to persuade the British government to support him.

The Zambezi expedition of 1858-64 was an expensive disaster. Livingstone, now a bestselling author and national hero, returned to Africa with a small party of men and two steamboats with which they hoped to navigate the great river. Unfortunately, Livingstone's charts soon proved to contain a glaring and crucial flaw: he had overlooked the Kebrabasa rapids, a turbulent stretch of water that would prevent any vessel from passing. Things went downhill almost as fast as the white water itself. The Shire River, investigated as an alternative route, proved to be equally impassable, and the expedition was eventually recalled by the government. Meanwhile, Livingstone's latest missionary outposts, remote and vulnerable by their very nature, were becoming embroiled in tribal warfare. His wife, Mary, who had come back to support him, died of malaria in 1862. His dream was turning into a nightmare.

It was a weakened man who returned to Britain to produce a narrative of his journey. With the profits from his writing, and perhaps with a private sense of foreboding, Livingstone managed to secure enough money to place in trust for his children before he turned his anguished eyes back towards Africa. His reputation was in ruins, and he could see only one way of restoring it. He would explore the water systems of central Africa, between Lake Nyasa and Lake Tanganyika, find the source of the Nile*, and bring the slave trade to an end. Not much to ask.

In 1866, with the financial backing of the government and his friend James 'Paraffin' Young, Livingstone found enough support to mount another expedition, albeit on a much more modest scale than the last. To give him more authority he had been appointed Britain's 'Roving Consul' in central Africa, and if the title had a slightly frivolous ring to it, this was certainly not a reflection of Livingstone's state of mind. He was on his own, both physically and mentally – apart, that is, from the teams of loyal African people who were willing to go with him as porters and guides. This was his last attempt, a plunge into the dark with a guttering candle.

Five years later, against considerable odds, a journalist by the name of Henry Morton Stanley (see p.247) fulfilled the dreams of a nation and the hopes of a particularly ambitious newspaper publisher by locating David Livingstone at Ujiji on the shore of Lake Tanganyika. Scarcely any news had been filtering through to the outside world, and the general opinion was that the explorer was either lost or dead.

When Stanley arrived, Livingstone was in a poor state. Fever and dysentery were taking a severe toll. His thoughts were confused and he was losing track of time; his explorations had become increasingly rambling and inconsistent. He rallied at the sight of Stanley and his appetite temporarily returned, but he would not leave Africa. Instead, he implored Stanley to carry his message to the world.

Livingstone could not know that his dream was on the verge of being fulfilled. Nor would he live to see it. When he died in February 1873, his servants took his embalmed body on a nine-month journey to the east coast, and a ship bore him home for the last time. He was buried in Westminster Abbey on 18th April 1874. Less than six weeks after his death, the British government brought pressure on the Sultan of Zanzibar to end the slave trade in East Africa. At least in death, if not in life, Livingstone could rest in peace.

In 1884, when Stanley rose to address the Scottish Geographical Society at its inaugural banquet, he shared his last memories of the man whom he had tracked across a mostly uncharted continent, and in whom he had sensed a kindred spirit.

> I have never forgotten, nor will I ever forget, the sad feeling that came over me as I parted with the old man... in 1872, and how each of us would have liked to stay longer. As I dropped his hand, and saw the departing form, a presentiment came over one that I should never see him again, and still there was the hope that I would, because he was stout in form, he was firm of will, he was resolute in determination. Perhaps I hoped, I prayed - if an earnest wish can be called a prayer - that he would have been preserved, and still there was the dread fear. As I was coming down the Congo, with only the Atlantic Ocean for my goal, I thought many a time of the cheering words he used to tell me, how one day the attention of Europe would be directed thither. Somehow or other these dreams perpetually haunt me. I seem to see through the dim, misty, warm, hazy atmosphere of Africa always the aged face of Livingstone urging me on in his own kind, fatherly way. 'Don't you think, Mr Stanley,' he would say, 'that some day there is a hope for this old Continent? Don't you think that some day the people of Europe will be awakened to what really is in Africa?'[2]

During his lifetime, it is estimated that Livingstone travelled over 29,000 miles. He mapped his journeys and kept detailed diaries. When his supply of notebooks ran out he would use a newspaper, turning it ninety degrees and covering the printed pages with closely written script. He described wildlife encounters and made intuitive observations about various kinds of tropical diseases, including parasites spread by tsetse flies. While it is true that his geographical discoveries helped fuel Africa's exploitation by western countries, he is also remembered as a passionate humanitarian. He has been called 'Africa's first freedom fighter'.

In 1901 Livingstone's daughter, Agnes Livingstone Bruce, endowed the Royal Scottish Geographical Society with a medal in memory of her father. The Livingstone Medal was struck in gold, bearing a portrait of the great explorer on one face and on the other a depiction of the Spirit of Civilisation bearing the torch of progress and the olive branch of peace. It has been awarded periodically to worthy recipients who have upheld Livingstone's humanitarian principles in the field of exploration and research.

* The source of the Nile was still under debate, although John Hanning Speke in 1858 had claimed that it flowed from Lake Victoria and was later proved correct.

1. Henry M. Stanley, *The Autobiography of Sir Henry Morton Stanley* (1909)
2. Donald G. Moir 'The Royal Scottish Geographical Society 1884-1959: Early days of the Society', *Scottish Geographical Magazine* (1959) 75:3, 131-142

Sir Henry Morton Stanley

African explorer
BORN: 28th January 1840 (Denbigh)
DIED: 10th May 1904 (London)
§
RSGS Gold (Scottish Geographical) Medal, 1890

Six years after Livingstone entered into Africa I came to Edinburgh and told the good people that I had found Livingstone. Some believed me; some didn't. I was told that some people used to button-hole one another in the street, and ask 'Do you believe that fellow Stanley found Livingstone?'[1]

ON THE EVENING OF 6th December 1884, Henry Morton Stanley was enjoying a glass of port and a cigar. He had come to Edinburgh from Berlin at the invitation of Mrs Agnes Livingstone Bruce, the daughter of the man he had last seen twelve years ago by the shore of Lake Tanganyika and whose tortured face had haunted his idle moments ever since. He had delivered the inaugural lecture to the newly formed Scottish Geographical Society, and performed the official opening of its rooms in Queen Street. Now, as the guest of honour at a lavish banquet in the Waterloo Rooms, he felt he could afford to relax.

Livingstone was long dead by then, of course, and that Stanley had 'found' him was no longer open to question. His remarks no doubt provoked gales of laughter, but behind the mask Stanley was still scouring his own soul, locked in the agonising process of trying to find himself.

I was not sent into the world to be happy, nor to search for happiness. I was sent for a special work.[2]

In 1846, when a Welsh boy called John Rowlands was only six years old, he was dressed in clean clothes by the family he had been lodging with, taken by the hand and walked the 8 miles or so from Denbigh to St Asaph. His guardian rang the bell of the workhouse and left him on the front doorstep. For the next ten years, knowing neither love nor friendship, he lived in a dark world of deprivation and abuse.

Few parents would wish their child to experience life this way but for Rowlands there was no alternative. Born out of wedlock, he had been abandoned shortly afterwards by his mother. His presumed father was dead, as was his maternal grandfather. With no family to take care of him, Rowlands experienced a harsh and loveless beginning. From it sprang a deep sense of betrayal; he learned that strength was essential for survival and that he could trust no one but himself.

If the inmates of the workhouse ever had a chance to leave, their prospects for getting on in the world were not great. Added to this, they had a dread of future confinement which was probably why Rowlands, once he was on the outside, kept on running. Aged seventeen, he was granted permission to go to Liverpool to beg employment with a relative. He shifted despairingly from one hopeless job to the next, until one day, delivering meat for a butcher, he found himself on the dockside where sailing ships were unloading exotic cargoes of spices and silks. Knowing he had nothing to lose and all to gain, he yielded to impulse and signed up as a cabin boy on a ship bound for America.

Life as a cabin boy was, predictably, not all it was cracked up to be. The young boys on board were beaten and abused. Rowlands learned that this was a regular practice, with the expectation that they would run away at the first port of call without waiting for their wages. In February 1859 he jumped ship in New Orleans, where he experienced one of the defining moments of his life. It is therefore frustrating, but typical of Rowlands, that this moment is blurred with contradictions. According to his autobiography, he met a cotton trader called Henry Hope Stanley on the dockside; their chance encounter led to a job which developed into a close relationship, and after a few months Stanley declared his intention to adopt the boy as his own.

> It was the only tender action I had ever known, and, what no amount of cruelty could have forced from me, tears poured in a torrent under the influence of the simple embrace.[3]

It is an irresistible image but, sadly, may be based largely in fiction. Biographers have subjected Rowlands's many and varying stories to the closest scrutiny, and found more plausible that the young lad wanted to free himself from his scarred childhood and start again, using a name culled from one of the rich merchants of New Orleans. Survival, after all, what was he was best at. He began to call himself Henry Stanley, and added the middle name of Morton much later, in 1872.

The American Civil War failed to claim him even though he fought on both sides, having been captured as a Confederate soldier and recruited into the Union Army. By the end of the war, Stanley had discovered a flair for writing and it was this journalistic skill, combined with his fearless sense of commitment, that held the key to his fortune.

His calling, when it came, could not have been more finely tuned to his talents. In 1869, concern was growing over the fate of the Scottish missionary, David Livingstone, who had disappeared in central Africa. The newspaper that could break the news of his discovery was sure of worldwide acclaim. But who could find him? To stand any chance of success, Livingstone's rescuer must be tough and resilient, a man with nothing to lose. As a journalist with the *New York Herald*, the role fell to Stanley.

Stanley struck inland from Zanzibar in March 1871. After nearly eight months of tracing Livingstone's last known footsteps and following word-of-mouth reports he succeeded in tracking down the elusive missionary, who was ailing but still alive. The two men passed four months together by the shore of Lake Tanganyika. Stanley was able to send a jubilant message to the world that his task had been accomplished. There was only one problem. Livingstone, whose heart was set on stopping the slave trade, would not leave Africa. Stanley now found himself with a much more important mission: conveying Livingstone's urgent plea to humanity. It was a second calling, this time from Livingstone himself, to raise public awareness on a global scale and stop the cruelty.

Fame and fortune awaited Stanley's return to civilisation, but in 1874 he chose instead to plunge back into the unknown, this time with the aim of tracing the Congo River. This expedition, which would solve one of the last remaining mysteries of Africa's interior, demanded almost superhuman stamina and resilience. It took the best part of three years. Of Stanley's party less than a third survived to emerge at the river's mouth on the west coast. For the epic journey, Stanley received widespread acclaim.

Shocking tales about the party's brutal treatment of Africans soon began to tarnish the glory of his success. Although not all of these were ascribed to Stanley himself, it is once again difficult to know whether his reminiscences are entirely accurate. In a letter to *The Times* dated 8th December 1890, he wrote that he had learned 'by actual stress of imminent danger... that self-control is more indispensable than gunpowder', and claimed that 'African travel is impossible without real, heartfelt sympathy for the natives with whom one has to deal.'[4]. He understood Livingstone's principles and held the man in great esteem. Still, the rumours persist. Stanley, who had known cruelty since birth, remains an enigma.

Having launched himself into the sea of life like a ship without an anchor, by the age of forty Stanley had built a reputation honoured by monarchs and statesmen. The irony was that, even as his name echoed along the corridors of power, he was still on a personal mission find his own sense of belonging and fulfilment. When he addressed his hosts at the RSGS banquet and gently derided them for their doubt in his abilities, he must have wondered what challenges were left for him. He need not have worried. His people-finding skills were soon going to be in demand once again.

In the late 1880s, one of the issues gripping the imagination of the British public was the plight of a man called Eduard Carl Oscar Theodor Schnitzer, better known as Emin Pasha. This German-born physician had succeeded General Charles Gordon as Governor of the province of Equatoria in southern Sudan, but Mahdist uprisings and the withdrawal of Egyptian garrisons meant that the region was cut off by hostile forces. At first, the peace-loving Emin protested that he had no need to be rescued, but the fact remained that he was isolated from the outside world and public concern was growing.

Henry Morton Stanley was the only man for the job. One of

the Vice-Presidents of the RSGS, Sir William Mackinnon, pledged £10,000 of his own money towards the much-publicised Emin Pasha Relief Fund, and several other members followed suit with smaller donations. In 1886, when Mackinnon approached Stanley about a relief mission, the explorer professed himself ready to depart at a moment's notice.

Stanley devoted three years of his life to tracking down the besieged Pasha and persuading him to leave. He succeeded against considerable odds, although there was a serious setback when, having reached the safety of Bagamoyo, Emin managed to mistake an open upper floor window for a balcony and stepped through it. While he recovered in hospital from a head wound, Stanley sailed back to Britain to a rapturous welcome. Crowds flocked to see him in London, and when he boarded a train for Edinburgh he nearly brought King's Cross Station to a standstill:

> A railway engine happened to be stationary on the off side of Mr Stanley's carriage, and in a few minutes it was simply swarming with engine-drivers, stokers, and railway porters... When Mr Stanley took his seat in the carriage, the first thing he did was to stick his railway ticket in the front of his hat – an act which gave rise to considerable amusement among the crowd, and led one Cockney spectator to describe the traveller as 'a free and easy old chap.' As the train steamed out of the station, Mr Stanley put on his gold spectacles and settled down in a corner to read a newspaper.[5]

The RSGS never needed any persuading to throw a banquet, and Stanley soon found himself addressing another august gathering in the Waterloo Rooms. This time there was a distinct African theme, with a 'tropical forest' of palm trees behind the Chairman's seat and specially painted menu cards promising delicacies such as White Nile Soup and Pigeon Cutlets à la Congo. During his lengthy address to the Society, in which he described his mission in grand and dramatic style, Stanley took a brief but interesting diversion into natural history, with a description of the dense jungle through which he had forged a path.

252

... underneath the thick impervious shades is the impenetrable undergrowth, often of such close growth that you fancy you could travel best above the tops, rather than through it. Imagine the forks of each tree crowded with little conservatories of orchids and ferns, and the great horizontal limbs burdened with grey-green lichens with leaves as large as prize cabbages, and drooping growths of epiphytes, or air plants, and hosts of tendrils with their delicate points swinging ceaselessly about, and here and there great swaying walls and nodding towers of vines, around the flowers of which the wild bees hum, and the fierce wasps dart, and brilliant butterflies sail in myriads.[6]

It was a vivid and colourful picture, revealing perhaps a hidden poet in Stanley's carefully suppressed Welsh roots. If he had not been tortured by the raw emptiness that had haunted him since childhood, he might have enjoyed considerable success as a writer. His descriptions also fed the Victorians' craze for exotic plants, and it is a fair bet that some listeners went home and started planning an extravagant tropical glasshouse.

The credit for Stanley's geographical discoveries, including the mapping of the Congo River, should go not just to him but also to his many assistants and followers who accompanied him on his expeditions, going through untold suffering on his behalf. As for Stanley himself, what remains is the truth of a man driven to undergo physical trials which perhaps only he could have entertained, and which he had in fact been replaying ever since his admission into the workhouse as a six-year-old child: a battle of the will in which his mind urged his body to ever-greater feats of endurance, with no opt-out clause and no respite.

The recipient of the Society's first Gold Medal in 1890, Stanley always had a fatherly interest in the RSGS, having been present at its 'birth', and taking a close interest in it thereafter, allowing his fame to draw national attention to the institution and to geography as a whole.

1. H. M. Stanley, address to RSGS, December 1884, from Donald G. Moir 'The Royal Scottish Geographical Society 1884-1959: Early days of the Society', *Scottish Geographical Magazine* (1959) 75:3, 131-142

2-4. Henry M. Stanley *The Autobiography of Sir Henry Morton Stanley* (1909)

5. *The Scotsman*, 10th June 1890

6. Henry M. Stanley 'The Emin Pasha Relief Expedition – Address to the Society', *Scottish Geographical Magazine* (1890) 6:7, 337-353

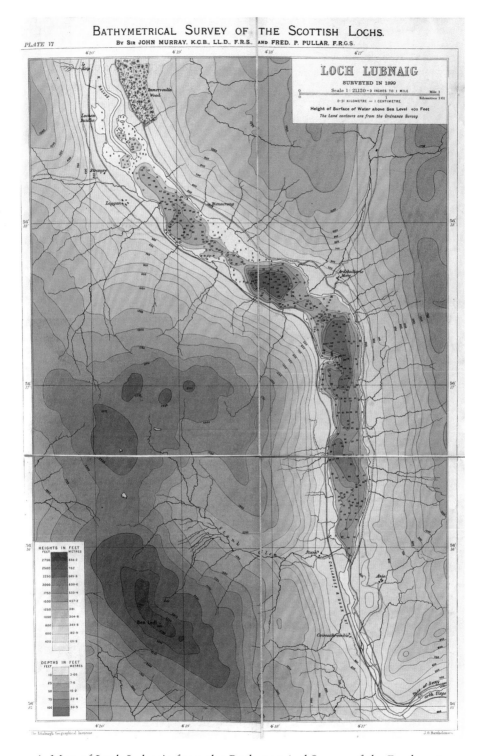

1. Map of Loch Lubnaig from the *Bathymetrical Survey of the Fresh-water Lochs of Scotland*, undertaken by Sir John Murray and Laurence Pullar and produced by Bartholomews of Edinburgh 1897-1909.

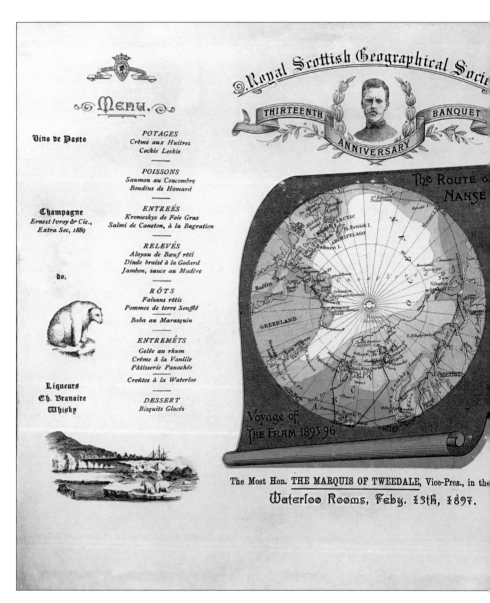

Royal Scottish Geographical Socie[ty]

THIRTEENTH — BANQUET
ANNIVERSARY

Menu.

Vino de Pasto

POTAGES
Crême aux Huîtres
Cockie Leekie

POISSONS
Saumon au Concombre
Boudins de Homard

Champagne
Ernest Ivroy & Cie.,
Extra Sec, 1889

ENTREÉS
Kromeskys de Foie Gras
Salmi de Caneton, à la Bagration

do.

RELEVÉS
Aloyau de Bœuf rôti
Dinde braisé à la Godard
Jambon, sauce au Madère

RÔTS
Faisans rôtis
Pommes de terre Soufflé

Baba au Marasquin

ENTREMÊTS
Gelée au rhum
Crême à la Vanille
Pâtisserie Panachée

Croûtes à la Waterloo

Liqueurs
Ch. Branaire
Whisky

DESSERT
Bisquits Glacés

The Route o[f]
NANSE[N]

Voyage of
The Fram 1893-96

The Most Hon. THE MARQUIS OF TWEEDALE, Vice-Pres., in the

Waterloo Rooms, Feby. 13th, 1897.

2. Menu from RSGS celebratory banquet held in honour of Fridtjof Nansen
in Edinburgh in February 1897.

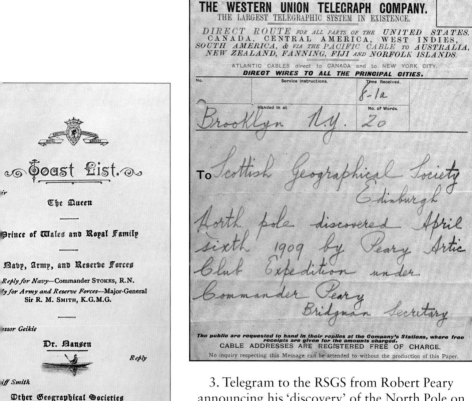

3. Telegram to the RSGS from Robert Peary announcing his 'discovery' of the North Pole on 6th April 1909.

4. Tickets to a lecture by Robert Falcon Scott entitled 'Furthest South' in St Andrew's Hall, Glasgow, on 14th November 1904.

5. The Rainbow Falls in the Tsangpo Gorge, named by Kingdon Ward.

6. LEFT: The Falls of the Brahmaputra, located in the narrowest and deepest section of the Tsangpo Gorge. Heard but not seen by Kingdon Ward.

7. Dungle Phuntsok, grandson of the Mönba guide who led Frank Kingdon Ward and Lord Cawdor, points out the route the explorers took in 1924.

8. *The Times* Everest Colour Supplement of 1953, signed by Sir Edmund Hillary and other members of the Everest team including team leader Sir John Hunt.

9. W H Murray at the entrance to the Girthi Gorge on the 1950 Scottish Himalayan Expedition. The excursion was instigated by Douglas Scott, who took this photograph.

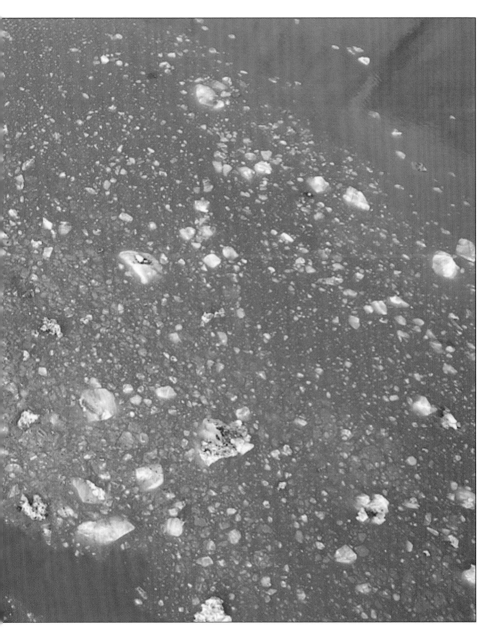

10. Aerial view of the *Northabout*, the vessel in which
Sir David Hempleman-Adams and his crew circumnavigated
the Arctic ice in 2016 to highlight the effects of global warming.

11. Sir Chris Bonington on Shivling in the Gangotri Himalaya, 1983.

12. Wangari Maathai.

13. Dick Balharry indulging his passion for wildlife photography.

14. Sir David Attenborough receiving the Scottish Geographical Medal (2011) and Honorary Fellowship of the RSGS, with Sir David Hempleman-Adams, Vice-President of RSGS (left), and (right) Professor Iain Stewart, President of RSGS.

15. Børge Ousland picks his way over pack ice near Sredny in Arctic Russia, in preparation for his North Pole expedition of 1994.

16. Børge Ousland's skis spanning a narrow crevasse in the ice sheet during his trek to the North Pole in 1994.

17. Karen Darke hand-cycling in the Tibetan Himalaya.

18. Rosie Swale Pope pulling her specially-designed cart through Alaska in November 2005, on her round-the-world run.

19. Craig Mathieson holding an RSGS flag at the South Pole
on 28th December 2004.

Joseph Thomson

African explorer
Born: 14th February 1858 (Penpont, Dumfriesshire)
Died: 2nd August 1895 (London)
§
RSGS Silver Medal, 1892
One of the Society's first four Honorary Members

Chi va piano va sano
Chi va sano va lontano

He who goes gently goes safely
He who goes safely goes far (Thomson's personal motto)

IN MAY 1879, at Behobeho in modern-day Tanzania, a young man from Dumfriesshire faced the most important decision of his life. Joseph Thomson was an eager but untried explorer aged twenty-one; just a few months before, he been appointed geologist and naturalist on Keith Johnston's *East African Expedition*. The post was the fulfilment of a dream, and Thomson was acutely conscious of the honour, particularly given his young age. Despite his boyish appearance, the Royal Geographical Society in London had seen his potential and he was desperate to prove them right. He knew there would be challenges, but could not have predicted this.

Keith Johnston lay dead, a victim of malaria and dysentery. The party, which numbered about 150 men, was now bereft of a leader and they looked to Thomson for a decision. The trek had barely started, and hundreds of miles of dangerous unmapped country still lay ahead. Would he turn around and retrace his steps to the coast – or would he carry on?

The carefree boy who had haunted the valleys and hills of southern Scotland suddenly felt the weight of the world on his shoulders.

The youngest of five sons of a respected stonemason and quarry owner, Joseph Thomson grew up with a love of the great outdoors and a restless curiosity about the natural world. He explored the country-side around his home with youthful energy and when he discovered

256

the works of eminent Scottish explorers such as James Bruce, Mungo Park and James Grant, he started dreaming about distant lands. He was little more than eleven or twelve when the details of Stanley's proposed expedition to rescue David Livingstone were published in the newspapers. Tearfully, he pleaded with his parents to let him go. He would find a way onto the ship, he assured them earnestly, if they would just give him enough money to get there.

Less than ten years later, the fresh-faced boy known to his friends as 'Joe' was a promising student of geology and mineralogy under Professor Archibald Geikie at the University of Edinburgh (see p.170). Geikie noticed Thomson's intellect and also admired his character, recalling his 'frank open-heartedness', effervescent humour and his remarkable talent for mimicking his peers, which sent his friends into gales of laughter. To Geikie's mind, this showed 'a versatility of adaptation and a knowledge of men and manners'. When Keith Johnston asked him to recommend a geologist for his forthcoming expedition, Geikie did not hesitate to put Thomson forward.

Now, in an unfamiliar and hostile country, faced with less than average chances of survival, Thomson could not hesitate either. He decided to take control of the expedition as Johnston's successor and pursue its official goal to find a potential trade route from Dar es Salaam to Lake Nyasa and Lake Tanganyika.

> If you want... to get some idea of what an African road is like, I would advise you to go out into some moorland place after rain, and march up and down in one of the drains for two or three hours. If there is a loch near at hand, vary your walk with a ramble into it, and now and then perambulate over some piece of dry ground. The effect will be highly realistic.[1]

Thomson was under no illusions about the severity of the challenges that lay ahead, even though he could not possibly foresee what shape they would take. The staple camp diet of 'fowls and rice' he accepted cheerfully enough, keeping a cob or two of Indian corn in his pocket for snacking while on the move. The African porters were headed by

Chuma, the man who had helped to bear Livingstone's body to the coast six years earlier, and his experience and steady judgement could be relied upon. The swampy ground hampered his party's progress. There was a more unpredictable threat, however, and that was the inevitable encounter with African tribes, many of which were known to be hostile.

The first real test of Thomson's nerve came a few days after he had assumed leadership. With just one word, 'Mahenge', whispered urgently down the line of porters, the expedition nearly turned into a rout. Some Mahenge warriors had been sighted ahead, and everyone knew an encounter with one of their hunting parties could lead to a bloodbath.

In barely controlled panic, still in the cover of trees, the party came to a halt. Fingers were poised nervously on the triggers of rifles as Thomson walked quickly to the front, unarmed – and stepped out to greet the warriors with a smiling face and words of friendly greeting. The Mahenge, stopped in their tracks, saw no fear in the face of the stranger, only the expectation that his welcome would be returned. They responded in kind. Within a few minutes the tension was transformed into harmony.

It was in this spirit that Thomson successfully led the expedition onwards to Lake Nyasa and ultimately to Lake Tanganyika, which was reached on 3rd November. He explored its shores with great thoroughness and confirmed Stanley's earlier theory about the Lukuga River, which is fed by the lake. The river's variable flow had long been a puzzle for geographers; it had been sluggish and partly dammed when Stanley had seen it, but Thomson saw it in spate, and his observations helped to prove that the variation was caused by seasonal fluctuations in the level of the lake.

Fourteen months later, on 10th July 1880, Thomson's party emerged at Bagamoyo on the east coast. It was a triumph that owed nothing to bloodshed. Thomson had succeeded through his own unfailing, stubborn optimism which saw something to appreciate in every awful situation. He had survived close encounters with crocodiles and lions, and had axes wielded over his head and arrows pointed at his heart by suspicious warriors who mistook him for a slave trader.

Throughout it all he had managed his men with decency and fairness. Nothing dimmed his spirit. Now that his achievement was known, a long career of brilliant exploration lay ahead him.

Had Thomson been born in the same mould as Stanley and other renowned African explorers who saw violence as an unavoidable necessity, and who did not question the exploitation of the continent and its people by European countries, his fame might have been much greater than it was. But Thomson was different: a man who saw human life in all its vividness of diversity. It is both tragic and ironic that during the next ten years of his life he was hired by acquisitive nations to push into unknown African territory in order to find trade routes and to prospect for minerals and forge agreements with tribal chiefs in favour of his employers.

In a paper read to the Royal Scottish Geographical Society in January 1886, Thomson expressed his distaste for the common belief that the African people were living in bleak ignorance of the benefits of 'civilisation', and would therefore welcome the arrival of sophisticated European culture with open arms. He gave his listeners a stark and probably unpalatable warning: so far, the Africans' contact with European traders had resulted in nothing but their degradation, and he could see no prospect of change. Their traditions, their skills and their independence had been swept away as they laboured to harvest products such as palm-oil for export. Although these men had not previously sought riches in the way that westerners did, the dubious incentive of material wealth was in fact proving to be their downfall. Some then turned to imported alcohol in an attempt to forget their lost identity.

The bitterness must have been doubly acute for Thomson, as his work, conducted with the eagerness of a pioneer, had helped to seal the fate of regions such as the Congo which had been the subject of the Berlin Conference just over a year before. Furthermore, having trodden for thousands of painful miles across Africa's uncompromising landscape, he knew that the untapped fertile lands, plentiful crops and lucrative trade existed only in the fevered minds of statesmen and the dangerously misleading rhetoric of newspaper columnists. Attending to a number of regions in turn, he listed the evidence, pointing at the poor soils, the unsuitable climate, the impossibility of access, the lack of transport, the absence of a workforce. Whole empires were being built on sand. He could see this with clarity, yet his words were tinged with the sadness of someone who knew that only time would prove him right. The real tragedy was that Africa had won his heart.

> With all its faults, or rather short-comings, Africa is the one Continent on this earth which incessantly occupies my thoughts by day and my dreams by night. If I had consulted only my own interests, I should either have joined the chorus of optimists or held my peace. I might have argued that if I painted Africa in such depressing colours, the world would turn round and say, 'Well, if it is as bad as you say, why should we trouble ourselves about it, and send men like you to explore and travel there? In future you had better stay at home.'[2]

It took courage and a steady mind to voice such a controversial opinion; Thomson revealed that he had been condemned by one critic as 'weak-minded, irresolute, and senile'. His sentiments were certainly not shared by Henry Morton Stanley (see p.247), who sat at the same table as Thomson when both men were guests at the Royal Scottish Geographical Society's inaugural banquet. Over the crisp linen in the Waterloo Rooms, Edinburgh, an exchange of barbed compliments began with Stanley, who rose to acknowledge a toast. Having meandered through a long celebratory speech, he concluded by urging the Society not to forget its countryman, Mr Thomson. Rather daringly, and possibly fuelled by copious helpings of brandy, Stanley added that if the Society ever had a severe or dangerous mission, he trusted that they would despatch Mr Thomson on it.

Thomson was only twenty-six and had every respect for the nation's hero, but he would stand no nonsense. Rising from his seat, he expressed his regret that 'the romance had gone out of African exploration' and that Mr Stanley was now 'wandering about in the Congo, loaded with cotton goods and Birmingham ware.' While his audience silently pondered the vulgarity of anything emanating from the Midlands, he concluded that 'if this sort of thing were to go on, he would prefer to go to [the] North Pole, and be done with Africa.'[3]

It was rather ironic that Thomson was called upon to go to the aid of Stanley a few years after this little episode, while Stanley was in search of Emin Pasha in Southern Sudan. Although the expedition, for which the Royal Scottish Geographical Society provided a great deal of financial and moral support, was a triumph for Stanley, before he re-emerged with the reluctant governor there was a worrying lack of communication from him. In September 1888 Joseph Thomson was asked if he would go and seek him out. He agreed and returned home from a trip in the Atlas mountains to receive further instructions. Much to his disappointment, he soon found that his services were not required. Stanley might have been glad about that, although he had more pressing things to worry about.

So too did Thomson, whose repeated exposure to tropical diseases was taking its toll on his otherwise vigorous constitution. On his last expedition in 1891, under instructions from the British South Africa Company to explore the Barotze country, he was so weak that he had to be carried over 700 miles and was strong enough to return home only after six months of nursing at a mission station. There may well have been complications; an interesting insight is given in the *Scottish Geographical Magazine* by John George Bartholomew, who revealed that while riding a mule in Morocco, Thomson was thrown onto the pommel of his saddle, and the resulting injury brought on a disease from which he never recovered.

After his return to Britain, a severe cold led to pneumonia. Despite rallying several times and travelling to South Africa and Italy to recuperate, Thomson could not regain his health. The young man who had shown such extraordinary spirit and so much prophetic wisdom, died in London at the age of thirty-seven, having assured his brother, a church minister, that he had faced death for many years and was not alarmed by it. True to his personal motto, he had gone gently, and he had gone far.

My fondest boast is, not that I have travelled over hundreds of miles hitherto untrodden by the foot of a white man, but that I have been able to do so as a Christian and a Scotchman, carrying everywhere goodwill and friendship, finding that a gentle word was more potent than gunpowder, and that it was not necessary, even in Central Africa, to sacrifice the lives of men in order to throw light upon its dark corners.[4]

---

1. *Joseph Thomson, African explorer* by Rev J. B. Thomson (1897)

2. Joseph Thomson 'East Central Africa and its Commercial Outlook', *Scottish Geographical Magazine* (1886) 2:2, 65-78

3. Donald G. Moir 'The Royal Scottish Geographical Society 1884-1959: Early days of the Society', *Scottish Geographical Magazine* (1959) 75:3, 131-142

4. *Dumfries & Galloway Standard*, 15th September 1880

Fanny Bullock Workman

Mountaineer
Born: 8th January 1859 (Worcester, Massachusetts)
Died: 22nd January 1925 (Cannes, France)
§
Fellow of RSGS, 1898

We left Askole on the 16th of July [1899]. Two hours' march
brought us to the beginning of the glacier, where all paths cease,
and the tiresome moraine work common to all great glaciers
begins.[1]

I N 1899, WITH THE elderly Queen Victoria on the British throne,
William McKinley in the White House, and the term 'suffragette'
yet to be invented, it is unlikely that many women on either side
of the Atlantic would have been sighing about the tedium of moraine
work*. But then, not all women were Fanny Bullock Workman.

Born in 1859 to a wealthy family in Worcester, Massachusetts,
Fanny Bullock enjoyed all the advantages of an expensive education,
first with private tutors and then at schools in New York, Paris and
Dresden. At the age of twenty-two, she married William Hunter
Workman, a successful physician and amateur geologist twelve years
her senior. The couple went on regular expeditions to the White
Mountains of New Hampshire where Fanny discovered a natural
aptitude for climbing that ideally suited her vigorous energy. Eight
years later, when William gave up work because of ill health, the
odds were stacked against an active retirement but Fanny was not
prepared to dwindle her life away between parlour and sickbed. Dr
Workman, lazily shaking out his newspaper on the front porch and
wondering if the frost had caught his hydrangeas, was in for a bit of
a shock.

A complete lifestyle change was needed and, as fate would have
it, the ideal opportunity fell straight into Fanny's lap. Travel was
a fashionable tonic for those who could afford it, and in 1889 she
and William used the combined wealth of inherited estates to move

to Germany, where the sparkling challenges of the Alps were easily accessible. William quickly recovered his health and Fanny ticked off some of her ambitions by climbing the Matterhorn and Mont Blanc. No constrictions, whether social, physical or mental, could stop her now; the world was at her feet and, with boundless enthusiasm, she set about finding a way to explore it.

In the late nineteenth century the safety bicycle was rapidly eclipsing the penny-farthing in terms of efficiency and ease of use. Riders could put their feet on the ground when they came to a stop, which was a pleasing development. Cycling was seized upon by both men and women as a liberating new pastime and, with the roads still relatively free of motorcars, the pleasures of cycling could be enjoyed in safety and tranquillity. Bartholomews of Edinburgh, the renowned map-making firm, spied the potential and launched a series of county maps for tourists and cyclists, but John George Bartholomew (see p.317) might have been surprised at the route which the Workmans were planning to take. Fanny and William were the proud new owners of two 'Rover' bicycles, steel-framed with solid rubber tyres, and in 1895 they set off on a 2,800-mile jaunt across Spain.

Afterwards, the Workmans recounted their experiences in a book called *Sketches Awheel in Modern Iberia*. In this way a pattern was set that would shape the rest of their lives; the pair would go on prolonged and arduous expeditions such as climbing mountains, then write books and travel around Europe giving lectures. They enjoyed considerable success and popularity. Fanny was certainly not shy of stepping into the limelight as a guest speaker at geographical societies and other academic institutions.

In 1897 the couple embarked on a cycling excursion around India that took two and a half years. The summer heat drove them up into the mountains, where Fanny had her first sight of the Himalayas. She was both enthralled and inspired. The promise of those unscaled peaks was enough to persuade the Workmans to cast aside their beloved bicycles and forge ahead on foot into a land of cool shady ravines and dazzling white summits.

It was this adventure Fanny shared with RSGS audiences when she gave a number of lectures entitled 'Amid the Snows of Baltistan' in December 1900. She described how a party consisting of herself, her husband, a Swiss mountain guide, and about fifty servants and porters, trekked from Srinagar in Kashmir towards the pass of Skoro La at 17,000 feet. At Skardu they were informed that it was too early in the year to cross the Skoro La. The Workmans, with typical stoicism, resolved to 'open the pass for the season' as if it were a simple matter of cutting some invisible ribbon. After all, someone had to do it.

The going was tough from the outset. The party had to ford the Askor Torrent twelve times before reaching the base of the pass, but Fanny was undaunted. A flimsy rope bridge thrown across the Braldu River, spanning a width of 270 feet, was described as 'one of the longest and most trying in the country', but she showed no trace of nerves. At Askole, a village which stood 'in the last dot of green on the ragged edge of a world of rock and snow', the Workmans called a halt to gather more provisions and hire more porters.

Two weeks later they were grappling with the séracs and crevasses of the Biafo Glacier – a serious consideration for any mountaineer, especially a woman encumbered by long skirts and with no previous experience of Himalayan climbing. Fanny appeared to be invincible; altitude sickness did not affect her, possibly because her progress was necessarily slow, and she was game enough to tackle anything – an attribute borne out by her many summit photographs.

In her lecture to the RSGS she described the ascent of three peaks, the highest of which was Koser Gunge at 21,000 feet:

> There at last we saw the final peak, a high snow cone with a blue ice cornice, emerging from a cloud... The distance seemed great, insurmountable. We descended, crossed the basin and attacked the slant in zigzags...[2]

The Workmans went on to make seven more expeditions to the Himalayas. In 1906, aged forty-seven, Fanny ascended Pinnacle Peak (22,736 feet) in the Nun Kun massif, setting an elevation record for a female mountaineer which was not surpassed until 1934.

Despite her lectures and extensive writings, Fanny is something of an enigma. Isabella Bird had a similarly indomitable spirit, and her writing is vivid with all the colour of her emotions. Freya Stark, unstoppable in her own way, expressed herself with all the joyful abandon of a poet. In contrast, Fanny's personality does not shine through her writing. As she relates her remarkable achievements, only occasional glimpses are visible: respect for expertise in guides and porters; impatience at delays, especially when caused by ineptitude or sluggishness; occasional hints of satisfaction at a notable success; and overtones of a staunch and unyielding determination that would have made a great army general in any era. She saw some of the world's great wonders, and experienced many fascinating cultures and customs but never seemed to fully immerse herself, preferring to stand back and watch from a safe distance – and her commanding attitude meant that people treated her with caution.

A clue may lie in Fanny's close-guarded personal life. She lost an infant son, Siegfried, shortly after moving to Germany; her surviving daughter, Rachel, was not allowed to hamper Fanny's wandering spirit. She may have known herself unsuited to motherhood and directed her energy into other channels to escape the inevitable criticism; perhaps her unflinching attitude hides a fear of being judged, especially in a field dominated by men. In William she seems to have found a kindred spirit. They were superb organisers, and money was never an issue, but their solid partnership must have been built upon mutual respect and understanding.

Many of the Workmans' books are written in the third person plural, an unusual choice which was also favoured by Mildred Cable. The effects are vastly different, however. Mildred had a gift of seeing her journey as if from above, and her writing is imbued with the benevolence and gentle wisdom with which she viewed the world. The Workmans are more pragmatic and business-like, recounting their experiences with the detachment and precision of military surveyors on reconnaissance duty. In Fanny's eyes, no doubt, they were blazing a trail for other travellers to follow, and their guidebooks were intended as a valuable source of reference. An emotional response would have been completely out of place.

There was, however, one red-hot cause for which Fanny was

unafraid to drop her guard, and that was the women's suffrage move-ment. In July 1912, she was photographed on the Siachen Glacier in the Karakoram, at a height of nearly 21,000 feet, holding a newspaper bearing the headline 'Votes for Women' – possibly the journal of the Women's Social and Political Union. Fanny knew how to create a stir and in this instance she cared nothing for the consequences. Throughout her life she was an ardent supporter of women's rights, and with this brilliant piece of propaganda she set an unprecedented example of what women could do.

The Workmans' exploration of the Siachen Glacier, the longest in the Karakoram, was perhaps their most significant achievement. A paper describing their expedition was published in the *Scottish Geographical Magazine* in 1913; Fanny, who could wither a recalci-trant servant with a look, seems to have been plagued by unreliable porters. Despite the 'perfidious actions' of the only headmen avail-able, and the 'prodigious pilferings' of the Saltoro Valley porters, she managed to stand on two new points of the north-east Karakoram water-parting, and her companions made a full survey of the Siachen Glacier.

Through sheer determination and self-belief, Fanny Bullock Workman secured herself a reputation as a geographer, though her surveying methods were not always immune from controversy. She was fiercely competitive, and when fellow countrywoman Annie Smith Peck staked a claim for the highest summit attained by a woman (Huascarán in Peru), Fanny sent her own team of surveyors to re-assess the height of the mountain and prove her wrong. She was resilient and adaptable, fiercely outspoken, terrifyingly capable, often leaving a litter of exhausted porters in her wake. Squalid conditions did not daunt her, which is just as well as she endured plenty, but the oppression of women, whenever she saw it, roused her to anger.

After Fanny's lecture to the RSGS at the Albert Hall in Aberdeen on 10th December 1900, the Chairman, John Clarke, expressed admira-tion for her recent lecture tour of Europe, where she had given her presentations in fluent French and German. The *Aberdeen Journal*, describing the evening's event, gave careful credit to the lantern operator, whose job of controlled combustion was still quite a new feature of Society lectures, and one which was guaranteed to draw enthusiastic crowds.

> The lecture was very well illustrated by limelight lantern views, the lantern being manipulated by Mr Stott, of Messrs Walker & Company, Bridge Street, Aberdeen. The slides showed the snow-clad peaks, three of which were explored and named by the party, the morraines [sic], glaciers, crags &c; while several picturesque cloud effects upon the mountains were applauded... At the close of a most interesting lecture, Lord Provost Fleming proposed a hearty vote of thanks to the gifted and courageous lady who had lectured to them so entertainingly that evening.[3]

With the outbreak of the Great War, the Workmans' love affair with the Himalayas came to an untimely end. They still had much to celebrate, however. Fanny had received France's highest literary title – *Officier de L'Instruction Publique* – and awards from geographical societies were being showered upon her. In 1898 she was the second woman, after Isabella Bird, to receive a Fellowship of the RSGS. More enduringly, she took a pick-axe to the marble halls of exclusive masculinity. Her 'Votes for Women' image is still a potent symbol of female emancipation.

> *Moraine is the term applied to a haphazard mix of rocks and sediment, deposited by a glacier in mounds or ridges. The moraine at the end of a glacier (terminal moraine) can be quite steep-sided and extensive. It is likely that this is what Fanny is referring to, as she would have had to climb it in order to reach the glacier itself.

1-2. 'Amid the Snows of Baltistan' by Fanny Bullock Workman FRSGS MRAS
  Scottish Geographical Magazine (1901) 17:2, 74-86
 3. *Aberdeen Journal*, 11th December 1900

Hannah ('Annie') Royle Taylor

Missionary-explorer
BORN: 7th October 1855 (Egremont, Cheshire)
DIED: 9th September 1922 (Kensington)
§
Lecturer at RSGS, 1893

IN DECEMBER 1893, Annie Taylor gave a lecture to the Royal Scottish Geographical Society entitled 'My Experiences in Tibet'. She explained there were three routes from the Chinese border to the Tibetan capital of Lhasa. The official road, used by Mandarins and official couriers, offered rest-houses where fresh horses could be hired. The second was the traditional Tea Road or Ga-Lam, dotted with encampments where meat could be bought. The third, called the Si-ning Lam, started in the Chinese province of Kan-su and converged with the Tea Road a few days' journey from Lhasa.

If she had been discovered on any of them, she would probably have been executed.

Annie's account may read like an early tourist guide, but neither she nor her listeners were under any illusions about the welcome awaiting foreign visitors to Tibet in the late 1800s. Once a powerful presence in Central Asia, Tibet had a long history of conflict. Over successive centuries the riches of this vast mountainous region had drawn the acquisitive eyes of its neighbours, including the rulers of the Mongol Empire and the Qing Dynasty of China. By the mid-nineteenth century two new contenders had appeared on the horizon: Russia, whose territories were hovering ominously to the north-west; and Britain, anxious to protect its imperial interest in India, which lay to the south. Tibet, still a protectorate of China in name at least, reacted by closing its borders to all foreigners and offering brutal punishment to intruders. Peace-loving Buddhist communities were roused into violence by fear.

On the face of it, this made Tibet one of the least attractive countries in the world to visit. There were, however, many people ready to challenge this view. Explorers such as Sven Hedin skirted around the perimeter and across the border in disguise. British officers Henry Morshead and Frederick Marshman Bailey risked their lives when they disappeared into Tibetan regions on a clandestine survey mission of the Himalayas. Mapping uncharted territory was a European obsession, and most explorers had an eye out for natural resources that would enhance the wealth of their empires. If trespassing carried the death penalty, that just gave the adventure an extra spice.

Annie Taylor was not a map-maker, nor did she ever masquerade as one. She had a plan of a different kind. Rather worryingly it involved not only entering Tibet but reaching its capital, the 'forbidden city' of Lhasa. Annie was a missionary, fired with the holiness of the gospels, and she dreamed of bringing the Christian message to the Dalai Lama himself.

Born in 1855 in Egremont, Cheshire, Annie was the second child in a wealthy family of five sons and five daughters. Her father, John Taylor, was a director of the Black Ball shipping line, whose packet ships plied regularly between Liverpool, America and Australia.

At the age of seven Annie was diagnosed with valvular heart disease, and because her doctors believed that she would not live beyond childhood they advised her parents not to trouble her with study. Annie was therefore not given a proper education. By her own admission she could do as she liked, which could not have endeared her to her siblings. She astonished everyone by surviving and, at the age of sixteen, declaring her intention to live a very demanding life indeed.

Annie was first touched by the idea of following a devoutly Christian life at a Congregational chapel. She was sensitive, despite being spoilt, and paid careful attention to the scriptures. She saw herself as one of the sinners mentioned so often in the prayers. She was prompted to pick up the Bible in earnest, and absorbed its teachings into her very core. To the considerable alarm of her father, she abandoned most of the pleasures young girls of her age indulged in – horse-riding, dancing, theatre-going – and prepared to devote her life to Christ.

The options for women wishing to enter religious service at that time were fairly limited. It was impossible for them to be ordained as ministers, so if they wished to do anything practical one of the popular alternatives was missionary work. The China Inland Mission was particularly keen to engage single women, many of whom were perhaps attracted by the prospect of doing something valuable while escaping the confines of a society they found uncomfortable. Annie seems to have had the kind of restless energy which sought a more demanding outlet than the well-trodden path of parties, marriage and motherhood; when she heard a recruitment address by a visiting missionary she announced her intention of answering the call.

Her father did all he could to prevent her. Trying to appeal to her better nature, he accused his daughter of being selfish. When that failed, he stopped her allowance, believing that the short sharp shock to her finances would be enough. Annie needed medical training before she could proceed with her application, so her father initially refused to pay the fees; Annie responded by selling her jewellery and renting a room in London while she worked in hospitals and taught at Sunday schools. By the time her training was complete, she was twenty-eight; she had never wavered from her purpose and her father, relenting a little, offered to pay for whatever comforts she might need on her voyage. Believing that her passion would fade after her arrival in China, he also gave her letters granting passage on a ship back to England or on to Australia, where he had a second home.

In one sense at least, Annie's father was right; after a couple of years of missionary work she found herself discontented in China. But that was only because she had heard of the unexplored potential of Tibet.

Annie spent months living in various towns on the Tibetan border, braving the suspicious glances of local people and learning the language spoken in Lhasa. She had a daring plan for a journey westwards across Tibet, passing through Lhasa and coming out in Darjeeling. Under no illusions about the perils involved, she cut her hair short in the style of a Buddhist nun to avoid detection and dressed in the loose-sleeved garments of a Tibetan. Annie had never been afraid to travel alone, but now found herself blessed with a loyal companion: a young Tibetan named Pontso had come to her for medical help while fleeing a cruel master. Motivated by gratitude, Pontso was willing to accompany Annie to Lhasa itself, risking the death penalty should he be caught.

Annie's party consisted of three Tibetans (including one woman), two Chinese men and sixteen horses. They carried cooking pans, bedding, cloths for barter, gifts for chiefs and warlords, and enough food for two months. On 2nd September 1892 they left Tau Chau in Kan-su Province and crossed into Tibet through fertile fields dotted with bustling villages and temples. Soon they reached the region of the Drog-pa ('black tent people'), and as they climbed higher the trees and shrubs gave way to a barren wasteland.

All roads into Lhasa were notoriously dangerous, not just because of the altitude and bleak weather. Bands of Mongol brigands would descend on trading caravans to steal horses and goods, murdering travellers who put up a fight. The first attack on Annie's party came just a few days after they had crossed the border; thieves took several horses and a large proportion of their luggage. One of Annie's companions was robbed of all his belongings and had to retrace his steps back into China.

Having crossed the Ma-chu River on a raft made from interwoven branches and four inflated bullock skins, Annie's little party encountered the Golok people, whose chieftain was a woman. Although the Goloks shared the Mongols' appetite for violence and pillage, Annie was entertained with great hospitality. She was fascinated to see women with amber and cowrie shells in their long plaits of hair, wearing earrings of silver and coral. The Golok men, she observed, wore one massive piece of jewellery in the right ear. When Annie left, she was given an escort of two warriors until she arrived in safer territory.

The weather conditions were already severe, with frequent snow-storms. One of Annie's party, a Chinese man named Leucotze, died of exposure. The caravan halted while he was buried in the frozen earth. At night, Annie heard wolves howling around his grave.

> All Tibetans drink tea. They boil it, branches and all, in water with a little soda and salt, and before drinking add butter, barley flour (which is called tsampa), and dried native cheese.[1]

The town of Jyekundo was known for its tea merchants, who would trade their produce for Tibet's rich exports of wool, hides and furs, gold dust, and mercury. Annie observed that the tea was compressed into bricks about fourteen inches long. Eight bricks were then sewn into a skin, which were loaded onto yaks for transport into Lhasa. In a land where tea was so widely available it must have been frustrating to find that, at high altitudes, water boiled while it was still tepid. Annie had to drink her tea quickly to prevent a crust of ice forming on the top. The effects of the elevation were taking their toll in other ways too, and Annie would wake in the night, gasping for breath. She was undeterred. At Christmas, she even managed to conjure a pudding from the supplies of flour, sugar, suet and currants that she had brought with her.

On 31st December 1892 they crossed the Bo-chu River and entered the district of Lhasa, with the city itself only a few days away. With hindsight, Annie admitted that she should have left her horses there and continued on foot, taking a less conspicuous route and arriving at the gates of Lhasa discreetly. At that time, however, she was in a weakened condition, and the constant menace of brigands persuaded her to stay on horseback and keep to the well-trodden path. A few days later she was arrested, having been betrayed by two of her companions, a man named Noga and his wife, who had deserted her a few days previously and gone on ahead to warn the authorities about her presence. Officials had been summoned from Lhasa to question her. Filled with dread, she awaited their arrival.

Annie knew the only thing that could save her life was her attitude. Submission, which could be interpreted as guilt, was not an option. Military chiefs and magistrates arrived and tents were pitched, ready for a tribunal. When Annie was called before them, she was accused of stealing. Holding her ground, she demanded justice and courtesy; she complained at the standard of food she was offered and drew a verbal picture of herself as a religious teacher with powerful connections and a legitimate reason to be travelling through Tibet. When she was told that she would be sent back to China unaccompanied, with only her exhausted horses and meagre supplies, she raged and accused them of sending her to her death, either through starvation, exposure, or violent attack. She argued also for the lives of her two remaining companions, Pontso and Penting, who would most likely be beheaded for helping a foreign intruder if they were taken to Lhasa. Annie's father, who had engaged her in so many verbal battles, might well have been proud.

Grudgingly acquiescent, Annie's captors granted her release along with Pontso and Penting. For her return journey they gave her food, an old tent, two fresh horses, and some silver rupees; they also gave her a guard of ten soldiers to protect her from bandits. It was as much as Annie could reasonably have expected, but her little party was still in grave danger. Two days into the return journey, the soldiers, obviously satisfied that they had done their duty, left them with a caravan of traders who were heading the same way. Although there was safety in numbers, Annie was not prepared to travel at the plodding rate of heavily loaded yaks, so insisted that she and her two companions ride on ahead. It was a daring and potentially disastrous decision.

At a monastery which Annie had passed on her outward journey, and where she had received friendly treatment, the attitude of the lamas was now openly hostile. They had been told that Annie was a witch who could see through mountains and locate all the sources of gold – a poisonous rumour originating from Noga and his wife, which had now spread far and wide. Most wanted to stone the strangers and throw their bodies into the river; they were only prevented from doing so by the more rational arguments of the head lama. Annie, looking at the ranks of suspicious faces still watching her little encampment, thought it wise to move swiftly on.

Tibet was now in the grip of winter, so the three travellers camped each night on the snow; ironically, they risked sunstroke on the high mountain passes. As the drifts became impassable, they were forced to make a detour and lead the frightened horses down a glacier. Both horses succumbed to the cold, but Annie and her companions struggled on even as wolves haunted their path. In February they reached Jyekundo, where Penting took his leave and made his way home to Gala. Annie and Pontso completed the last leg of the journey together, staying in village houses wherever possible but on many occasions sleeping in the open air.

> My bed was either on the ground in the lee of a pile of luggage, or, if I chanced to find one, a hole, the sides of which protected me from the fierce icy blasts... A piece of felt to cover the ice at the bottom of the hole made my couch, and a warm sleeping bag into which I crept formed my sleeping clothes.[2]

On 12th April 1893 they reached China. Annie gazed in heartfelt gratitude at a fertile landscape of green grass, apricot trees and fields of growing corn. At last, she was safe. In seven months and ten days she had travelled 1,300 miles across some of the most inhospitable terrain on Earth.

When Annie was welcomed by the Royal Scottish Geographical Society in Edinburgh and Glasgow she would almost certainly have been accompanied by Pontso, although no mention is made of him in the reports. Annie gave a collection of Tibetan artefacts to the Kelvingrove Museum and to the National Museum of Scotland. She used her lecture tour to find recruits for the Tibetan Pioneer Band, a new missionary centre of her own, and returned to Sikkim in February 1894 with nine new members – five Scotsmen, two Norwegians, one Swede, and one Englishman. It was an ill-fated venture and the group broke up within a year, with some of the members joining the China Inland Mission.

Annie made no further attempts to reach Lhasa. She could, however, claim to be the first European woman to enter Tibet. After her mission centre disbanded she moved with Pontso and his wife to Yatung, a town on the border with Sikkim where she established a small trading store. She had kept a diary of her travels, but it was thanks to the efforts of a missionary named William Carey that her story was transcribed. In 1904, after the British invasion of Tibet, Annie helped to nurse the wounded in a hospital in the Chumbi Valley and secretly hoped that her dream of easy entry to Lhasa would become a reality. She was disappointed, as the action only served to heighten Tibet's defensiveness (see Younghusband p.177). The story of her later life remains unclear, but it is believed that the violence against the Tibetans sent her into a state of depression. In 1907 she was brought back to Britain by her sister, and her last years were spent in an institution.

Annie's story is filled with endurance and grim determination, but according to William Carey, who published her journals, she laughed about many aspects of her adventure. Her face was rosy and roguish, betraying a vivacious nature; she was 'a busy little gypsy boiling her obstinate Christmas pudding under the lee of the hill'[3]. Annie might have been pious, but she was still vibrantly human.

1-2. Annie Taylor, 'My Experiences in Tibet', *Scottish Geographical Magazine* (1894) 10:1

3. *Adventures in Tibet: including the diary of Miss Annie R Taylor's remarkable journal from Tau-Chai to Ta-Chien-Lu through the heart of the 'Forbidden Land'*, William Carey (1902)

FIELD MARSHAL HORATIO HERBERT KITCHENER

Cartographer, military commander and British cabinet minister
BORN: 24th June 1850 (Ballylongford, County Kerry)
DIED: 5th June 1916 in shipwreck of HMS *Hampshire* off Orkney
§
RSGS Livingstone Medal, 1915

IN JUNE 1916, when the news came that Lord Kitchener was dead, the nation was stunned into silence. Hushed crowds gathered around newspaper stands to stare at the headlines in disbelief and a creeping dread settled among the forces at the western front, who feared that Britain had now lost the war.

Sir Arthur Conan Doyle found words to describe what everyone saw and felt. Kitchener's death, he wrote, left behind 'the memory of something vast and elemental, coming suddenly and going strangely, a mighty spirit leaving great traces of its earthly passage'[1].

If Kitchener's parents had been able to read those words, they would have been surprised. Contemporaries who had known him as a youth would probably have rolled about laughing. But Kitchener was the Secretary of State for War, a responsibility which brought with it not only the duties of a cabinet minister but the weight of a country's expectations and the awful burden of millions of young men's lives. He must have had to shut off human empathy and consider only success and defeat, not life or death. Although reluctant, he was perceived by the public as a god of war.

The story of the man beneath the mantle is slightly different.

As a child and then a youth, Herbert Horatio Kitchener was reserved and shy – no doubt the result of a rigorous upbringing in a house ruled by a disciplinarian father. He was not a brilliant scholar;

280

at the Royal Military Academy in Woolwich he struggled to achieve even the average marks required of a Royal Engineer. He was difficult to get to know, distant, although not unpopular; none of his colleagues thought him cut out for a distinguished career, let alone greatness.

Aged just twenty-four, Kitchener was commissioned by the Palestine Exploration Fund to carry out a topographical survey of the Holy Land. Existing records of the region were sketchy at best, making this a long and daunting task, but he welcomed it.

> The Survey of the North of Palestine... covered 1,000 square miles of country; during a single month the extent of country surveyed had been 350 square miles; 2,773 place-names were collected, and 476 ruins were mentioned – some with special plans. At every village a record was compiled of the number and religion of the inhabitants, remains of ancient buildings, character of the neighbourhood, and nature of the water-supply. Special notes were made of the geology and archaeology of the country, and photographs were taken of the more important sites.[2]

Kitchener was meticulous in his approach, often questioning up to twenty people before he was satisfied that a single place-name had been transcribed correctly. He then had them all double-checked by a guide and a scribe. He was particularly impressed with the Roman roads, and noted they might serve a useful purpose in the future: 'Over a most difficult country such as this it excites admiration to see the way that difficulties were got over with the least possible expenditure of labour. Should Palestine ever be re-opened to civilisation, these roads will form the basis of the principal lines of communication through the country...'[3]

Overall, Kitchener's research party met with little hostility, but on one occasion his camp was attacked by band of Muslim rebels. Armed only with his cane, he saved the life of his fellow officer, Claude Conder, and between them they beat off a gang which vastly outnumbered their own men. Conder wrote, 'I must inevitably have been murdered, but for the cool and prompt assistance of Lieutenant

Kitchener, who managed to get to me and engaged one of the club men, covering my retreat.'[4]

While in Palestine, Kitchener met a French archaeologist, Clermont-Ganneau, who described him as tall, slim and vigorous, capable of headstrong acts. 'A frank and most outspoken character, with reserves of winsome freshness. His high spirits and cheeriness were in agreeable contrast to the serious, grave characters of some of his comrades.'[5]

In Jerusalem, Kitchener came across a dealer who was doing a roaring trade in 'ancient Moabite' pottery. These apparently rare and highly collectable items were being snapped up by German connoisseurs, but Kitchener had seen his fair share of archaeological treasures and knew a forgery when he saw one. Having made some discreet enquiries, he identified the purveyor of these so-called ancient artefacts and surprised him at his workshop. His story no doubt amused dinner-parties all over the Empire.

On 2nd October 1877, in Jerusalem, Kitchener wrote to the Chairman of the Palestine Exploration Fund: 'I am sure you will be glad to hear that the Map is an accomplished fact, and six years' work has been finished... the work in the south was 340 square miles. The fact is we had to work hard; the water was so bad, being salt and the colour of weak tea, and our bread all went mouldy.'[6]

Having done such a splendid job in Palestine, Kitchener was promptly despatched to Cyprus on a similar mission. He was asked to investigate the condition of the people, and found a scenario that distressed him: 'They have nothing to eat; their children cry for food, and they have nothing to give them; they live on vegetables, but very shortly there will be no more to be had. They have no houses, and sleep under trees.'[7] Kitchener demanded that the Turkish government act immediately, 'for the safety of the district, and prevent these people from dying of want.'[8] The climate, lack of roads, language barrier and the occasional hostility of the islanders all caused a headache for the surveyors, even before they saw the tangled labyrinth of ridges and valleys running down from the Troodos mountains. None of that stopped Kitchener from enjoying himself. In Nicosia, he cut quite a dash as a horseman, and a trophy he won in a steeplechase became one of his most prized possessions.

Kitchener was in Cyprus between 1879 and 1882. The resulting map, drawn on a scale of an inch to the mile, was pronounced to be 'a very finished specimen of the art of Cartography'. His fun and high jinks in Cyprus seem to have been the natural destiny of most young servicemen of that era, but at least one inhabitant of Cyprus had an uncanny knack of foresight.

> Kitchener's room in Nicosia was kept as far as possible in the state in which it had been while he occupied it, the owner, a Greek, declaring his belief that the young English officer would one day be a very great man.[9]

Kitchener joined the Egyptian Army as a Captain and rose rapidly through the ranks to succeed Lord Grenfell as the Sirdar (Commander-in-Chief). In 1898, three years after the massacre of the Anglo-Egyptian garrison in Khartoum, Kitchener defeated the Mahdist forces and rebuilt the city as a centre of government.

Three years in command of British forces in the Boer War, seven years in India, and a return to Egypt as Consul-General was a formidable military record. In 1914 Horatio, now proudly bearing the titles Field Marshal and Earl Kitchener of Khartoum, suddenly found himself facing a dilemma. Storm clouds were gathering over Europe and after forty years of military command away from British shores, he was being pressed into service as the Secretary of State for War.

He was not a politician, he told them, but his aura of greatness drew support, and he was obliged by his sense of duty to accept. His celebrity outshone his ability; he won the heart of the nation while leaving his cabinet peers, who had to deal with him at first hand, rather less convinced. Although irascible and difficult, he was among the few who predicted a long war. His campaign for voluntary enlistment was one of his lasting glories; the irony was that it hurled millions of young soldiers into a war machine they could not have imagined nor foreseen. It was a responsibility few men could have borne.

Kitchener's competence was called into question several times. He was largely blamed for the 'shell crisis' of 1915, when it was found that British forces at the front line had insufficient ammunition. The simple reason was that Britain was not geared towards producing arms in such quantities, over such a long period of time. The Prime Minister, Herbert Asquith, feared a public backlash should Kitchener be dismissed. In the end fate saved him the necessity. In June 1916, the HMS *Hampshire*, was skirting the west coast of Orkney as it carried Kitchener to a secret meeting in Russia when it struck a German mine. It sank within fifteen minutes. Out of more than 600 on board, only twelve survived.

> His methods did not suit a democracy. But there he was, towering above the others in character as in inches, by far the most popular man in the country to the end, and a firm rock which stood out amidst the raging tempest.[10]

A hundred years after his death, Kitchener's wartime legacy has eclipsed his geographical achievements. In particular, his recruitment campaign was a work of timeless genius. Generations of graphic designers return to his original message, 'Your Country Needs You', and his heavily moustached face still stares commandingly out of all kinds of posters. Less well known was his private life, partly because he had in effect married the nation to which he devoted his duty. He had no wife, no family, and disliked his own company; having steeled himself to deal with war, he likely found it impossible to face the reflections of an idle mind. It is interesting to speculate on the nature of the man; he loved beauty in flowers and landscapes, collected fine porcelain, and enjoyed a witty joke.

In 1915 Lord Kitchener was awarded the Livingstone Medal by the Royal Scottish Geographical Society 'in recognition of his topographical work in connection with the survey of Palestine, and as Director of the Survey of Cyprus; also in recognition of his signal services to the State.'[11]

1. Tribute by Sir Arthur Conan Doyle, published by the War Office, 1916, and reproduced in *Lord Kitchener, his Work and his Prestige* by Henry D. Davray, 1917

2-9. *The Life of Lord Kitchener* by Sir George Arthur (1920)

10. *The First World War, 1914-1918* by Lieutenant Colonel Charles à Court Repington (1920)

11. Minutes of RSGS Council meeting, 5th July 1915

Evangeline French   Francesca French   Alice Mildred Cable

Missionary-explorer	Missionary-explorer	Missionary-explorer
BORN: 1869	BORN: 12th December 1871	BORN: 21st February 1878
(Algeria)	(Bruges)	(Guildford)
DIED: 8th July 1960	DIED: 2nd August 1960	DIED: 30th April 1952
(Dorset)	(London)	(London)

§

RSGS Livingstone Medal, 1943

O N 20TH OCTOBER 1933, *The Scotsman* carried a news item entitled 'Through Central Asia – A Missionary in the Desert':

Miss Mildred Cable, a missionary of the China Inland Mission, was the speaker at the inaugural lecture for the session of the Royal Scottish Geographical Society, the lecture being illustrated by coloured pictures from photographs taken by herself. Miss Cable has lived in China for 32 years, the last ten of which have been spent among the oases of the Gobi Desert, and in Chinese Turkestan. Her subject was 'Central Asian Towns and Types'...
Miss Cable had crossed the Gobi Desert four times – journeys on camels or in mule carts which proceeded at a speed of four miles per hour. She had therefore had ample opportunity to study the subject upon which she would address them.[1]

Ample opportunity, indeed, yet in her lecture Miss Cable had carefully downplayed the most exciting parts or else omitted them altogether. An evangelist who devoted her life to the wellbeing of others, it was not in her nature to beat her own drum. She was addressing an academic institution, after all. She focused on the landscape and people, and her interesting discoveries of archaeological remains. The story that she did not tell was flushed with colour and drama, and shared by her two dearest friends. So closely entwined in their

287

mission and mindset were the three that they called themselves 'The Trio'.

Sitting together for a rare portrait, Mildred Cable and Eva and Francesca French look serene and composed, the ideal of elderly maiden aunts who might enjoy crochet or collect snuffboxes. This is an illusion. When they travelled around northern China in the early 1900s, their arrival was often met with hostility and shock. They received death threats on a regular basis. All they had to defend themselves with was a wagonload of Bibles.

The daughter of a Guildford draper, Mildred Cable had studied pharmacy and human sciences at University College, London. As a child, she had been schooled by a succession of severe governesses and forbidden to read fairy tales in case they polluted her soul. It was her father's wish that she should dedicate her life to God as a foreign missionary and when she set sail for China in 1901, aged twenty-three, she carried with her a broken heart. Having had to choose between her faith and her fiancé, her Christian beliefs had won out. Unable to look back, she decided to look forward.

Evangeline 'Eva' French was nine years older than Mildred, and a good deal more rebellious. The eldest of three daughters, she had been an acute source of anxiety at the convent school in Geneva where she was educated, climbing the highest walls and edging her way across crumbling parapets while the nuns watched with goggle-eyed horror. Her parents' life was no easier; when her youngest sister, Francesca, was born, a housemaid locked Eva in a cellar as a punishment for being noisy. Emerging a few hours later, tearstained and unrepentant, she waited for her moment to steal the baby away and promptly dumped her in a patch of nettles.

When Mildred Cable arrived in China, Eva was already there, having survived multiple near-catastrophes with her spirit of adventure undimmed. She had once described herself as an 'embryonic Bolshevist', but thanks to a moment of pure spiritual revelation she was now driven by a strong zeal for Christianity, and had answered the call of the China Inland Mission in Shanxi Province. A few years later Francesca joined them, obviously having forgiven her sister for the nettle incident and keen to lend her support to the mission.

At the school in Hwochow, they became known as the 'three-in-one teachers'. The Trio rapidly became absorbed in their teaching work, but soon the edge of the challenge began to soften and they found themselves drawn towards something more demanding. If they really wanted to spread the message of the Gospels in the vast regions of northern China, they would need to travel. They packed their books and pamphlets into a mule-drawn cart, and set off on their humble quest.

None of the women expected an uneventful journey, as the landscape they were venturing into was far from peaceful. Suspicion and hostility often greeted their arrival in a strange village, but they had a way of winning trust with their gentle patience. They organised prayer meetings and taught people about the gospels, renting rooms where they could. They cared little about their own comfort.

Passing through portals in the Great Wall, they crossed and re-crossed the Gobi Desert, tracing ancient trade routes and exploring places of astonishing beauty. They marvelled at the Lake of the Crescent Moon, hidden among the sand hills, and gazed up at a cliff into which were carved the thousand-year-old Caves of a Thousand Buddhas. The vast wilderness held its own mysteries; their guide informed them that spiralling dust spouts were the spirits of dead people, and at night they listened to the eerie cries of the desert that came from no earthly being. Their faith was undisturbed by such phenomena, but something even more sinister was on the horizon.

In the autumn of 1932, Mildred, Eva and Francesca were travelling through lands being terrorised by a merciless warlord. In a country of despots, this was not remarkable, but the extreme violence of Ma Zhongying had earned him the nickname 'The Thunderbolt'. The usually impassive Sven Hedin (see p.125) had encountered him several years before and likened him to the fourth horseman of the Apocalypse.

Their home at that time was a rented house in the City of Sands (Dunhuang). Quietly, they retreated there and waited. Before long, a band of brigands arrived at the city gates, demanding that the defence forces hand over the keys and surrender their weapons. It was inevitable that the city would capitulate, and equally inevitable that the

conspicuous foreign ladies who had been holding Christian services
would receive an 'invitation' to an audience with Ma Zhongying.

Mildred, Eva and Francesca were fully aware that such an invitation was usually one-way. When they were summoned they made
one stipulation: they would not be separated and would travel to his
headquarters in their own cart, with their own servant. Alongside
them walked two hundred prisoners, many tied together with ropes.
The 80-mile journey took several days, and they prayed as they went.
There was little else they could do.

Ma Zhongying was in his early twenties, tall, slender and elegant,
his body exquisitely perfumed and his bearing deceptively noncha-
lant. When he received them, he was lounging on a dais spread with
rugs, flanked by heavily armed guards. Flames from a brazier lit up
the weapons that hung on the walls. He seemed preoccupied with a
man who had displeased him for some slight offence, for which he
would be shot. Somebody had dared, foolishly, to plead for the man's
release; Ma Zhongying complained petulantly at the inconvenience.
Then his attention turned to the three women before him. He had
just sustained a gunshot wound, he told them, and was fearful
because it was not healing. He knew they had medical knowledge,
and commanded them to take a look.

One of them produced some disinfectant and treated it with shaking
fingers. He flinched at the sting of it. Their first audience was over.

For several days the women were 'guests' of Ma Zhongying,
subsisting on poor rations and waiting to learn their fate. They knew
that if they begged for their release too boldly or too soon, they
would be refused, and once a decision was made, he never changed
his mind. The three found an unlikely ally in the warlord's Chief of
Staff, who advised them of the best time to appeal and came to them
a few days later with the news that they would be allowed to leave.
There was one condition: their captor would see them one last time.

Ushered into Ma Zhongying's presence, the three missionaries
submitted quietly to his message of farewell and then rose to go,
determined that no action of theirs should jeopardise their safety. But
Mildred could not help herself. Clutching her copy of the New Testament and the Ten Commandments, she advanced on the reclining

despot and made him a gift of them, advising him to have a care for his immortal soul.

Back in the City of Sands, they could breathe again but were still not at liberty to continue their journey. While Ma Zhongying held power, his soldiers guarded the town's entrances day and night. Believing that God would find a way, and with grain rations already dwindling, they began to stockpile food in preparation for a dash to freedom. Eight months later, leaving their house in careful disarray as if intending to return, and with reserves of flour carefully stashed in their sleeping bags, they sneaked out of the south gate as the townspeople slept.

They made a good choice of cart-driver, who was an honest man and knew the desert well. Aware that speed was of the essence, he still took great care to find the safest places to ford rivers, and navigated expertly around quicksand – but even he could not disguise the wheel tracks.

When the scouts caught up with them, Mildred stared them calmly in the face. They demanded to see the travellers' special permit; she knew that they had none. She also knew the men were quite likely illiterate. Careful not to betray her panic, she turned to Eva and asked her to find her passport. The scouts perused this in wonder for a few long minutes, then saluted the little party with respect. The Trio were allowed to carry on.

As she lay under the stars and tried to sleep, Mildred reflected on her faith and the dangers that still awaited them. They had passed through scenes of awful destruction and death, the inevitable aftermath of battle. Several more days of anxious travel lay ahead before they would reach safety. Eva and Francesca were asleep, exhausted with the physical and mental strain of their flight. Although none of them bothered about their appearance, Mildred knew they looked grimy and dishevelled, and was privately glad they had no mirror. Finally, as the morning star rose in the lightening sky, she slept.

The Trio survived to share many more adventures, which they later recounted in their many books. When they returned to Britain they brought with them an orphaned Chinese girl whom they had adopted as a daughter. Their later years must have seemed tame by comparison. In the foreword of *Something Happened* (1936) their address is given as 'The Willow Cottage, Wessex' for all the world as if they lived in a Thomas Hardy novel.

Mildred Cable, Francesca and Eva French were the guests of the Royal Scottish Geographical Society in Edinburgh in December 1943, when they were awarded the Livingstone Medal. 'In her lecture entitled 'The Gobi Inhabitants and Oases', Miss Cable told of the amazing variety of scenery to be found in the land called 'desert', and illustrated her lecture with lantern slides made from her own photographs and beautifully coloured.'[2]. She may not have spoken of her dealings with Ma Zhongying, but she was probably still praying for his salvation.

---

1. *The Scotsman*, 20th October 1933
2. *The Scotsman*, 12th December 1943

Frederick ('Eric') Marshman Bailey

Himalayan explorer
BORN: 3 February 1882 (Lahore, India)
DIED: 17th April 1967 (Stiffkey, Norfolk)
§
RSGS Livingstone Medal, 1921

WHEN THE NAME OF Frederick Marshman Bailey was engraved into the roll of honour on the Menin Gate of Ypres as a fallen hero of the Great War, one of his mother's friends sent her a sympathetic postcard. She took it straight to the office of the War Graves Commission and demanded that her son's name be removed because he was still alive.

Polite surprise greeted her complaint. There could be no mistake. The names had been double-checked, and all those on the list were undoubtedly dead. But he is still alive, she protested. Alive and well, and staying in Lhasa with his friend, the Dalai Lama.

Immediately detecting a mother driven half-insane with grief, the officials soothed her with platitudes and probably made her a cup of tea while they called a taxi. She saw that further remonstrance would be pointless, but she was right: Bailey was indeed alive.

If there is a James Bond of geographers, it is Frederick Marshman Bailey. Born in Lahore, India, in 1882, he was the son of a Lieutenant Colonel in the Royal Engineers; though he was known as Eric, he must have been a madcap youth because his friends called him 'Hatter'. When the RSGS, announcing a forthcoming lecture by Bailey in 1921, said he had done 'a good deal of interesting travel', they were not joking. Most of the time, it was to places where he definitely should not have been.

In the late 1800s India was still ruled by the British Empire, and the young Bailey was destined to follow in his father's military footsteps. He trained at Sandhurst and served in the 17th Bengal Lancers then the 32nd Sikh Pioneers; he accompanied Francis Younghusband's 1904 Expedition (see p.182), and the following year he was posted as British Indian Trade Agent to Gyantse in Tibet. But he was not going to settle down into a safe diplomatic career. Crossing borders into forbidden territory became his speciality, and he stepped boldly into one of the most spectacular political landscapes of the nineteenth century.

The 'Great Game' was a period of dark threats and prolonged sabre-rattling between Britain and Russia. The rivalry was all about wealth and power. Russia was pushing her boundaries ever closer to the glittering wealth of British India, while Britain nervously tried to maintain control of the access routes through the Himalayas. The tension had been simmering for many decades; the Great War and the Bolshevik revolution served only to raise the stakes. Central Asia was in turmoil. Neither side knew what the other was doing, and in the absence of any kind of intelligence, communication held the key to victory.

Bailey was fluent in many languages, which the British Indian Government recognised as being very valuable indeed. Early in his career he had been examined in Tibetan by the man who inspired the character of Hurree Chunder Mookerjee in Rudyard Kipling's *Kim*. He also had first-hand experience of travelling through unknown and potentially hostile terrain. In 1913, accompanied by Captain Henry Morshead of the Survey of India, he had trekked for 1,500 miles through uncharted territory on a quest to map the course of the Tsangpo Gorge.

> The very nature of the country and peoples amid which the explorers moved precluded the possibility of communication between them and the civilised world. I gather that Mrs Bailey heard nothing from her son between June 5 and November 17 – an anxious time! Still, on November 2 a friend well qualified to judge wrote to me: 'Young Bailey will turn up all right, you will see.'[1]

It seemed Bailey could survive against the odds, and had a talent for reappearing unscathed when most people thought he was dead. He was already an explorer, soldier and diplomat, and he was about to become a secret agent. In 1918 he was despatched to Tashkent, capital of the newly formed Soviet state of Turkestan. He described the reasons for his posting, with considerable understatement, to the RSGS in 1920.

> Major Bailey said that during the last year of the war German intrigues in Turkestan gave the Indian Government cause for a good deal of anxiety. For that reason the Government of India sent a mission, of which he was in charge, to Turkestan to talk frankly with the Bolshevists and see if they could come to an understanding.[2]

Coming to an understanding with the Bolsheviks was an optimistic goal, to say the least. Marooned in Central Asia's vast, inhospitable region of mountain and desert, Tashkent was a city controlled by fear. The ruthless new leaders of Russia's working class patrolled the streets, seizing houses and property at random, and shooting anyone who offered resistance. Bailey disappeared undercover, in an attempt to discover the threat that Russia posed to India.

The finer details of Bailey's life in Tashkent have to be teased out of his writing like seeds out of cotton wool. When he wrote *Mission to Tashkent* in 1946, much had to be omitted for reasons of confidentiality. What remains is a rather dry account that lacks excitement or emotion. Bailey himself was a study in reticence; without this quality, he would certainly have died. Switching identities like a chameleon, he was able to observe the dangerous machinations of the Bolshevik militants while somehow managing to send reports back to base. He began by posing as an Austrian officer.

> I had several narrow escapes of being caught, and had to change my name and get fresh papers several times. One couple with whom I lived really believed I was an Austrian, and kept bringing me tit-bits of information that they thought I should like to know...[3]

The duties of a secret agent involved befriending people who might be of assistance, and Bailey had an uncanny instinct about whom to trust. After two months in Tashkent he received, through unreliable sources, a message from British authorities commanding him to get out. He suspected an attack on the city was imminent so, boldly wearing his Austrian uniform, he got hold of a cart loaded with hay and drove it out towards the north-east with a friend who had promised him refuge at his farm. Holed up at the farm with a Russian-Polish cavalry officer and a Russian general, both of whom were 'wanted' and on the run for unspecified reasons, Bailey took stock of their combined weapons. They planned what to do in the event of an attack, and set about cutting firewood.

How does a British spy, lying low and waiting for the Bolsheviks, pass the time? Bailey chose to study the finer points of cooking pilau. Vegetables and mutton were in plentiful supply, and he found a big iron cooking pot in the kitchen. In *Mission to Tashkent*, he compares the merits of putting the carrots in before or after the onions, and observes that both take longer to cook than the meat. He fries everything in butter and explains that the diced meat – in this case, a sheep's tail –- should be added after the vegetables. The rice, washed in cold water, must go in last, along with a handful of sultanas, if available. For best results, the dish should be covered for a few minutes and kept hot, and only stirred when diners are ready to eat.

If he had thought of opening a take-away, he might have changed the course of history.

November turned to December, and a baffling array of mysterious comrades came and went. Then one snowy morning Bailey was alarmed by the sound of barking. Grabbing his rifle, he went outside to find a one-armed Russian soldier whose hunting dogs had cornered a wild boar; the Russian had fired seven shots at it, but his gun was misfiring. Bailey killed the beast, and, with convincing coolness, introduced himself as a Hungarian sausage-maker. It was a brilliant gamble. Pleasantly surprised at the convenience of his profession, the Russian allowed Bailey to keep half of the pig for himself.

Judging that the emergency had passed, Bailey returned to Tashkent, and for over a year he evaded capture. But by this time the

Cheka – the Bolshevik secret police – were on his trail and actively seeking to kill him. Bailey's response was to leave his lodgings and find somewhere else to stay under another new identity, deliberately leaving his toothbrush behind. The Cheka, arriving hot on his heels, examined it suspiciously. When Bailey failed to return, they concluded that he had been murdered, because, in their estimation, no one of Bailey's calibre would be so careless as to forget his toothbrush. This subtle deception bought Bailey enough time to save his life — but the net was closing in, and his nerve was about to be tested to the utmost.

He could see only one way to get himself back across the border to safety. The Cheka wanted to find him, so he would help them look.

Assuming yet another disguise, Bailey arranged an interview with the Cheka and assured them of his considerable talents. Impressed, they gave him a mission. He was to go to Bukhara, a town which was outside Bolshevik control, and seek out a dangerous Anglo-Indian spy. Without twitching an eyelid, Bailey heard the name of his quarry: Frederick Bailey. His plan had worked. He was being hired to look for himself.

Three hundred and fifty miles away in Bukhara, Bailey made some convincing attempts to find himself before sending an assistant back to Tashkent with the news that he must have escaped. He then lost no time in making a dash on horseback for the Persian border, struggling through snowstorms and escaping by the skin of his teeth from the gunfire of Bolshevik patrols. In *Mission to Tashkent* he recalled that the sight of the sunrise gleaming on a range of snow-covered mountains, which he knew were in Persia, brought a sense of relief impossible to describe. He did not escape alone but, true to form, he does not name his travelling companions.

It seems impossible that Bailey ever had the time or opportunity to make observations about the landscapes he passed through, but during his colourful career he made many valuable contributions to geographical science. On his trek into Tibet with Henry Morshead he collected over 2,000 bird skins from 270 species, which he deposited in the British Museum; he discovered the habitat of the Tibetan Eared Pheasant (*Crossoptilon harmani*) and described the breeding of the Ibisbill (*Ibidorhyncha struthersii*). The Tibetan blue poppy,

Meconopsis baileyi, is named in his honour, as he pressed some of its flowers in his notebook on one of his expeditions.

Bailey's father, also called Frederick, was Secretary of the RSGS, and Bailey was educated at the Edinburgh Academy. He received the Order of the Indian Empire, and the Viceroy of India described him as 'an absolutely first class man'. His mother was likely not so flattering when she saw him again after his party with the Dalai Lama.

In 1921 Frederick Marshman 'Hatter' Bailey was awarded the Livingstone Medal by the Royal Scottish Geographical Society 'in recognition of the admirable geographical work he had done on the Upper Brahmaputra and in other parts of Central Asia.'[4]

---

1. 'Captain F. M. Bailey's latest exploration' by Lieutenant Colonel A. C. Yate, *Scottish Geographical Magazine* (1914) 30:4, 191-197
2. *Aberdeen Journal*, 18th December 1920
3. 'In Russian Turkestan under the Bolsheviks' by Major F. M. Bailey, *Scottish Geographical Magazine* (1921) 37:2, 81-99
4. Minutes of RSGS Council meeting, 16th December 1920

MARION ISABEL NEWBIGIN

Geographer, biologist, lecturer and author
BORN: 1869 (Alnwick)
DIED: 20th July 1934 (Edinburgh)
§
RSGS Livingstone Medal, 1923
Editor of *Scottish Geographical Magazine*, 1902-34

On the seashore at a frequented resort, as the tide flows one may see splendid sand castles rising above the level surface, with moats and towers, lofty walls and all the devices that the ingenuity of their youthful builders can suggest. When the tide ebbs at most a slight irregularity of the surface, smoothed by the action of the waves, marks the site of the vanished edifice. With such worn-down castles we may compare the mountain remnants of Europe...[1]

I T IS EASY TO SEE HOW Marion Newbigin's books with their fluid prose won her so much respect in the field of geographical science. In the late 1800s and through the first three decades of the twentieth century, she inhabited a sphere largely populated by men and contributed a lifetime of work that helped to define the study of geography. Her professionalism won great respect from the foremost scientists of her time, and as a teacher she sparked the interest of younger generations to whom she made geography both accessible and enjoyable.

Marion was studious and disciplined but nowhere does her character appear forceful. In fact, throughout her writing, her character rarely emerges at all. Yet her list of qualifications, posts and awards is astonishing for a woman of her time. The world was still highly sceptical about the education of women, so where did she gain the confidence, not only to succeed but to excel?

The answer may lie with her father's unorthodox views on education. James Leslie Newbigin, a pharmacist in Alnwick, Northumberland, had three sons and five daughters. While he encouraged his sons to choose a career and become independent in their teenage years, he felt his daughters should have the benefit of education for as long as possible. For the girls this was a remarkable opportunity, despite the question of where that education could be obtained. Until the early 1900s few universities in Britain would admit women, and even fewer allowed them to graduate. Luckily, the Edinburgh Association for the University Education of Women offered a respectable alternative to female students barred from the universities themselves.

Marion studied in Edinburgh and in 1890 she passed the matriculation exam for the University of London. This scheme, the first of its kind in the UK, allowed women students to gain degrees while studying at one of the handful of universities that had taken the step of allowing women through their doors. In 1891, aged twenty-two, Marion entered the University of Wales in Aberystwyth to study chemistry, physics, biology and mathematics. She was awarded a BSc (Hons) degree in zoology in 1893, and five years later she gained a DSc, becoming only the university's second woman ever to do so.

Now admirably qualified, Marion soon found a position on the team of scientists who were examining and recording the findings of the *Challenger* expedition, a four-year voyage around the oceans of the world which had returned to Britain in 1876. Based at Millport Marine Biological Station, she undertook new research into the natural pigments of plants and animals, and published a book, *Colour in Nature*. In 1897 she became a lecturer at the Edinburgh School of Medicine for Women, and in her spare time she undertook a wide range of extra work including marking examination papers and teaching at Patrick Geddes's summer schools (see p.323).

Marion's move from biology to geography was likely encouraged by Professor James Geikie (see p.174), whose lectures she had attended as a student in Edinburgh and who must have recognised her potential. So began Marion's most enduring and arguably significant role – as Editor of the *Scottish Geographical Magazine*, the academic journal of the RSGS. Not only did she collect and edit contributions from a diverse range of scientists, but she actively sought submissions from brilliant newcomers to the field, ensuring that the magazine became one of Britain's most highly respected geographical journals.

Marion herself was a regular contributor to the magazine, and her diverse offerings include: 'Constantinople and the Straits: the Past and the Future'; 'Ice Ages and the Geological History of Climate'; and 'The Kingussie District: a Geographical Study'. Her writing is concise, clear and highly organised; it is only in her many books that she allows her imagination a little more freedom.

In the Introduction to *Frequented Ways*, for example, Marion sets out a delightful argument for the appeal of European countries to the well-seasoned traveller. As a generation of explorers were opening up exotic travel to an eager public, it became fashionable to dismiss the more familiar destinations – the Alps, Norwegian fjords or the Mediterranean – as unbearably boring. After all, Thomas Cook were already taking parties of tourists to France, Switzerland and Italy so it was hardly the stuff of pioneering adventure.

> ...since the visiting of foreign lands has thus ceased to be a mark of what was once called 'elegance,' the really superior person is apt to feel that distance, difficulty or great cost can alone justify a journey...[2]

Marion allows herself a little fun, but still has some words of comfort for aspiring travellers who 'are liable to have their judgement warped by the ceaseless journalistic chatter about colonies and dependencies'[3], and consequently feel deprived. She proceeds to give a systematic analysis of the virtues of Europe, and compares its diverse yet relatively compact geography with that of other continents. British travellers are reminded that magnificent glaciers can be found at Chamonix, only a day's journey from London by sea and rail, whereas a resident of Montreal, for example, would have to travel over 2,000 miles in order to see one. Volcanoes are likewise conveniently accessible; the distance from London to Naples, for views of Vesuvius, is only 1,300 miles, and indeed many inactive volcanoes exist even closer to home, in the Auvergne, the Eifel, and the Lowlands of Scotland.

> The very fact that Arthur's Seat rises in solemn majesty above the city of Edinburgh has helped to make that city a home of geologists, has led to the enrichment of human knowledge.[4]

As Marion goes on to evaluate and explain the distinctive geographical features of selected European regions, she allows her passion for travel to slip through. She visited these places herself, of course, and took many of the photographs in her books; she was also a keen mountain climber. Her case for exploring Europe with fresh eyes and seeking the thrill of new discoveries in well-charted territory is irresistible.

With her strongly independent nature and passion for learning, Marion was a lifelong supporter of the women's suffrage movement. How ironic was the twist of fate when, in 1916, the University of Edinburgh finally yielded to pressure and granted female students full access to its courses in medicine. Marion would have been torn between delight and regret; a victory for women's rights rendered her teaching post at the Edinburgh School of Medicine for Women no longer necessary, and she found herself out of a job.

In much of her writing, Marion had the clear-sightedness to step back from the political scene of the early twentieth century, where the British Empire still distorted thinking on politics and race. She preferred to take a more objective view of geography. Where it bordered on anthropology, she challenged the accepted idea that racial characteristics were fixed and hereditary, reflecting the environment in which they had arisen. Physical differences in race, she argued, were of little importance under modern conditions, and she daringly suggested that race was being used as a political tool. In the austere and smoky chambers of gentlemen's clubs this must have been about as welcome as an overdose of snuff.

During the latter part of her life, Marion shared her home at 2 Chamberlain Road, Edinburgh with three of her sisters, who had pursued successful academic careers of their own. Marion never married and had no children; nevertheless, she still held some strong and insightful views on children's early education, warning against cramming their minds full of facts in every field of science. Instead, she recommended that they should be inspired with an appetite for learning, and be made aware of all the many sources of information available to them in libraries, societies and museums. As teachers, she said, we should 'be content to open doors, to give peeps of attractive vistas'[5]. It is a sentiment her contemporary, Sir Patrick Geddes, would have agreed with wholeheartedly, even though his abhorrence of paperwork was poles apart from Marion's diligence.

20th July 1934 was a special day in the calendar of the RSGS. This was the Society's 50th anniversary, and to mark the occasion a garden party was held in the grounds of George Heriot's School, Edinburgh. The event was eagerly anticipated, and Marion devoted many months to preparing a jubilee edition of the *Scottish Geographical Magazine*. On 20th July, however, sad news arrived in the offices of the RSGS: Marion had died at her home that morning. Her death was entirely unexpected, and the Society's celebratory mood was dampened by the loss. Her obituary in the Magazine paid tribute to her many achievements, and added that her dry wit and warm friendliness would be sorely missed.

Marion Newbigin's name is not linked with any great feats in the field of exploration. She is rather one of the quiet inspirers – confident in her own abilities, fascinated by the natural world, and passionate about kindling that fire of fascination in others. She may have remained in the shadows, but by all accounts she had strong opinions and was fearless in speaking her mind. She wrote for an astonishingly wide audience, and it is impossible to tell how many young explorers gained their first taste of geography from her text books.

A delightful insight into her talent comes from the rather unfortunately named *Man and his Conquest of Nature* (1912), in which Marion demonstrated that the spread of humanity across the globe was strongly influenced by environmental factors. In Chapter 1 she describes three travellers, presumably students of natural history, descending from the heather-clad slopes of the Grampians with curlews calling overhead and remnants of snow glistening in the lee of the hills. The walkers come across a schoolhouse with a small gaggle of children playing outside. Strangers being an uncommon sight, the children stop and stare with open curiosity, and that curiosity is returned by the walkers.

> ...the travellers suddenly realized that the poets had deceived them about the purple mountains and the tumbling streams. Mountains are good, and streams are good, but not so good and not so interesting as man.[6]

Was Marion one of the travellers? We will never know, and that is just as she would have wished. More importantly, with this simple passage she has caught our imagination and led us into the field of human geography.

Marion Newbigin was awarded the Livingstone Medal of the RSGS in 1923, 'for her numerous contributions to geographical science, based largely on her own observations'[7]. She was the first female recipient of this award. In her honour, the Newbigin Prize was introduced in 1938 and is awarded periodically to authors who have made an outstanding contribution to RSGS publications.

1-4. *Frequented Ways* by Marion Newbigin (1922)

5. Marion I. Newbigin 'The Study of the Weather as a Branch of Nature Knowledge', *Scottish Geographical Magazine* (1907) 23:12

6. *Man and his Conquest of Nature* by Marion Newbigin (1912)

7. Minutes of RSGS Council meeting, 28th June 1923

ROSIE SWALE POPE

Marathon runner and philanthropist
BORN: 2nd October 1946 (Davos, Switzerland)
§
Fellow of RSGS, 2011

WHEN ROSIE SWALE POPE woke up in the middle of the night to find a wild boar stuck in the ropes of her tent, she decided to call him Eric. This was mainly to calm her nerves as she stared at him, her heart pounding as she tried to decide what to do next. Camping in the German forest, she had quickly discovered, led to close encounters with all kinds of wildlife, some of them more alarming than others. But Eric, having brought Rosie's bivouac abruptly down on top of her, merely looked apologetic and rather confused in the light of her torch. He waited patiently as she cut him free, then scampered back into the darkness with a twist of his tail and a scornful snort.

As Rosie surveyed the tangle of canvas that used to be her tent, she was glad that dawn was not far away. Philosophically gathering her things together, she resolved to put white ties on the guy ropes in future so that wild animals could at least steer clear of them. Although she was shaken, her sense of humour was soon flowing back. She had faced her first test of nerve! She knew that there would be more to come, in environments a hundred times more threatening than this – because, just a few weeks earlier, she had set off from her home in South Wales with the intention of running all the way around the world.

For many people, journeys of exploration are born out of curiosity or fascination, some overwhelming urge that compels them towards new discoveries. Instead, the idea for Rosie's extraordinary adventure came to her in the darkness of grief, as she mourned the death of her beloved husband, Clive, who had been suffering from cancer. Rosie was already an accomplished marathon runner with some of the world's most gruelling races under her belt. She cast around in her mind for something to do, a new challenge that would draw attention to the disease and hopefully raise money for medical research. When the thought of running around the world sneaked into her head, it galvanised her with excitement and fear. It would, she decided, be a joyful endeavour rather than a mournful one. For Rosie, running was a means of communication. It stimulated the senses, taught her about her soul, brought her closer to nature and made her more aware of life itself. She could not have guessed how many thousands of people would be inspired to communicate with her too.

For such an immense and potentially dangerous expedition, careful planning was essential. Rosie would be alone, and even though she would carry a satellite phone through the vast uninhabited areas, her clothing and equipment would have to be world-class; she was depending on it for her life. Her route would take her right around the Northern Hemisphere — through Holland, Germany, Poland, Lithuania, Latvia, and Russia, including the vast wilderness of Siberia. And that was just the first leg; having crossed the Bering Strait, she would continue down through Alaska and Arctic Canada, turning east to cross the US, before heading home to Wales via Greenland, Iceland, Fair Isle and Scotland. It would take her the best part of five years. On 2nd October 2003, her fifty-seventh birthday, she set off, sped onwards by an emotional but uplifting farewell in her home town of Tenby.

The quality and efficiency of Rosie's support team was second to none. By cleverly sending parcels ahead of her, they had managed to trim down her carrying load to the barest minimum while keeping her stocked up with food supplies and replacement gear. Rosie's high-tech bivouac, which would be the only membrane between her and all kinds of night-time visitors, weighed only two pounds and two ounces. She would be running through the foulest winter weather, so she needed a dependable system to keep the innermost layers of her tent dry at all times and a sleeping bag to protect her in some of the coldest places on Earth. She had planned her food rations carefully; she would melt snow on a small stove for drinking and cooking. Her budget was tight, but she knew how to be frugal. Physically and mentally, she was prepared. There was, however, still an unknown element to deal with: the human one.

In Lithuania, she found, people who appeared to have nothing went out of their way to help her with small gifts of kindness; she was offered food, shelter, or a bed for the night by cottagers who lived such a meagre existence that they deserved charity themselves. Rosie was touched. She had come expecting to be the giver, not the recipient. In Poland on Christmas Eve, she was gathered into a family's home and offered a place at their table. Houses that looked forbidding on the outside often held a warm welcome within. She also discovered that pride could co-exist with poverty when she lost her purse on a lonely route through Russia and a fellow traveller returned it to her, refusing to accept a reward even though he seemed to be in desperate need. In the end, Rosie put some money in a little bag and tied it to the collar of his dog, hoping she would be far enough away when it was discovered.

Of course, not everyone was so benign. In the forests or on the roads that ran through them, Rosie encountered men whose dire poverty had driven them to violence. Two of them, working together and carrying knives, tried to lure her away into the woods; she escaped by throwing herself across the path of an oncoming juggernaut, missing it by inches but using the alarm to distract her attackers and make good her escape. Another man, ostensibly selling apples by the roadside, held a blade to her chest and demanded that she hand over her phone. He broke down as she talked to him soothingly, and once again she seized the moment and ran. But late one night, with her tent pitched and all her gear on the ground, evasion was not so easy when a wild-looking woodman appeared out of nowhere, bellowing ferociously and waving an axe. Unbelievably, it turned out that he was shouting for joy; having stumbled across Rosie's little tent at night, he wanted to invite her to a vodka party. The alcohol was already flowing freely, and it took all of Rosie's inventiveness and

310

tact to decline his offer. In the morning, she found that he had left her a parcel of sausages, bread, and a small bottle of vodka.

In the bleak wilderness of Siberia Rosie was shadowed by a pack of feral dogs. She had been warned about them. They were starving and had no fear of man. Unable to shake them off, and surrounded by their snarling faces, in desperation she threw them her last loaf of bread which they bounded after with joy. She was relieved at their disappearance, but they soon returned. That night, sensing a presence outside her tent, she peeled back the flap to see them all slumbering on the ground around her. Catching her eye, one of them raised his head and lazily wagged his tail. Rosie was almost moved to tears; they were guarding her through the night. With kindness, she had won their loyalty and their trust.

Incredibly, with so many near misses and so many Bohemian night-mares, Rosie's enchantment with the deep forests stayed with her throughout her trek. She loved lying and looking at the stars through the trees as the owls were calling, then listening to the blackbirds sing in the first light of dawn. She loved the little black beetles that shone with iridescence in the light of her torch, and gazed with awe at the footprints of a bear that had prowled around her tent in the snow. She was not unaware of danger – she was acutely conscious of it – but she could always see a way around it and talk herself into a more secure frame of mind. This, perhaps more than any other skill, was the secret of her survival.

One hazard that Rosie had not seen coming was a bus, which hit her as she was running near Lake Baikal in Siberia, knocking her uncon-scious on the road. Never one to dwell on misfortune, she insisted that the driver was the kindest and most generous of all bus drivers because he painstakingly collected all her scattered belongings and returned them to her in hospital. In fairness, she had been weaving all over the road, her body giving in to pneumonia while her mind fiercely propelled it onwards. Medical attention came not a moment too soon.

In September 2005, nearly two years after she first set out, Rosie was approaching Magadan on the east coast of Russia. She was on her twenty-fourth pair of shoes, and these alone had covered 1,500 miles. They were so worn that she was picking bits of tyre rubber off the roadside and gluing them to the soles. Her route had taken her along the 'Road of Bones', a grim path of ghost towns, derelict concentration camps and disused gold mines; before she reached the coast she was waylaid by a group of elderly and frail-looking men, veterans who were once Guardians of the Roadworks, keen to offer her gentle hospitality like the last knights on a crusade for the human spirit.

As she crossed the Bering Strait to Alaska, Rosie still had another two years of running ahead of her. She would face temperatures as low as -62°C, she would have to bear the brunt of gales tearing into her tent, and she would have to carry a pistol to scare away bears. It is tempting to think that she might have been able to talk even them out of any premeditated violence.

Sometime during the first year of Rosie's epic adventure, the world began to appreciate the scale of her challenge. Through the hum of publicity, which was far greater than Rosie had ever dared to believe, she was spreading awareness of cancer and saving lives through early recognition and treatment. All along her path she was receiving messages as well as sending them. 'Travel with your heart, not your feet' was the advice given to her by the driver of a black limousine who slowed down to speak to her in Siberia before mysteriously vanishing into the distance. Rosie was certainly travelling with her heart, although her feet were taking most of the strain.

After surviving so many physical hardships, it was both cruel and ironic when Rosie very nearly fell at the final hurdle. She had expected an easy homecoming to Wales, the final leg a mere stroll compared to her previous exertions, but with the finish line almost in sight she woke up one morning and found herself unable to walk. X-rays revealed two stress fractures in her legs. As she recovered in hospital she fretted with a restlessness that she had not known in Russia or the wilds of Arctic Canada. Her determination, as ever, found a solution, and on 25th August 2008, four years and ten months after she set out, she limped triumphantly back into Tenby to a joyful reception.

In her books and interviews, Rosie comes across as a charming blend of courage, vulnerability, wisdom and youthful energy. Craziness gets attention, she says, revealing that behind the apparent naiveté is a strong will and an unshakeable sense of purpose. She refuses to acknowledge the accepted 'laws' about growing older and continues to push her body and her mind to places where most people half her age would hesitate to go. She scoffs at the idea that running solo is harder or more dangerous for women; a woman travelling alone is often safer, she says, because she is not perceived as a threat.

For Rosie, running has become a metaphor for life, teaching her to treat every experience as an adventure and a miracle. In an age of ever-decreasing distances she has certainly redefined slow travel, and proved beyond doubt that the pleasure is in the journey, not the destination. She has three simple rules: bless the ground that you sleep on; pick up litter as if it is bank notes; and never miss a chance to be happy. Probably, as long as her legs will carry her, she will keep sprinting cheerfully across boundaries, smiling at strangers.

VISIONS
FOR
CHANGE

John George Bartholomew

Cartographer and geographer
Born: 22nd March 1860 (Edinburgh)
Died: 14th April 1920 (Sintra, Portugal)
§
RSGS co-founder and first Honorary Secretary
(with Ralph Richardson)

It is an easier matter to dream dreams of ideal projects than to realise them. Then the real work begins...[1]

IN THE LATE NINETEENTH century the popularity of the 'safety bicycle' was at its height, luring many would-be explorers out of their armchairs and into the saddle for some pioneering adventure across counties and – in some cases – continents. Motorcars were still a rare sight on British roads but for those intrepid enough to trust themselves on two wheels, the great outdoors held the promise of pleasurable discovery. Cycling clubs sprang up, turning the activity into a regular social event. All cyclists needed was a set of reliable road maps.

In Scotland, one enterprising cartographer was already starting to produce them.

As a boy, John George Bartholomew escaped reprimand for blotting his school copybook by reshaping ink stains into miniature maps. He was, after all, the fourth generation in a well-respected Edinburgh family of map-makers, beginning with George Bartholomew in 1806. George's son, John Senior, set up his own business in 1826, and Bartholomew's became a map-making institution. With this background, no one could punish John George for cartographic endeavour, however imaginative. His great-uncle Henry is said to have engraved the map of Treasure Island for Robert Louis Stevenson, after all.

After completing his education at the Royal High School and the University of Edinburgh, John George joined his father, confusingly known as John Junior, at John Bartholomew & Son. By the age of twenty-eight he had taken over the company's management and soon proved he had a flair for business. With an instinct for crowd-sourcing astonishingly ahead of its time, he hit on a brilliant way of keeping Bartholomew's road maps updated. Around that time, the Cyclists' Touring Club of Great Britain numbered over 60,000 members. John George invited cyclists to submit their detailed findings to him in return for a generous discount on the price of his half-inch maps. Soon, Bartholomew's offices were receiving bundles of letters full of valuable eye-witness accounts that gave their road maps the vital advantage of newness and accuracy. John Bartholomew & Son might not have had satellite imagery, but they had the next best thing.

Although John George was passionate about geography, he cherished another ambition as well. With the public clamouring to hear news of famous explorers returning from previously uncharted regions, he could see the need for something more than a set of freshly updated maps. As the blank spaces in the continents were being filled in, cartography was advancing in leaps and bounds. Thrilling tales of discovery added colour and excitement to the fast-advancing science of geography. Here were stories that needed to be told, and people were keen to hear them. Geographical societies were already springing up all across Europe and John George saw no reason why Scotland should not have one of its own. It would be a platform from which knowledge could be shared, and from which the study of geography could be encouraged.

> It was at North Berwick on a Sunday afternoon in the summer of 1884 that the project of forming a Scottish Geographical Society was proposed to Mrs Bruce.[2]

John George was in the fortunate position of having a wide and influential circle of friends. One of them was Agnes Livingstone Bruce, daughter of the celebrated explorer David Livingstone (see p.239). He visited her at her home near North Berwick in East Lothian, and as they walked on the beach, he told her about his dream for a Scottish Geographical Society. He felt the idea had little prospect of realisation, because 'it had been proposed before and discouraged by various kind friends.'[3] Mrs Bruce disagreed. Her eyes alight with enthusiasm, she assured him that her father would have welcomed it. Her husband, Alexander Low Bruce, whose counsel was eagerly sought when they returned to the house, greeted the idea with cheerful optimism. Before midnight a prospectus had been drafted. The next day, leading Edinburgh geologist Professor James Geikie gave the idea his wholehearted support.

In this way, John George Bartholomew was both a spark and a guiding light in the early days of the Royal Scottish Geographical Society. Far from wishing to steal the glory for himself, he earnestly welcomed a succession of guest lecturers in the form of eminent explorers and scientists, and worked with a team of influential Council members and office-bearers to ensure that Scotland's new geographical society grew in scope and stature. John George 'may be said to have had a genius for friendship'[4]; he knew the importance of all the relationships he was developing.

Many of the visiting explorers were returning from the polar regions, so it seems fitting that John George was responsible for giving Antarctica its name. Although the term 'Antarctic', meaning 'opposite to the Arctic', had been used by writers since the first century AD to describe the uncharted regions around the South Pole, the name 'Antarctica' first appeared in 1886 when John George prepared a map to accompany a report to the Royal Scottish Geographical Society by the oceanographer Sir John Murray (see p.111). The following year, Antarctica was clearly labelled on Bartholomew's *Handy Reference Atlas*.

Bartholomew collaborated with Sir John Murray to produce the maps from the *Challenger* expedition, and in the early 1900s he worked with Murray again, in the publication of his *Bathymetrical Survey of the Fresh-water Lochs of Scotland*. The accompanying maps illustrated the depth of the lochs in plan and cross-section, and included some of the surrounding land. They were also beautiful works of art and stand as fine examples of the layered shading of contours: soft greens and browns indicated low-lying areas; darker browns were used for high ground; white indicated mountain summits; water depth was illustrated by carefully graduating tints of blue. This system was an innovation that John George had worked passionately to establish, and from 1880 onwards it became a much-loved feature of Bartholomew's maps. He used it to great effect in the *Survey Atlas of Scotland*, published in 1895 by the Royal Scottish Geographical Society.

Throughout his life, John George never enjoyed robust health but such was his commitment to his work and to the Society that he had helped to establish that he regularly sent advice to its Council from his sick bed. He used his skill and vision to publish some truly inspiring maps, fully justifying his appointment in 1910 as Cartographer to King George V. This royal appointment continued to be held by Bartholomew's, through three successive monarchs, until 1962.

John George's successor was his eldest son, John 'Ian' Bartholomew, who was born in 1890. Ian inherited the large and supremely efficient print workshop in Duncan Street, and in April 1926 he welcomed a particularly exciting visitor through its porticoed doors. T. E. Lawrence, otherwise known as Lawrence of Arabia, arrived unannounced on a motorcycle. His purpose was to discuss some alterations to the map which Bartholomew's were producing, illustrating the route of his 600-mile march across the Arabian desert in 1917 for inclusion in his forthcoming memoir, *Seven Pillars of Wisdom*.

Ian Bartholomew served in the trenches during the First World War and was awarded the Military Cross in 1915. When approached in the early 1940s with an idea to help British prisoners in the Second World War, he naturally gave his wholehearted support. The request came from Christopher Clayton Hutton, a key figure in a new government department called MI9 who was known as an eccentric genius. His idea was to produce small-scale maps of parts of Europe and insert them secretly into innocent-looking items such as board games that were being sent to British prisoners of war by MI9, masquerading as a charity. The maps would assist any escapees to find their way back to Allied lines, and they were printed on silk, which was far more durable than paper.

Ian Bartholomew readily agreed, waiving any fees for the use of his maps; he kept the matter so secret that he mentioned it to no one, including his sons.

> Adventure has gone into the map-maker's art, and there is a sense of adventure in it still.[5]

The Bartholomew family's illustrious contribution to map-making continued when Ian's son John Christopher became Cartographic Director in 1953. The company was later sold, but Bartholomew's name and mapping traditions are perpetuated by Collins Bartholomew, today a subsidiary of HarperCollins.

Flicking through the *Scottish Geographical Magazine* or the newspaper archives of the RSGS, it is impossible not to come across the name Bartholomew in some capacity: as a Secretary or President of the Society, as the author of an academic paper, as a croupier (assistant chairman) at one of the early banquets, or as a host congratulating the recipient of a medal. The close bond between successive generations of Bartholomews and the RSGS was one of mutual appreciation and support, and in 2000 this relationship was celebrated with the introduction of the Bartholomew Globe, an award that is bestowed 'for excellence in the assembly, delivery or application of geographical information through cartography, GIS* and related techniques'.

* Geographic Information Systems

1-3. J. G. Bartholomew 'Mrs. Livingstone Bruce and the Scottish Geographical Society', *Scottish Geographical Magazine* (1912) 28:6, 312-314

4. Obituary of J. G. Bartholomew, *Scottish Geographical Magazine* (1920) 36:3, 183-189

5. *The Scotsman*, 24th March 1956

Sir Patrick Geddes

Philanthropist, naturalist, teacher
BORN: 2nd October 1854 (Ballater)
DIED: 17th April 1932 (Montpellier)
§
RSGS Council member, 1895 & 1896

There have been two sorts of great travellers. First, of course, those who sail round the world, or climb higher and higher upon its mountain peaks, who venture farther into the icy North, deeper into the tropical forest than any who have gone before. Yet the other kind travel also, and that far further, in their chairs and in their dreams.[1]

AT THE AGE OF TWENTY-SEVEN, Patrick Geddes went totally blind. It was 1879 and he was in Mexico, carrying out zoological research. He had always been a strongly visual person, finding lessons in the simplest of natural forms, but now the only images he could see were mental ones. As he sat in a darkened room with his eyes bandaged, he found himself groping for light within his own soul.

Patrick Geddes was born in Ballater in 1854, the fourth son of an officer of the Black Watch. Most of his young life was spent in Perth at his family home on Kinnoull Hill. Alexander and Janet Geddes were staunchly religious: Alexander named their home 'Mount Tabor' after the hill in Galilee where Christ was said to have appeared to his disciples, transfigured with radiant light. For Patrick, the strictures of the Church fell on deaf ears. From the summit of Kinnoull Hill he looked down on Perth and the winding River Tay, a landscape spread out beneath him like a living lesson in geography, and began to evolve his own vivid philosophy about the Earth, its inhabitants, and its communities.

The attitude of Alexander and Janet Geddes towards their children's education was delightfully organic. Their garden was full of flowers, vegetables and fruit, and on Sunday afternoons the whole family would walk around the beds and borders, examining every new leaf and studying the emerging blossoms. In allowing him to help plant potatoes, which had to be spaced at regular intervals, Patrick's father gave him his first lessons in mathematics. He was, however, less than enthusiastic about his son's first attempt at a botanical garden, which involved digging up some shrubs and supplanting them with weeds salvaged from the vegetable plot. When Patrick was older, Alexander took him on walking tours around Scotland, exploring the valleys of the Dee, Don and Spey, nurturing his open and questioning mind.

Biology, botany, geography, geology – Patrick was interested in everything, and refused to accept the divisions between the disciplines. His all-encompassing view of life saw links rather than boundaries and his enthusiasm overflowed into enthusiastic rapture about the world around him. Talking came easily to him, whereas sober and methodical study did not. His first week at the University of Edinburgh, where he had enrolled to read botany, turned out to be his last. Science was about life, not dry and dusty specimens in a laboratory. He was unrepentant.

At this point, it is possible that his parents began to despair of their son's future career. Banking seemed like a good option, but after just eighteen months as an apprentice in Perth, where he proved a dependable if uninspired employee, he quit his post without a moment's regret. Patrick was capable of filling a mould if he had to – he was simply uninterested. He had more important things to do.

A spell at the Royal School of Mines in London was inspired largely by the wish to learn from the biologist Thomas Huxley, whose writings Geddes found particularly inspiring. He learned the skills of dissection and microscope work and grudgingly passed an exam, which was probably the first and last he would ever take. He earned himself an appointment in the laboratory of J. Burdon Sanderson at University College London, and had a surprise encounter with a bearded and elderly Charles Darwin, whose enthusiasm for microscopic pond life surpassed even Geddes's own.

Communication was a skill that Geddes refined into an art form. He used it to make a network of contacts with the great minds of Europe, attending lectures, absorbing knowledge and, above all, finding opportunities. This is how, in 1879, he devised a tailor-made expedition to Mexico, gaining sponsorship from the British Association to carry out palaeontological and zoological research. His brother Robert was already out there, a rich and successful banker in Mexico City. It must have seemed as though nothing could possibly go wrong. Yet only a few months later, his eyes were bandaged and useless, his dreams ebbing away.

Geddes's natural instinct was to see solutions instead of problems. This sudden and inexplicable illness forced him to seek solutions within himself, and they came in vivid flashes of understanding. Navigating by feel around the house, his fingers touched a window with nine panes of glass and his mind started down a new avenue of thought. These small squares, each leading to the next in a repetitive pattern, formed the basis for a new theory. Geddes saw them as containers from which one concept would naturally flow into another. He had found what he called 'a thinking machine', symbolising the ways in which people interact with each other, with their immediate environment, and with the planet. It was an elegant illustration of his idea that everything was, in fact, linked; people's thoughts and actions affected their environment, and their environment had an impact on their own wellbeing. A few weeks later his physical sight returned and with it came a new way of looking at the world.

Returning to Scotland, Geddes took up an appointment in the botany department at Edinburgh University, and in his spare time he set about transforming other people's lives. On noticing the deplorably squalid conditions of Edinburgh's Old Town and the ill health of its inhabitants, he not only dreamed up a remedy but actually moved there in order to experience it from the inside. Luckily his wife, Anna, was as strong-minded as he was, and soon they were scrubbing and painting their run-down flat in James Court, just off the Lawnmarket.

That was just the beginning. Geddes organised the community into groups and set them about cleaning and repairing their living quarters. He led by example and would often be seen in an old nightshirt, painting bright colours over dirty walls. Anna set up sewing classes while her husband's work spread outwards into all the tenement blocks and dingy courtyards; wherever there was enough space he would squeeze in a small park or a garden. He rejuvenated Riddle's Court, converting it into a students' hostel for the university, and breathed fresh life into the buildings that are now Ramsay Gardens.

Although Geddes turned out to be the patron saint of Edinburgh's Old Town, he was still a wildcard in academic circles. He wanted to teach, but his refusal to specialise in one subject earned him a degree of suspicion which no amount of enthusiasm could make up for. When he failed to gain the Chair of Botany at the University of Edinburgh, a generous benefactor endowed a part-time Chair of Botany for him at the University of Dundee. Meanwhile Geddes established his own summer school in Edinburgh, based in an old canal barge which his pupils called 'The Ark'. Offering lessons in social evolution, psychology and practical botany, this annual event attracted students from all over Britain, Europe and America, and it helped to inspire many young scientists and explorers including William Speirs Bruce (see p.51).

Once Geddes had conceived an idea in his head, no will in the world could convince him it was impossible. The most spectacular example came in 1915, while he was in India. His creativity in town planning had just won an award at an international exhibition and as a result Lord Pentland, the Governor of Madras, wanted his advice. The city of Indore was in desperate need of help. Its buildings were ramshackle and filthy, and lack of sanitation had allowed disease to become rampant. Geddes walked around its streets in quiet contemplation, then went to the ruling prince of Indore with an idea: he would like to be put in charge of the town's forthcoming Diwali festival, and to be made Maharajah for the day. The prince must have smiled at the bare-faced audacity, but gave his consent.

Geddes had realised that he would never succeed in reshaping the town unless he won the hearts and minds of its people. He made a public announcement that he was designing a grand pageant, the like of which had never been seen before – but the procession would pass only through the cleanest streets. Naturally, no one wanted their street to miss out on the excitement, so his challenge provoked a whirlwind of washing, sweeping, painting and mending. Trees were planted in courtyards and around temples; six thousand cart loads of rubbish were removed from the town. When 'Geddes Day' arrived, the people were happy, excited and ready to be entertained. And they certainly were not disappointed.

Diwali festivals traditionally celebrate the triumph of darkness over evil. In his interpretation of the theme, Geddes allowed his imagination to run riot. The entire panoply of life was represented as a moving, living picture. First came the symbols of military power: the State's infantry, artillerymen and horsemen in gleaming splendour; then a display of rich harvest, including gods of rain and sun. This was followed by a tableau of disease and poverty with figures dressed as strange, sinister animals, models of derelict houses and even some grotesquely huge mosquitoes. Representing the plague was a six-foot-long rat with a moving swarm of 'fleas' around him in the form of locusts, dyed black and mounted on quivering wires. In his wake came four hundred sweepers, dressed in spotless white and brightly turbaned, accompanied by garlanded white oxen.

Geddes cleverly included visual depictions of his proposed changes in the form of model houses, libraries, museums and theatres, and all the craftsmen who would build them; he even invoked a new goddess for the occasion, that of Indore City herself, her throne adorned with a street plan showing the improvements that would be made. He had wanted Lakshmi, the goddess of prosperity, to ride through the streets on a white elephant, and was disappointed to find that no white elephants were available. He promptly set about whitewashing one from head to tail, so that the animal shone with snowy brilliance in the sunshine*.

The whole event was a masterpiece, a concept of jaw-dropping brilliance that precisely and wholeheartedly achieved its goal. In the evening, marked by the ceremonial burning of the pestilential rat, Geddes was heralded as the town's saviour. In the weeks that followed, disease disappeared from the streets of Indore. In its place came a new sense of pride and wellbeing.

To describe Patrick Geddes as a scientist is to miss the point of his work. He was a revolutionary, a natural phenomenon. He has been compared to Leonardo da Vinci, in the sense that his vision was not properly recognised in his own time; few people could fully appreciate his perspective and even fewer, it must be said, could withstand his infectious enthusiasm. One of his acquaintances complained that clearing up after his demonstrations was like trying to put the lava back into a volcano.

> It can be hardly too strongly insisted that nature teaching begins neither with knowledge nor discipline, but through delight; the former is but premature until the latter be assured.[2]

When he became a father, Geddes taught his children the important connections between heart, hand and head, and how to open their eyes and see. In later life he set up the *Collège des Écossais* in Montpellier, France, with an educational garden where students of all nationalities could be taught outdoors. He was, at heart, a passionate and gifted teacher, and it is only now, years after his death, that his lessons are beginning to be heard.

As an early Council member and frequent lecturer at the RSGS, Geddes helped to shape and energise the fledgling society. The Geddes Environment Medal was introduced in 2009, to honour people who uphold his principles in their own work.

*Whitewash would not have been a particularly healthy coating for the elephant so it was hopefully washed off afterwards.

---

1. *The World Without and the World Within – Sunday Talks with my Children* by Patrick Geddes (1905)
2. 'Nature Study and Geographical Education', *Scottish Geographical Magazine* (1902) 18:10, 525-536

George Hubert (Sir Hubert) Wilkins

Polar explorer, aviator, pioneering film-maker
BORN: 31st October 1888 (Mount Bryan, South Australia)
DIED: 30th November 1958 (Framingham, Massachusetts)
§
RSGS Livingstone Medal, 1931

A HURRICANE WAS HOWLING in the Antarctic, screaming through the masts of the little ship and tossing her around like flotsam on a ferocious sea. As the crew battled with the rigging, a giant wave crashed over the deck, washing one of them overboard. Horrified, the men shouted his name above the wind and stared into the raging waters, but it was no use. He was gone. A few seconds later, another huge wave broke across the ship, dumping the sailor back on board. He was drenched to the skin, but unharmed. Life still had unfinished business with Hubert Wilkins.

If there was an award for escaping the jaws of death in a variety of ways each more astounding and apparently impossible than the last, Sir Hubert Wilkins would be the most decorated man in the history of exploration. He walked away from a series of aeroplane crashes; he ran for his life across an Arctic ice floe that was breaking up all around him; he was shot at by German planes while clinging onto an observation balloon with his fingertips; he was placed in front of a firing squad three times, and three times he was miraculously spared. Incredibly, that is just the tip of the iceberg.

Wilkins was acutely aware of his extraordinary capacity for survival, and began to sense the presence of something greater, as though he had a hidden purpose. His friends believed he was charmed, and his colleagues would stand open-mouthed when he reappeared, large as life, long after he had been given up for dead. Leaders of expeditions from Shackleton to Stefansson and Lincoln Ellsworth, all astute judges of character in their own way, singled Wilkins out. They saw him as a remarkable man, who could be depended upon for capability and strength of character and whose company they would be glad to have again in whatever extreme conditions they were asked to endure. Yet today his name has dropped from public awareness so completely that most would struggle to name just one of his achievements.

It may sound like an enormous injustice, but Wilkins would most likely say, if he could, that anonymity is what he always wanted.

Hubert's father, Harry Wilkins, used to claim that he was the first-born son of South Australia, as his birth came just three days after the official proclamation of the Province of South Australia in 1836.

Harry and his wife, Louisa, children of a handful of courageous settlers, had struck inland and built a house on the parched grass-lands beneath Mount Bryan. Sheep farming was their plan, but they were risking everything in a climate that was unknown, untried, and would ultimately prove disastrous for livestock and agriculture.

Born on 31st October 1888, Hubert was Harry and Louisa's thir-teenth and youngest child. He played with the children of Aboriginal people – camping with them, eating their food and sharing their stories. Maybe this is when he learned to 'see' with all his senses, to feel the Earth and his connection to it as living things. Had his family prospered, he might never have moved away from that place, but life was about to propel him on a journey that would never really come to an end.

In 1901, a summer of exceptional drought brought ruin and immi-nent starvation to the farmers around Mount Bryan. Hubert, aged just twelve, was horrified by the plight of both humans and animals, and felt himself powerless to help. He saw his parents broken. He vowed to find a way of forecasting the weather so that farmers would never have to experience such suffering again. In the years to come, fate would lead him up some very strange paths but this one enduring quest governed his life.

As an apprentice to an electrical company, Wilkins was on a job laying cables in Adelaide when he was called in to fix the wiring in a theatre. He was still an impressionable lad, but when he asked to see the projector in action he knew straight away that film-making was what he wanted to do. Moving pictures were taking the world by storm, and he wanted to be a part of it. He secured not just a part, but a leading role in the industry: having acquired the skills, he was offered work at the Gaumont Film Company studios in London, where photographers risked their lives on a daily basis in pursuit of newsworthy subjects. Taking risks was something that Wilkins would develop into an art form.

In the early 1900s, the aerodrome at Hendon in North London witnessed a startling array of contraptions taking flight in the hands of pioneering aviators, some of whom were mad, and some of whom were utterly insane. Wilkins, typically, could not merely stand and watch; he wanted to take the first moving pictures from the air. He got talking to a pilot who immediately offered him a ride. It was a generous offer, and Wilkins hesitated only for a moment when he found that the plane, a French-built Deperdussin, was a single-seater. Clambering up in front of the cockpit, he sprawled precariously over the front fuselage and gripped the bracing wires as the propeller roared into life just inches away from his nose. The flimsy-looking aircraft had just received a powerful new engine which threatened to rattle out of its housing, but the pilot, whose dashing reputation had nothing to do with health and safety, solved that little problem by getting Wilkins to wriggle backwards and forwards to balance the weight. It would be fair to say that both pilot and passenger were grateful to be alive when they touched down again, several heart-stopping minutes later.

Wilkins was shaken but undeterred. He took flying lessons himself, and became an expert pilot and navigator. Slowly, like the features in a darkroom photograph, the elements of his life story were starting to appear.

Covering the Balkan War as a newsreel photographer, Wilkins needed every ounce of his survival skill when he was captured by Turkish forces. He was bullied in the hope that he would admit to being a spy. He knew that they had no proof and so maintained his innocence on three successive mornings in the face of a firing squad, while other victims fell around him. As his captors debated what to do with him, he was saved by an armistice and released.

Shortly afterwards, Vilhjalmur Stefansson recruited his services on the *Canadian Arctic Expedition* of 1913-16, and when he came back he was despatched to the Western Front as official photographer of the Australian forces. He refused to carry firearms, but was commended by officers for his bravery and integrity. One of his photographs was taken in mid-air as he was lifted off his feet from the force of a shell; dusting himself off, he was relieved to find no severe injuries. He kept the picture as a memento, alongside his Military Cross and Bar.

In 1919 Wilkins wrote a letter to his mother which even she, accustomed as she was to his hair-raising adventures, must have read with some concern. He was planning to compete in an air race from London to Australia, for which the prize was £10,000. The victor was assured of world media attention as revolutionary new airline routes were opened up; not that Wilkins cared for the publicity, as his mother well knew. It was to her, he said, that he owed his impulse to be of service to his fellow men. He carefully neglected to tell her there were no real airfields between India and Australia, and no plane had yet been built with a range that was required for the last leg of the flight. In view of this, it was probably a blessing in disguise when Wilkins and his crew found themselves plummeting towards the ground in their stricken Blackburn Kangaroo, somewhere over Crete. Miraculously surviving the emergency landing, they came to rest in a muddy ditch, next to a lunatic asylum. Wilkins probably chose not to tell his mother about that, either.

Meanwhile, Wilkins's long-term plan was never absent from his mind. Inspired by a perception of the Earth as if from space, he imagined the northern and southern hemispheres with air currents circulating constantly between the Poles and the Equator. He was convinced that the Poles held the key to predicting global weather patterns. This was the era of great airship voyages and he had already noticed the potential of these ponderous giants in the field of scientific exploration. He had been badgering manufacturers – without success – to allow him to take one to the North Pole. They thought he was crazy.

The call to join Sir Ernest Shackleton's fourth expedition to the Antarctic (see p.43) on board the *Quest* came at a perfect time. Wilkins's official title was cameraman and naturalist, but the opportunity allowed him to shift his focus to the southern ice and look for suitable sites for meteorological stations. He was also excited by the prospect of flying a small aeroplane in the Antarctic. His mother received another letter full of earnest assurances about his comfort and safety.

Sadly, conditions and fate conspired against the voyage from the outset. Bad weather hampered the battered little ship, and her slow progress dragged the expedition behind schedule so the aircraft could not be collected in South Africa as planned. Then in January 1922, as the *Quest* lay in port at Grytviken in South Georgia, Shackleton died. His heartbroken crew buried him on the hillside and erected a memorial cairn in his honour. Wilkins, as stricken as the rest, filmed them building it.

On his return to Britain, Wilkins was offered a three-month mission as a newsreel photographer in Russia, where a programme of famine relief was being organised by the Society of Friends. The blood of the Tsar and his family had scarcely dried in Yekaterinburg before another evil stalked the land: people were dying in their millions from disease and famine. Wilkins's task was to make a film about the society's efforts, with a full remit to shock the western world into action. It would be dangerous work, so to give himself an air of authority he grew a black beard to rival that of Lenin.

Throughout Russia, Wilkins discovered scenes of unspeakable suffering. Desperation was driving people to all kinds of crime. At Buzuluk, a city on the Samara River, a gruesome rumour reached his ears; in this region alone it was estimated that around half a million people were starving, and there was a dark story of an old woman's house at which many people had inexplicably disappeared. The implication was that they had been killed and eaten. Wilkins, always curious, could not ignore such a story, so he gathered some meagre supplies of food and set off to investigate. About half an hour later he woke on someone's porch with a painful lump on his head and signs of cannibalism evident around him. As he dizzily took stock of his surroundings, he could hear a number of people arguing noisily over his fate. He was saved only when they saw that he had brought food; he promised faithfully to bring them some more.

Wilkins travelled to the Kremlin for an interview with Lenin shortly afterwards. The purpose of the meeting remains unclear, but a connection with British Intelligence is a possibility. Having witnessed so much human suffering at first hand, it is tempting to wonder whether Wilkins favoured the Russian leader with some characteristic Australian frankness. In any event, he was allowed to leave.

1928 marked two of Wilkins's most recognisable achievements in geography and exploration. On 15th April 1928, in the company of the renowned American aviator Carl Ben Eielson, he took off from Barrow, Alaska, in a modified Lockheed Vega with its Wright J-5 engine specially adapted for flying in the intense cold. After twenty hours in the air, and some rather breathless calculations involving maps and fuel gauges, the pair landed in Spitsbergen, having completed the first flight over the Arctic – although their route did not take in the North Pole. Their shared near misses strengthened their friendship. In the outpouring of celebration that followed, Wilkins received a knighthood from King George V.

He did not rest on his laurels, however. In December that year, with the financial backing of newspaper tycoon William Randolph Hearst, he turned his attention to the Antarctic.

Wilkins's forty-hour, 1,200-mile flight in the Antarctic, accompanied once again by Eielson, crossed previously uncharted territory and made newspaper headlines around the world. As the landscape unfolded beneath them, Wilkins sketched the topography, naming new landmarks with breathless speed. This achievement came shortly after his engagement to Suzanne Bennett, a beautiful Australian actress newly arrived on Broadway. Suzanne was one of the few who understood his true nature, and she lovingly endured separations that amounted to many more years apart than they ever spent together.

In 1929 Wilkins returned to the Antarctic, keen to expand the possibilities of exploration by air. As he searched for potential landing strips, he realised with amazement that the floating ice field had receded by almost 600 miles in the space of a year. He told a news journalist that the dwindling ice was impacting upon climatic conditions around the world, and his prediction was supported by a severe drought that summer in the United States. His foresight was unrecognised at the time.

As an explorer, especially in an age that appreciated flamboyant heroics, Hubert Wilkins had none of the qualities that would have gifted him lifelong fame. He was gentle, kind, thoughtful, self-effacing to a fault. Stefansson, frustrated by his refusal to accept praise, described him as 'aggressively modest', yet those who knew him spoke of a strong magnetism that came not from ego but from deep within his soul.

Perhaps the clearest insight came from the Aboriginal people in Wilkins's homeland. In 1923, commissioned by the British Museum to record the dwindling wildlife of northern Australia, he effectively vanished from the face of the planet for two and a half years, trusting to his wits and bushcraft for survival. The experience brought him close to the people who had lived on the land for centuries, and who had seen a stream of occasional visitors – missionaries, traders, surveyors – come and go. They were acutely intuitive and could smell insincerity in the wind, but found Wilkins to be like no other stranger they had met. They noticed how he would sit with them, composed and quietly observant. Something about him attracted them. They would take turns to sit with their arms about his shoulders, and would tell him how comfortable they felt to be around him. Coming from people who were at one with nature, this is the finest tribute of all.

Nearly sixty years after Wilkins's death, his vision of co-operative weather prediction on a global scale is a reality. With the benefit of satellite imaging we have learned to step back from the Earth and view it from a distance, as he could do in his own mind. All we have learned only proves that Wilkins was ahead of his time. Polar meteorology now plays a vital part in our understanding of climate change. His wish has come true; perhaps it was only a case of waiting for technology to catch up with his vision. Yet he is not touched by fame. It is as if he removed the shadow of himself – his human identity, which is transient according to Aboriginal culture – and stepped aside in order to let his dream catch the light instead.

THOR HEYERDAHL

Ethnographer and adventurer
BORN: 6th October 1914 (Larvik, Norway)
DIED: 18 April 2002 (Colla Micheri, Italy)
§
RSGS Mungo Park Medal, 1950

I T COULD HAVE BEEN just another embarrassing moment in the life of a shy young man. Thor Heyerdahl – Norwegian, tall, handsome, but painfully self-conscious – had gone to a graduation ball against his better judgement and was now regretting it. He was trying to make small talk to a pretty girl with direct blue eyes; she was a stranger, and their conversation was stilted at best. Beneath the constraint Heyerdahl sensed an attraction, and he thought desperately of his secret plan. He wanted to leave behind 'civilisation' with its materialistic greed. In desperation, he blurted out an outrageous proposal. What did she think about going back to nature?

Three years later, in 1937, Heyerdahl was standing on a beach with the same girl: Liv Torp. She was now his bride. Scattered around them were trunks containing, among other things, her wedding gown and his dinner jacket, but these were of no use to them now. Eight and a half thousand miles from home, on a remote island in the South Pacific, they were about to start another life in a paradise that Heyerdahl had been dreaming of almost since birth.

In the 1930s, the task of telling two sets of parents that you wanted to spend a lifetime in another hemisphere, deliberately marooned from most forms of contact, cannot have been an easy one. Heyerdahl had a passion that knew no fear and a vision that would always find a way. For years he had been planning, poring over maps of the world's oceans, looking for an island that would suit his particular dream. Born with an open-eyed wisdom, he saw the perfection of nature and longed to live in harmony with it. He distrusted the older generation, who were inventing new weapons and talking about war; it seemed to him that mankind had boarded a train with a one-way ticket to disaster, and he wanted to jump off.

Heyerdahl put together a scheme that was breathtaking and mad in equal measure. His ambition was clear: he wanted to live on a Pacific island untouched by 'progress'. However, he was forced to confront the practicalities, and he needed funding to do it. His university professors suggested a sponsored research project. Heyerdahl would settle on a volcanic island, one which had been created only recently in geological terms, and discover where the animals had come from to colonise it.

There was one major obstacle. Not only did Heyerdahl need his parents' consent, but he also needed them to pay for the tickets. With the help of his tutors he won their support, but Liv's parents proved more difficult to convince; knowing nothing about Heyerdahl's chosen island, they consulted an encyclopedia to discover that it once had a reputation for cannibalism. What fate were they sending their daughter to? Thor's father, himself only a recent convert to the plan, stepped in to reassure them.

Thor and Liv's idyll on Fatu Hiva, one of the Marquesas Islands in French Polynesia was, in fairly rapid succession, thrilling, enchanting and challenging. After a year the couple admitted themselves defeated, partly by tropical diseases and partly by their interactions with the native people. Unfriendly and occasionally hostile, the islanders presented a cultural barrier that the Heyerdahls found impossible to overcome.

When they returned to Norway, Heyerdahl's obsession did not go away. He was fascinated by the origin of not only the wildlife, but also the people who had settled on those islands. Where had they come from? How had they got there? A far-fetched theory had intrigued him ever since he was a youth: the idea that the Polynesians had sailed from South America, and not from Asia, as was generally believed. It was a proposition that flew in the face of contemporary scientific understanding but, far from satisfying his curiosity, what Heyerdahl had seen of the Polynesian culture only served to add fuel to the flames.

The academic world was not receptive to Heyerdahl's theory, so he reasoned that the only way to prove it was to research it himself. Using centuries-old illustrations as reference, he decided to build a traditional raft from balsa wood, bamboo and other natural materials, and sail it from Peru to Polynesia. This is how the *Kon-Tiki* expedition was born.

The name itself was a flag Heyerdahl flourished in the face of his critics. According to an Incan legend, a sun god named Con-Tici or Sun-Tiki was worshipped by a race of fair-skinned people who lived on the shores of Lake Titicaca in the Andes. The god was attacked by a warrior chieftain and escaped over the sea to the west with his closest companions. Meanwhile in the eastern Pacific islands, the people had a tradition that a white chief-god named Tiki, the son of the sun, was the original founder of their race. Heyerdahl was in no doubt that these two gods were one and the same.

Finding the men to accompany him on his outrageous expedition was easier than Heyerdahl had expected. At the Sailors' Home in New York, where he had been eking out the remnants of his cash, he met Herman Watzinger, an engineer from Trondheim. Heyerdahl's invitations to three friends – Torstein Raaby, Knut Haugland and Erik Hesselberg – were met with enthusiastic acceptance. The sixth and final place was taken by Bengt Danielsson, a Swedish anthropologist who could speak Spanish.

From the moment that the balsa trunks were floated down the Palenque River, Heyerdahl's unusual boat-building project attracted great interest in the harbour at Callao. Bemused locals looked on as nine logs, the longest measuring 45 feet, were lashed together with hemp ropes. A small bamboo cabin was constructed on top, thatched rather jauntily with banana leaves. Two masts were cut from mangrove wood, and bamboo strips formed a makeshift deck. There was, of course, no engine; in fact, there was no metal anywhere in the construction. It looked like a floating cocktail bar.

Heyerdahl surveyed the vessel with pride, but visiting dignitaries took a slightly different view. Horrified by the risk, one diplomat asked whether Heyerdahl's parents were both living and when he was assured that they were, he uttered the dire prophesy that they would be grieved to hear of his death. Heyerdahl later admitted to having a few misgivings, but he would not be deterred. An amateur radio station was one of the few concessions that Heyerdahl had made to modern technology, and it allowed the team to reassure the Norwegian Embassy in Washington of their continued safety. Loaded with supplies of fruit and vegetables, tinned army rations and cans of drinking water, on 28th April 1947 the unlikely-looking craft was towed out into the open sea and cast off to make her way as best she could, propelled by the Humboldt current and the efforts of her optimistic crew.

For the first few days, in high seas with the ropes squealing under pressure and the vessel pitching like a cork, they battled to learn a skill that had been forgotten for centuries. The Spanish conquistadors who had illustrated their journals with pictures of traditional Peruvian rafts had omitted to include any instructions on how to sail them. But once the seas were calm, the magic began. Shoals of flying fish skimmed the waves, glittering in the sunshine, many of them landing on deck and supplying a delicious fish supper for the grateful men. At night, they gazed into the inky depths at strange sea monsters – huge squid and deep-water fish with eyes that glowed in the light of the lanterns. Being on a level with the water's surface gave them a perspective rarely enjoyed by any naturalist, and the quietness of their approach seemed to inspire curiosity in the most elusive of creatures.

Heyerdahl often expressed doubt that time actually exists except in the logical human mind. While floating on the serene blue ocean he must have been tempted to let go of the concept altogether.

The crew had estimated that it would take them ninety-seven days to sail 4,300 miles from Peru to Polynesia; and on the ninety-seventh day they arrived at Angatau, a small atoll in the Tuamotu islands. Beaching the raft proved hazardous and it was another four days before the *Kon-Tiki* struck a reef and was finally pulled to safety on Raroia atoll. Dazed with exhilaration, the men lopped the top off some coconuts and poured the contents down their throats. Then they stretched out their weary bodies on the soft sand and gazed up at the clouds.

The *Kon-Tiki* expedition was a huge success; on that point, Heyerdahl was adamant. By practical demonstration, he had proved his theory that the Polynesian islands were colonised by people from South America.

The scientific world disagreed. Archaeological and cultural evidence to back up his claim simply did not exist. Heyerdahl found himself in an unusual position: his voyage elevated him to celebrity status and his book sold over 20 million copies, but the doors to academic acceptance remained firmly closed. At best, he was regarded as a misguided, eccentric explorer who was infecting history with fantasy.

Far from sulking in obscurity, Heyerdahl followed the *Kon-Tiki* expedition with several more projects, each aiming to blow the cobwebs from a legend that was half-lost in the mists of folk memory. In 1970 he sailed from Morocco to the Caribbean in a papyrus boat, proving that the ancient vessels were more than capable of crossing the Atlantic. In 1978, a ship built of reeds bore him down the Persian Gulf and westwards across the Arabian Sea, tracing a route that may have been used 5,000 years ago by the Sumerians of Mesopotamia.

Looking back at his achievements in later life, Heyerdahl considered that he had proven beyond doubt that early civilisations had communicated with each other across oceans, and he felt the onus was now on the historians and anthropologists to prove that the seas isolated, rather than connected, these ancient mariners. With quiet humour, he acknowledged that he might never have pushed his first boat out from the shore if he had not been blissfully ignorant of the perils of the sea; his family, he revealed, came from inland Norway, with no seafaring blood in their genes. If he had been a sailor, he said, he would never have believed that he could cross the Pacific in the *Kon-Tiki*.

Although he had given up his seafaring adventures, Heyerdahl remained true to his creed of challenging the notions of the modern world well into his eighties. Shortly before he died he was working on a book in which he intended to show that the Norse god Odin had been a real-life person with Russian ancestry, and had founded a Scandinavian royal dynasty in the first century AD. A review of his research, entitled *Thor Heyerdahl's Search for Odin*, was published posthumously in 2014.

The Polynesian question continues to inspire debate. In 2011, nine years after Heyerdahl's death, Professor Erik Thorsby of the University of Oslo conducted some DNA testing on the inhabitants of Easter Island and came up with a startling result: Heyerdahl's theory held an important grain of truth. While the genetics showed that the people had originally come from Asia, Thorsby discovered that DNA from native Americans had been introduced sometime between the mid-thirteenth and late fifteenth centuries. There were two possibilities: some of the Polynesian settlers could have continued east towards South America, inter-married with the local people, and then, at some stage, doubled back; or some South Americans had sailed west to Polynesia and settled there among the native people. It is an intriguing conundrum.

If Heyerdahl's passionately held beliefs still divide scientific opinion, there can be no disputing the wisdom of his philosophy. Warfare, pollution, destruction of the natural environment... all these things troubled him very deeply. Like many visionaries before him, he had the gift of being able to stand away from the world and see the harm that was being done to it by human civilisation. He had no illusions, and he issued some stark warnings about what must be done. Men could shave and cut their hair, he once said, and women could paint their faces, but beneath the surface we are all the same. We cannot escape ourselves, and we must help one another to live in harmony with the natural world. Eighty years after he set foot on the shore of Fatu Hiva, his words still ring true.

In February 1951 the Usher Hall in Edinburgh was packed when Thor Heyerdahl was a guest of the Royal Scottish Geographical Society. After an enthralling lecture, which was illustrated by a film of the his most famous expedition, Heyerdahl was awarded the Mungo Park Medal by John 'Ian' Bartholomew, the Society's President, 'for his leadership, courage and enterprise in navigating the Kon-Tiki raft from South America to Polynesia.'

All references in this chapter from Minutes of RSGS Council meeting, 17th October 1950

WANGARI MUTA MAATHAI

Scientist, environmentalist and human rights campaigner
BORN: 1st April 1940 (Ihithe, Nyeri District, Kenya)
DIED: 25th September 2011 (Nairobi, Kenya)
§
RSGS Livingstone Medal, 2007

W HEN SHE WAS growing up in the highlands of Kenya, Wangari's mother told her to beware of stepping on a leopard's tail when walking in the forest. She reminded her daughter that her name, Wa-ngarī, meant 'of the leopard' in the language of the Kikuyu. Should she happen to encounter one of these beautiful creatures, instead of running away she should continue walking, and remind the leopard politely that, since they were one and the same, there was no reason for them to disagree.

Like many of the stories that Wangari heard as a child, this tale reminded her of her roots and identity, her connection with the land on which she was raised, her one-ness with the soil and every living thing that it supported.

It was always the women who told the stories. Women cultivated the land, planted and harvested the vegetables and fruit, collected the firewood and cooked the food. In the evenings, while they were waiting for their meal, the children would listen to the women's voices weaving tales that never grew old with time, and they were encouraged to tell stories of their own.

As one of her daily tasks, Wangari was sent to fetch water from the clear-running stream that issued from beneath a magnificent old fig tree. The water beguiled her and she would lose all sense of time as she stood in the shallows trying to catch strings of frogspawn. On wet days, she would sit beneath an arrowroot leaf and watch the raindrops pearling and falling from its edges.

It was a happy time. The landscape was green and the rivers flowed freely, irrigating the soil. Wildlife flourished in the woodlands. Wangari revelled in the abundance without realising that within a few years it would disappear, or that she, with the courage of a leopard, would have to fight to bring it back.

Wangari was born in 1940 in the village of Ihithe in the Nyeri District of Kenya. She belonged to the last generation of Kikuyu people who remembered their native country as it had been for centuries. Kirinyaga or Mount Kenya was a sacred place to which the Kikuyus offered thanks for the rains and the fertility of their land. Likewise, the fig tree under which Wangari had played as a child was revered, because her family knew that fresh water bubbled up from beneath its roots.

In the wake of the 'scramble for Africa', much of the continent had already been divided up by European countries eager to bring what they saw as the civilising influence of trade. Kenya was under British rule, and forest was being cleared to make way for tea and coffee plantations. Native Africans were recruited, largely involuntarily, into the workforce. Traditional methods of barter were replaced with western-style economies. People were moved out of their homes and displaced from the land they had occupied for generations. It was a carefully controlled way of removing power from the hands of the people, which also removed their sense of identity.

While the plantations overturned the Africans' physical world, a new influence came to work on their minds. With the new farmers came bands of European missionaries. Catholic sisters, benevolent and peaceful, insisted that God dwelt not in the high mountains but in the churches that they built, and this was the proper place for prayers to be offered. They set up schools to educate the children, teaching them to read and write in English. Little by little, the world of the Kikuyu was being washed away.

While she was still a child, Wangari's family moved from Ihithe to work on a farm operated by a British man. They were not treated unkindly, but in this respect they were lucky. Other families in other places did not fare so well. Discontent was growing.

There was another element at work: Kenyan men who were returning from the Second World War, where they had fought for Britain, were outraged to find their homes and their traditional livelihoods being taken away while their British comrades were receiving military honours and gifts of land. In 1952 the Mau Mau uprising began. This first armed liberation struggle against colonisation in Africa was led by the Land Freedom Army, which was made up of men from Kikuyu, Meru and Embu communities. By that time, Wangari was a student at St Cecilia's, a boarding school attached to the Mathari Catholic mission in the Nyeri hills. As British forces hit back at the insurgents with brutal force and persecuted their families, she was protected, at least, from the worst of the danger.

Despite her initial homesickness at the convent, Wangari flourished. She was a bright and energetic student, and in 1956 she was offered a place at the Loreto Girls' High School in Limuru, just outside Nairobi. Meanwhile her mother had returned from the plantation to live in her native Ihithe, and when Wangari went to visit her she would help to re-plaster the mud walls of her hut with a mixture of dung and ash. Wangari's bond with all her female relatives was particularly strong. Few Kenyan women received a proper education, so her achievements were regarded with pleasure and pride.

In 1960, Wangari was one of about 600 students who were selected to travel to America in the 'Kennedy Airlift', a pioneering project which was the brainchild of President John F. Kennedy, offering education to students from African countries. She spent four years in a Benedictine college in Kansas, then moved to Pittsburgh University to study for a master's degree in biology. She greeted each new opportunity with eagerness. Her ambition was entirely without self-importance; she wanted to enjoy life, accept new challenges, and learn about the world.

After years of unrest, 1963 brought independence for Kenya. The inauguration of the country's first president, Jomo Kenyatta, was greeted with joy. It was only the beginning of a very long road to stability – but no one wanted to look for pitfalls. The handover of power from Crown to State brought little change in environmental policy: the exploitation of the forests continued.

Wangari returned to Kenya in 1966 to take up a post at the University of Nairobi. She was overjoyed at being reunited with her family, but when she visited her homeland the devastation that she saw around her village filled her with sadness. The forests had been felled and the rivers that once ran clean and clear were now brown and sluggish, choked with soil that was being eroded from the bare earth. Even the once-revered fig tree had been uprooted. Families were desperate for firewood, and because their traditionally grown vegetables took a long time to cook over the open fire, the shortage made them turn to introduced foods that contained processed sugar and fat. This was having an alarming impact on their health and new diseases were arising as a result. For the Kikuyu and other Kenyan communities, the future had never looked more grim.

In retrospect, it seems that many diverse and potentially conflicting strands came together in Wangari's life just for the fulfilment of a specific purpose. She was emphatically a child of Africa, vibrantly aware of her identity. Her parents had raised her to believe that life gave no cause for fear, and encouraged her to dream and be creative. She had received a privileged and wide-ranging education with a focus on biological science. She had travelled and mixed with other cultures, and learned what it was to be open-minded and public-spirited. In America, she had seen people stand up fearlessly for what they believed in and receive respect for it, regardless of their skin colour. She began to perceive what a single black woman could do.

In her autobiography, *Unbowed*, Wangari remembers how beautiful it was to cultivate the land at dusk, when the breeze was cool and the hills were lit with gold. The elements of earth and water, air and sun emphasised her kinship with the soil. Life, she knew, was born out of the earth. She had seen at first hand the impoverished conditions in which Kenyan communities now lived. Deprived of their natural resources, they had lost touch with their environment. With the removal of the forests, their lifeline had been cut.

The answer, Wangari decided, was to restore the trees.

It began as a simple exercise. Wangari bought some tree seeds and persuaded some women to plant them in their local area. She offered to pay them a small amount for every seedling that survived, and to perpetuate the scheme she encouraged them to collect more seeds from the remaining forests. The species they planted were native to Kenya; too many exotic trees had already been introduced, and were of no value to the ecosystem. Soon, hundreds of seedlings began to sprout from small containers, and the news began to spread further afield. It was an idea to which every woman could respond; most of them were distraught by their inability to nurture their families. They needed no telling about their connection to the land but their voices were still fiercely suppressed. This, finally, was something positive that they could do, a step towards a better future.

Inevitably, the authorities had some serious questions to ask Wangari. Once the women started banding together and creating tree nurseries, officialdom woke up to the implications of people taking action on a large scale, unsupervised and unregulated. Foresters told Wangari that her women needed a diploma before they could plant trees. Wangari saw straight through that argument to the hidden politics beneath. She travelled around the communities, speaking to women, reassuring them, laughing and singing with them, and bolstering their self-respect. As long as they were polite to their official visitors, she said, nobody had the right to stop them. In 1977 she gave her venture a name: the Green Belt Movement.

Wangari was stepping where perhaps no other woman in Kenya at that time would have dared to tread, but she was well placed to garner support. She was, after all, the first woman in East and Central Africa to gain a doctorate degree, and the first woman to chair a department at the University of Nairobi. She was an active member of the National Council of Women of Kenya. Her success with the Green Belt Movement gave her a reputation that propelled her into the fearsome machine of Kenyan politics where she would have to withstand the scorn of men in government, whose insecurity fanned their rage.

The story of Wangari Maathai's political career is astounding from many points of view, primarily for the simple fact that she survived it. In 1978 President Jomo Kenyatta was succeeded by Daniel arap Moi but Kenya was still governed with an iron fist. As she spoke out for democracy and free speech, Wangari was repeatedly threatened, insulted and harassed. In 1992, when she led a four-day hunger strike in Nairobi's Uhuru Park to demand the release of political prisoners, her encampment of women was broken up by force and Wangari was beaten unconscious. But, little by little, the light that shone from her was reaching the rest of the world.

It would have been so easy for Wangari to cherish a sense of bitterness. She was a black woman in a world that discriminated against her race and her sex. Her convictions cost her dearly in her personal life, but she looked for a positive aspect in every dilemma. She never lost her capacity to dream, and never abandoned her belief that society is inherently good. When she smiled, which was often, joy radiated from her face. It shines also from the faces of the women whose lives she helped to restore. Standing beneath mature trees that they have nurtured, and which, in turn, are now nurturing them, they speak of a transformation in their lives, in their health, and the wellbeing of their families. Their pride in their identity has returned, and they will pass it on to their children.

Wangari Maathai received the Nobel Peace Prize in 2004. This accolade joined a long list of honours that speak of her lifelong commitment to justice, humanity and the environment. She represented the Tetu constituency in Kenya's Parliament from 2002 to 2007, and served as Assistant Minister for Environment and Natural Resources. She was Chairman of the National Council of Women of Kenya, and was named a UN Messenger of Peace in 2009. In 2010, in partnership with the University of Nairobi, she founded the Wangari Maathai Institute for Peace and Environmental Studies.

The Green Belt Movement has grown to become a powerful environmental organisation, and it continues to work towards improving the livelihoods of rural communities through tree planting and conservation. Thirty-five million trees now stand as a living testament to a woman who never let fear cloud her sky, a little girl with the heart of a leopard. Her message is clear: we are inextricably linked to our natural environment. We will survive only if we take care of it.

DICK BALHARRY

Conservationist
BORN: 3rd September 1937 (Muirhead of Liff)
DIED: 22nd April 2015 (Newtonmore)
§
RSGS Geddes Environment Medal, 2015

HOW DO YOU TRAIN KESTRELS to hunt for mice? Eleven-year-old Dick Balharry knew the answer, through keeping an assortment of wild animals in his back yard. Much to his satisfaction, he had succeeded in training not just one but a pair of kestrels to bring back rodents for him. In addition, he had two pet jays, three jackdaws and some brown rats. He looked on them all as personal friends, so saw no reason why he should not take them to school, lovingly stashing the rats in his desk. It was not a habit that greatly pleased his teachers, but, as he said himself, school was 'a bit of an impediment'[1] anyway, occupying valuable time he could be devoting to other things.

Dick Balharry was born in 1937 in a village called Muirhead of Liff, near Dundee. From an early age he was allowed the freedom to explore the local countryside of woodlands, marshes and fields, and his avid interest led him to build up many natural history collections. It was easy to see where his passion lay, but his first choice of career was so ill-suited to his nature that it demanded drastic action. At sixteen, having completed a year's training at a college in Dundee, he turned up for work at an engineering plant and was appalled by what he saw. For about twenty minutes he stayed in the factory with its noisy machinery and the stench of hot oil and smoke, and then he ran.

From that moment, and throughout his life-long love affair with

354

the Scottish hills, Dick Balharry proved just what can be achieved by following your heart and trusting where it may lead.

On that day at least, it took him on a long and unexpected journey. Unwilling to go home, and at a loss to know what to do next, Dick wandered into a local newsagent and bought a copy of the *Oban Times*. In the jobs section he saw an advertisement for an assistant gamekeeper at a place called Tighnabruaich. That sounded like a job he could do, but he had no idea where it was. Undeterred, he phoned the number and secured himself an interview later that day.

Blissfully unaware of the distance between Dundee and Tighnabruaich on the western arm of the Kyles of Bute, Balharry caught a bus to Glasgow and another to Otter Ferry on the bank of Loch Fyne. By the time he arrived it was eleven o'clock at night, but that did not deter him from hammering on the door of the laird's house with a curling stone that had been thoughtfully placed on the step. The owner opened it to see a dishevelled, red-haired youth who obviously needed somewhere to sleep. Dick had nothing much to recommend him, but something about his persistence must have made an impression because he was offered the job.

It was not necessarily a smooth path for Balharry from then onwards. The head gamekeeper, to whom he was responsible, turned out to be a hard-headed traditionalist extremely skilled at ridding the land of 'vermin' by means of snares, traps and bullets. Balharry must have found that aspect of the work extremely difficult. He adapted, however, by taking in some of the young animals that he was meant to be killing, and taming them.

Keeping a fox as a pet was a risky venture under those circumstances, but according to Balharry's own account it was a wickedly intelligent raven that cost him his job. Ravens, he discovered, are superb mimics. His pet raven, whom he named Rory, followed him around everywhere and learned to repeat the rather unflattering remarks uttered by the head gamekeeper and his wife, to whose house Balharry went for his meals. As they all sat down at the table, Rory would invariably exclaim: 'Get that dirty black [bird] out of here!' This might have gone no further than a delightful joke had Balharry not been invited for Sunday lunch with the local minister.

Rory, it turned out, was no respecter of the Sabbath. Balharry and his indiscreet friend would not be parted, so they found themselves looking for a new home.

Balharry's next employer proved to be his inspiration and mentor. Archie MacDonald in Glen Lyon was a real 'gentleman of the hills', with a deep-seated understanding of nature that quenched Balharry's thirst for knowledge. He learned to see not just a patch of woodland or a hill in isolation but to look at the landscape in its entirety, with its rich diversity of plants and animals, its seasonal changes and age-old rhythm of life. He studied the natural regeneration of Scots pines and learned that their existence stretched back over 9,000 years. Most importantly, he learned that nature was capable of nurturing itself, given the opportunity to do so. The problems arose when human intervention upset the balance.

Suggesting better ways for wealthy landowners to manage their estates was not a job for the faint-hearted, but Balharry was never shy of speaking his mind. In 1959 he was given a job with the Red Deer Commission, which focused his attention on shooting estates throughout Scotland. He was asked to deal with the effects of over-population, and he noticed that fencing animals out of woodland areas was never as effective as the landowners would have liked. For ease of stalking, deer were being kept away from forestry so that they remained on the open hill. Animals that transgressed the boundaries were seen as 'marauding', when in fact nature was just trying to reset the balance. Fences were alien to Balharry's way of thinking. With such a wide vision himself, he found himself wanting to teach it to others, to bring about a sea-change in the guardianship of the land.

In 1962, aged only twenty-four, Balharry was appointed warden of the Beinn Eighe nature reserve in Wester Ross. Now responsible for over 10,000 acres of mountain and pine forest, he could really stretch his legs.

A little over ten years previously, Beinn Eighe had become the first ever designated National Nature Reserve in Britain, mainly because it contained some precious fragments of the great Caledonian pine wood that once stretched across the breadth of Scotland. Over the millennia, this forest has dwindled to a fraction of its former size.

Scientists believe that the main factors were a gradual shift in the climate of north-west Britain around 4,000 years ago, which brought cooler, wetter conditions, and the impact of human activity which has led to huge swathes of the wood being cleared for timber and agriculture. The task of the Nature Conservancy was to protect the remaining trees and establish the optimum conditions to support natural regeneration. Their more immediate priority was to prevent the saplings from being eaten by deer.

This mission, simple though it sounds, was a tall order at a time when very little was known about Scotland's native woodlands and their ecosystems. Other government bodies such as the Forestry Commission had a presence in Wester Ross, and the Nature Conservancy was also working alongside private estate owners whose policy was to maintain high deer numbers to satisfy their sporting clients. From the slopes of Beinn Eighe, Balharry could see the physical pattern that the disparate parties made on the landscape: the bare hillsides that were being kept clear of trees, to facilitate stalking; the large tree plantations set up by the Forestry Commission; and the small woodland enclosures of the nature reserve. Each had a different attitude towards deer: the Conservancy tolerated a few deer in its woodlands, while the Forestry Commission was trying to exclude them completely. In contrast, the surrounding estates wanted as many deer as possible, including fine stags with trophy antlers.

There could be no easy solution. Balharry's great gift, however, was communication. Not only did he succeed in bringing estate owners together in order to count the deer population, but he helped establish an agreement to keep their numbers at a more natural level through culling. Only through this action would the ancient forests be given the breathing space to recover. Nature, as Balharry knew, would do the rest.

The weather and the landscape conspired to make Balharry's job at Beinn Eighe demanding, but he relished the hard work. His love of nature meant he was keen to get involved with observing and recording wildlife. In the company of visiting scientists he inspected golden eagle eyries, and was delighted to find evidence of wildcats on the reserve. He learned how to live-trap pine martens for research, and took the success one stage further, by breeding them in captivity.

There was another element to Balharry's vision, what he called 'public interest'. Visits to the national parks of America and Canada had shown him that public engagement could flourish alongside successful land management and game shooting. He wanted to see the same level of success at Beinn Eighe, and began to transform the public facilities on the reserve. He helped to install Scotland's first nature trail along the shore of Loch Maree, and this, together with improvements to the visitor centre and picnic site, helped to attract unprecedented numbers of visitors to Beinn Eighe. People were exploring the natural environment, learning about Scotland's landscape, and taking pleasure in what they found. It was a rare achievement for a place that few people had ever heard of.

Throughout his long career, Balharry brought the same enthusiasm and clear-sighted wisdom to other estates such as Creag Meagaidh, a Nature Conservancy reserve in Glen Spean, and Glenfeshie, a private estate in the Cairngorms. To begin with, neighbouring landowners and land managers were naturally cautious and protective of their own legacy. In addition, some scientists directly opposed Balharry's approach to reducing deer numbers. Dick was not a qualified scientist, but he understood the complex interaction between plant and animal species. Where his knowledge was lacking he actively filled the gaps by studying academic research papers. He was fearless in debate, and his sound practical experience and habit of plain speaking made him a formidable opponent. In many different fields, and across a wide cross-section of people, he won respect.

Balharry understood why his plans were so controversial. His answer was encouragement, a word which he reminded us meant 'the giving of courage', and he called for new incentives and rewards for landowners who were willing to reach for longer-term goals. In the short term, he was adamant that deer populations would have to be thinned, but the animals that remained would be able to forage in woodlands without having a devastating impact. The truth of his words became apparent over time. As the new trees started to grow, rare plants and wildlife began to return, like missing pieces in a long-forgotten jigsaw. Finally, people began to acknowledge the evidence.

Dick Balharry's gift was a vision that saw well beyond his own life span, and he expected others to do the same. His voice was eventually heard and welcomed, and he was given many opportunities to air his views: through his employment by Scottish Natural Heritage; by chairing the John Muir Trust; as chair of the local access forum for the Cairngorms National Park; and with the National Trust for Scotland, as a Council member and a brief spell as Chairman. He became a popular TV presenter and public speaker, with an unaffected warmth and passion that caught the hearts of his listeners. In particular, he loved to inspire young people to see the landscape with the same curiosity and wonder that he had known at the same age. He was not so much an explorer as a rediscoverer; the Scottish mountains have a long memory, and he helped them regain their wildness.

> The challenge I leave behind for those who follow is to clarify the vision, devise a method of formal recognition respected by all sides in the debate, give rewards on delivery of results and seek change through empowerment.[2]

In April 2015 in Glenfeshie, surrounded by friends and his loving family, Dick Balharry was presented with the Geddes Environment Medal of the RSGS. Aged seventy-seven, he was weakened by illness, but his passion for the mountains was still strong. The principles that he upheld are reflected in a paper he presented on that day, offering a persuasive strategy for the long-term management of the Scottish uplands. This was his legacy: a clear beacon of encouragement for government and landowners alike. Meanwhile, in the diverse landscapes of Beinn Eighe, Glenfeshie and Creag Meagaidh, his vision will flourish for many more human lifetimes.

---

1. Interview with Mark Stephen for BBC Radio, 27th April 2015
2. 'Delivering Change Through Vision, Empowerment and Recognition' by Dick Balharry, 2015

Sir David Attenborough

Naturalist, writer, broadcaster
Born: 8th May 1926 (Isleworth)
§
RSGS Livingstone Medal, 1989
Scottish Geographical (Gold) Medal, 2011
Fellow of RSGS, 2011

I know of no pleasure deeper than that which comes from contemplating the natural world and trying to understand it.[1]

F EW TELEVISION EVENTS CAN bring the country to a halt: a royal wedding, perhaps, or the Olympics. But every time Sir David Attenborough makes a new series, it seems that the entire British population tunes in to watch. This phenomenon has been going on for at least five decades.

Why is the nation so enthralled? It might be the fantastic filming, or the stunning locations, or the exciting, never-before-seen behaviour of wildlife which he and his team always succeed in capturing, often against the most daunting odds. While all these factors play a part, Attenborough himself is the extra ingredient. He speaks with a boundless enthusiasm which captures the imagination and sweeps the viewer along with him; he has an air of gentle authority, and his genuine fascination for all living things wins us over every time. The respect which Sir David commands is universal. He has been described as a national treasure, and it is easy to see why.

Looking back at the beginning of his career, it could all have gone very differently. In 1950, as a young graduate in animal science, Attenborough was recruited by the BBC for their television Talks Department. Interviewing people live on air was fraught with difficulty, not least because of the limitations of camera equipment at the time, and Attenborough, whose energy must have electrified the peaceful offices of senior management, tried to push its capabilities beyond what was physically possible. His early broadcasts appear

361

charming enough now, but in those days not everyone saw him in quite the same rosy light. One memo from the BBC described him as intelligent and promising, and conceded that he might well be producer material, but advised that he should not be employed again as an interviewer because his teeth were too big!

Luckily, Attenborough's ambitions did not lie in studio work. He was keen to travel, and hatched some ambitious plans for making wildlife programmes. All he had to do was persuade the BBC to give their backing.

So began *Zoo Quest*, which beamed images of exotic animals into people's living rooms on a weekly basis. Attenborough travelled with zoo collectors to far-flung corners of the globe, gathering live specimens which were then transported back to Britain where some became minor celebrities. Attenborough's quest for this or that species captured the nation's interest to the extent that even London bus drivers would stop him in the street and ask if he had found it yet.

Before long, Attenborough found himself on the trail of birds of paradise in Papua New Guinea, a search which would leave him frustrated for many years. In the 1950s, information about such destinations was scarce; few British people had been there, and even fewer knew anything at all about the wildlife. Attenborough confessed that, although his mind was full of tantalising possibilities, on a practical level he had no idea what to do when faced with a Komodo dragon or a Malay bear.

What was his secret? Nothing daunted him. The lure of adventure, the dream of exploring landscapes where no outsider had hitherto even set foot, the chance to film animals that had never been captured on camera – all of these prospects were irresistible. With his floppy blond hair and boyish smile, Attenborough charmed his way into the hearts of native people, many of whom had never seen a white man before. When his encounters with wildlife were screened on TV, the British public were equally enthralled.

> I hankered to return to New Guinea... there were still quite
> large patches of country where it could be truthfully said that no
> white foot had yet trod. There, thick rain forest blankets steep

mountains. There was only one way to explore such country and that was by walking, accompanied by a long line of porters carrying supplies. Maybe it was the last place in the world where that was still the case. That in itself made such an expedition worth filming.[2]

Attenborough was a natural film-maker, but his potential could well have been left untapped had he not made a conscious and rather risky decision about his career. Rising quickly through the BBC's illustrious ranks to become Controller of BBC2 and then Director of Programmes, he found himself being interviewed for the post of Director-General without having expressed any desire for the job. He was already discontented; he wanted to make programmes, not talk about them. In 1972 he handed in his notice and became a freelance broadcaster. Within weeks he was back in his natural habitat, filming an erupting volcano in Indonesia.

Starting with *Life on Earth*, the nine-series 'Life' collection which Attenborough began in 1979 is still revered today as an outstanding example of wildlife film-making at its best. Attenborough wrote his own scripts and helped plan the itineraries, and was joined on his adventures by world-class cameramen and sound recordists. Breath-taking sequences were captured using the very latest technology. In a revolutionary new approach to on-screen editing he could appear to be whisked from one continent to the next, sometimes mid-sentence. Aware that he was now a household name, he made sure that his personal appearances never dominated the show; the wildlife, in his opinion, should always take centre stage.

One of the most memorable sequences from *Life on Earth* was filmed in Rwanda in 1978. Attenborough had been given special permission to track a family of mountain gorillas, and intended to talk about the significance of their opposable thumbs. The animals took an unexpected interest, scrutinising his hair, face and hands while he remained spellbound and silent. It was almost as if they were casually making a natural history programme of their own. Attenborough kept his nerve, and his encounter made a deep impression on millions of viewers worldwide.

Still an avid broadcaster, Attenborough's most recent programmes have made full and brilliant use of sophisticated cinematography. *Life Story* was the first landmark series to be shot in Ultra-high-definition, treating viewers to the highest quality images ever seen in a wildlife documentary at that time. He has made several films in 3D, including *Galapagos* and *Flying Monsters*, focusing on the first animals with wings. Not surprisingly, over the years Sir David has amassed a diverse collection of natural history specimens and man-made artefacts. His 2011 documentary *Attenborough and the Giant Egg* reveals the charming story of how he was given the fragments of an egg laid by the extinct Elephant Bird in Madagascar.

There is no need to tell the British public that Sir David Attenborough's latest offering will be unmissable, because they know already. He delivers fascinating narratives with a gentle authority that makes for attentive listeners, while viewers are guaranteed spectacular footage thanks to the skill and dedication of his team. In 2014, more than fifty years after his first visit to the Great Barrier Reef, Sir David returned to make a three-part series about the planet's natural wonder, squeezing himself into a submersible and gazing with schoolboy eagerness at the abundance of brilliant marine life that surrounded him. Two years later, in 2016, the nation was riveted to its collective sofa once again when the series *Planet Earth II* was aired on BBC One. Once again the nation fell in love with the beauty and diversity of the Earth; on the morning after each episode, newspapers and social media channels were buzzing with appreciation.

Sir David Attenborough was a guest lecturer at the RSGS in 1964, when he spoke about 'Madagascar, its People and Animals' in Edinburgh and Glasgow. In 1989 he was awarded the Livingstone Medal 'for his contributions in not only expanding man's knowledge of the ecology of planet Earth but also his quite outstanding ability to communicate that knowledge to others.'[3] The RSGS hoped to bestow the medal on Sir David in person, but a delightful insertion in the Society's newsletter of June 1990 reveals that although he had hoped to attend, he had been called away at the last moment when 'earlier than expected, the optimum conditions for filming migrating moose in Alaska required him to be there.'⁴ More recently, Sir David was awarded the Society's Scottish Geographical (Gold) Medal for 2011.

With his first-hand experience of the Earth's life forms and habitats over successive decades, Attenborough has been a witness to change, for both good and bad. There can be few people more qualified to speak about the pressures humans are putting on the natural world. He has often expressed strong concerns about the effects of climate change and a burgeoning human population, and in May 2015 he was interviewed by President Barack Obama at the White House. Attenborough was characteristically modest and slightly awed by the honour, but he spoke with frankness and integrity about the measures that he believes must be taken to redress the balance.

The future of life on Earth, Sir David once said, depends on humanity's ability to take action, and we can only succeed if there is a change in our societies, in our economics and our politics. As we continue to celebrate his passion for the natural environment and its dazzling panoply of life forms, we should also uphold his wisdom.

1-2. *Life on Air* by Sir David Attenborough (2002)

3-4. RSGS newsletter *GeogScot*, June 1990

SIR DAVID HEMPLEMAN-ADAMS

Polar explorer, climber and adventurer
BORN: 10th October 1956 (Swindon)
§
RSGS Livingstone Medal, 1997
Scottish Geographical (Gold) Medal, 2012
Fellow and Vice-President of RSGS

WHAT DRIVES AN explorer to push himself past his apparent physical limits, when his mind and body are screaming at him to give up? What makes the essential difference between success and failure?

The answer, if there is one, is surely known to Sir David Hempleman-Adams. In 1998 he was the first person ever to complete the Explorer's Grand Slam, which consists of climbing the highest mountain on each of the world's seven continents and trekking to both Poles. He has flown a hot air balloon to the North Pole, and retraced Ernest Shackleton's epic journey after the loss of the *Endurance* in the Antarctic (see p.43). As one of Britain's greatest living explorers, he has likely set himself more challenges of physical endurance than almost anyone on the planet. Yet arguably his most significant expedition is one which he regrets being able to complete.

In the summer of 2016, David was the leader of a small crew who sailed a boat around the entire Arctic ice cap in one season. Travelling in a 48-foot aluminium vessel named *Northabout*, they set off from Bristol on 19th June and returned on 20th October. The entire voyage, which he named the *Polar Ocean Challenge*, took just 142 days. The speed of David's journey was achievable only because climate change is causing the polar ice to recede dramatically, so that seas which were once permanently frozen are now navigable in summer.

Arctic ice may disappear altogether in the summer months within the next few decades.[1]

David's passion for the world's most extreme climates began when he was growing up in rural Wiltshire. As a teenager who loved the great outdoors, he was inspired by the Himalayan expeditions of Sir Chris Bonington, Dougal Haston and Doug Scott. In 1972, aged fifteen, he wrote to Bonington to ask if he needed an extra porter on his next expedition. Bonington's reply, gracefully declining, contained a message of praise and encouragement which David never forgot.

Business studies were paving the way for a career in company management, but David knew that the mountains had unfinished business of their own. Climbing in the Alps, although exhilarating, fed his appetite for greater challenges. In 1993, thanks largely to his unstoppable energy, David found himself gazing out across a panorama of glistening white peaks from the summit of Everest.

In recent years the popularity of Everest as an extreme 'tourist destination' has soared, making this life-threatening tiger of a mountain seem more like a domestic cat. But no one should be fooled. To the Tibetan people, Everest is the home of capricious mountain gods, and it continues to claim the lives of novice and experienced climbers alike. Avalanches can occur suddenly and without warning; the Earth has its own rules, and changes them to suit itself. At Base Camp, located at 11,000 feet below the summit, David recalls hearing the mountain 'groaning' at night – an unnerving sound, caused by ice and rocks creaking in the freezing wind.

Since 1953, when Everest was first ascended by Edmund Hillary and Tenzing Norgay, the number of achievable 'world firsts' has been dwindling. The same principle applies to the North and South Poles, where any new world records now depend on factors such as the season, the time scale, the age of the person or an unusual method of transport. But records are still there for the taking, and David has a dazzling clutch of them. In addition to the Explorer's Grand Slam, he has also stood at the Magnetic North and South Poles and the Geomagnetic North Pole*.

In 1998, when David and his companion, Norwegian explorer Rune Gjeldnes, were making the slow and painful trek across the Arctic, they looked up to see the vapour trail of an airliner thousands of feet above. David was at a low ebb; the previous day he had fallen through thin ice into freezing cold water and although Rune had dragged him to safety he was demoralised and suffering from frostbite. There must, he thought, be an easier way of reaching the Pole. The vapour trail reminded him of an earlier explorer who took to the skies in an attempt to achieve his goal, and a new idea started to take shape in his mind.

Salomon Andrée, a Swedish physicist and engineer, attempted to fly to the North Pole in a hot air balloon in 1897. The bid was unsuccessful, and Andrée and his two companions perished. Far from being put off by the risks, David was inspired by their daring venture. As soon as he got home from the Arctic trek, he started to look into the logistics of ballooning. To honour the memory of the Swedish team, he steered away from insulated capsules in favour of a traditional open basket – the kind that, it had to be admitted, was more suited to carrying champagne parties over the Mendips.

With typical vigour, after and a lot of intensive research but only a few hours' practice, David challenged himself to break a few records, the first of which was flying over the Andes.

In May 2000 he was the first man to fly a hot air balloon to the North Pole, taking off from Spitsbergen and surviving for five days in the wicker basket, cocooned in an immersion suit while he was over the sea, and dependent on bottled oxygen as the balloon ascended to catch the winds that would propel him northwards. During that time he had precious little sleep, and his body and mind became exhausted: one morning, having dozed for a short time, he woke in complete confusion to find that he had one leg out of the basket, poised to leap into space! Even the descent after his success was heart-stopping, with the balloon crash-landing and dragging him for fifteen interminable minutes over ice ridges and into an expanse of open water, where he feared he would drown. Perhaps more than even his Everest ascent and his polar treks, David's North Pole balloon flight called on unknown reserves of mental endurance.

In 2007, when he set a world altitude record by flying a conventional hot air balloon to 32,500 feet, David drew a startling parallel between his balloon's capacity (42,000 cubic feet) and our own carbon footprint. On average, a single person in the UK is responsible for producing that volume of carbon dioxide in just ten weeks. His growing concern about human impact on the natural environment led him to think about new expeditions, and a few years later the idea of the *Polar Ocean Challenge* was born.

In organising the *Polar Ocean Challenge*, David's aim was to highlight the changes that are happening in the Arctic and the effects that they are having on the environment and communities. He has witnessed the changes at first hand, as a frequent visitor to the polar regions over a period of more than thirty years. Entire ecosystems are feeling the impact of warming seas; on land, vast regions of permafrost are thawing. David believes that it may still be possible to curb this progressive change, but if it is not, the priority must then be to 'navigate the future of the Arctic responsibly.' With the Northeast and Northwest Passages now regularly ice-free in summer, shipping companies are already tempted to exploit these shorter routes that link the Pacific and Atlantic Oceans via the Arctic, saving both time and money. But the summer season is short, and because of the remoteness it would be practically impossible to mitigate the consequences of unforeseen events such as oil spillage.

The rate of change is alarming. Only a few generations ago the ice posed a daunting barrier for ships, luring many explorers north in the hope of discovering the fabled seaways around the Arctic. Some, like Sir John Franklin, never returned. Roald Amundsen was the first to sail through the Northwest Passage, between 1903 and 1906; the first confirmed voyage through the Northeast Passage was achieved by Adolf Erik Nordenskiöld, from 1878 to 1879. Worryingly, the yearly rate of decline in Arctic ice seems to be speeding up dramatically. The *Northabout*, which was the boat David used for his expedition, navigated the Northwest and Northeast Passages in 2001 and 2004 respectively, and her crew remember that the passages were choked with ice. In 2016, it took only fourteen days to sail across the Northwest Passage and David reported no ice at all.

David has set up a charity called Wicked Weather Watch which aims to inform young people about climate change, working with schools to share the latest research and suggesting ways in which individual people can help to alleviate the impact. He feels a strong responsibility to educate, and hopes his own experiences will directly benefit the next generation.

Having achieved his Gold Award by the age of sixteen, David is now a Trustee of the Duke of Edinburgh's Award Scheme, and was chosen to lead their Golden Jubilee Appeal in 2006. He believes that people from any background should be able to experience the thrill of global adventure, and with this in mind he helped to establish the Youth Adventure Trust, which allows disadvantaged youngsters to embark on the holiday of a lifetime.

'I have been very lucky in being able to travel and do the things I have wanted to do. As I have got older I've decided it's time to give a little bit back... It is important to pass this on to the next generation, hopefully inspiring them to go out and see the world for themselves. You can do whatever you want to do if you put your mind to it.'[2]

*GEOGRAPHIC POLE: A fixed point marking the northern and southern tip of the axis around which the Earth revolves. This is where all lines of longitude converge.

MAGNETIC POLE: A point marking the northern or southern focus of the Earth's magnetic field. A compass at the North Magnetic Pole would try to point straight down, hence its other name, the 'Magnetic Dip Pole'. The Magnetic North and South Poles move in response to the convection of molten iron in the Earth's core. They are not necessarily antipodal, meaning that an imaginary line drawn between them need not pass through the centre of the Earth.

GEOMAGNETIC POLE: This point is calculated by considering the Earth's magnetic field modelled as a perfect bar magnet. In other words, it does not take into account the effects of convection in the Earth's core. Using this definition, a line could be drawn between the North and South Geomagnetic Poles.

1. Sir David Hempleman-Adams, lecture to RSGS in Stirling, 14th February 2017
2. Interview with the author at RSGS in Perth, 13th February 2017

Karen Darke

Paralympic cyclist, paratriathlete, adventurer and author
Born: 25th June 1971 (Halifax)
§
RSGS Mungo Park Medal, 2016

What is life if it isn't an adventure? I'm constantly amazed by what can be achieved if we set our heart and mind to it. It's all about finding belief, confidence, motivation and commitment. And, of course, friends. Then there are no limits.

EXPLORATION IS USUALLY understood as the ambition to discover new lands or revisit already charted regions for fresh scientific study. There is another, more personal, form of exploration, however, which is to do with human identity. We all want to experience the world on our own terms but what do we do when those terms change? Faced with great physical challenges, the human spirit is astonishingly resilient. This is perhaps the key to all exploration: the knowledge that at the heart of every obstacle lies a solution.

At the age of twenty-one, Karen Darke was a strong and competent climber. She had scaled the Matterhorn and Mont Blanc; she revelled in the wildness and the freedom of the mountains. Then in 1993, while climbing a sea cliff near Aberdeen, she fell.

Waking up in hospital three days later, Karen learned that she had a break in her spine at chest level. The lower half of her body was paralysed. She felt as if she was drowning in questions, all of which began with 'what if'. As she gazed up at her family and climbing companions and saw the unspoken grief in their faces, she acknowledged the irony of her conversation with a friend only a few days before; she would rather, she had declared, be dead than paralysed. Until now, she had always found fulfilment outside herself, taking pleasure in her physical capabilities. In a few brief seconds the world had changed. Now the quest had to start from within.

A glimmer of hope came from an unexpected source; the death

of a friend in a climbing accident, three months after her own fall, brought new sadness but also lit a spark of determination. She was alive. A whole host of unknown challenges lay ahead, but her spirit found new momentum.

On the television in hospital, Karen watched wheelchair athletes competing in the London Marathon and wondered whether she would ever do anything like it. She had always been a keen sports-woman, and while she considered the possibilities she realised that she still could be.

Within a few months she had entered herself in the Lake Vyrnwy Half-marathon. It was an act of faith, which some would have called foolhardy. There was only one other wheelchair competitor; from the start line he sped off into the distance on his three-wheeled racing vehicle. Karen was left to complete the course on her own, in her regular wheelchair. Instead of being disheartened, she realised how wonderful it was just to be outdoors, breathing the clear air in the silence of the forest. Her body responded with joy to the physical exertion and she felt liberated.

The next year, she completed the London Marathon.

It was the first step on a long road. With that achievement, Karen began to realise that the things she had thought were impossible were within her grasp. A change in perception and attitude was the secret. She dreamed of a bike that was designed to suit her body, and luck led her right to the man who could build one. Having resumed her studies in geology at Aberdeen, she was invited to speak at a conference in Australia, and she took the opportunity to contact an innovative designer who lived on the outskirts of Melbourne. A few months later she was united with a custom-made cycle that would change her life. It was a hand-pedalled recumbent tricycle, and a tandem, which Karen had specified because it would allow her to go on tour with a friend. Her companion would provide the leg-pedalling from the rear seat while Karen used her arms at the front.

Karen called it the 'Green Beast', and she and a girlfriend took it for a road trip around Harris and the Uists. They camped close to the white beaches of Berneray and were lulled to sleep by the surf. One day a group of kayakers took them on a paddling trip to the Monach

Islands where Karen soaked up the peace and the wildness that her soul had been craving. The bliss of adventure, she realised, was still possible. The vastness of the natural world brought both freedom and a sense of perspective.

The cycling tour of the Western Isles was confined largely to tarmac but in the months that followed, Karen discovered that the tricycle could cope with dirt tracks in the Cairngorms. With increasing confidence she started to look at more distant horizons. She had always wanted to visit the Himalayas.

It was a crazy idea. The logical part of Karen's brain bombarded her with warnings: it was irresponsible and dangerous, and the practical problems were immense. But the last couple of years had taught her that with time, patience and determination, anything was possible. She chose to listen to the quieter voice within, the voice that was reassuring and positive. How exciting would it be to cross the Karakoram mountains?

Karen got out the guide books and the maps, and then booked a flight to Kazakhstan with three friends. Their little convoy consisted of two mountain bikes, the tandem tricycle and a trailer for Karen's chair. They gathered supplies in Bishkek, the capital of Kyrgyzstan, then they took to the road. Unfortunately, the rough surface of the Central Asian roads took a far greater toll on their gear than the mountain tracks of Scotland; it seemed that every few miles an essential piece of metal would work itself loose and drop off. Within a few days, Karen's hand-pedal came apart and had to be stuck back in place with chewing gum. The group learned it was wise to tighten all the nuts and bolts on their bikes every night, but then they ran across a different problem. After camping in a grassy orchard by the roadside, they woke to find all their tyres were flat; the rubber had been punctured by fierce thorns that they had somehow missed in their tiredness.

To alleviate these trials, there were plenty of heart-warming pleasures. The Kyrgyz people were welcoming and friendly, extending generous hospitality to the travellers with their curious means of transport. Karen and her friends were offered naan bread and kumis – fermented horse milk – and invited to sleep on a colourful array of mattresses and blankets. As they approached the Dolon Pass, the road surface deteriorated still further. Beyond the town of Naryn they entered a landscape that was barren and windswept. Hot, dry days were succeeded by freezing nights, and Karen burrowed into her sleeping bag for warmth. Their diet was simple and basic, and they often had to ask local herdsmen to help them locate fresh water.

Karen had no complaints. She had overcome her practical worries, and found herself not just managing but soaring.

Once they had passed the critical checkpoint on the Kyrgyz-China border, the cyclists lingered for a while in the bustling town of Kashgar, refreshing their appetites at market stalls selling fresh vegetables and fruit. They repaired their bikes and replenished their energy for the next phase of their journey, which was the Karakoram Highway.

Rising from the Taklamakan Desert, the Karakoram Highway runs for 800 miles from Kashgar in China to Abbottabad in Pakistan, skirting Tajikistan and Afghanistan and passing beneath the majestic Karakoram mountains – of which K2 is the highest. Opened in 1979 and reaching an elevation of over 15,300 feet, it is one of the highest roads in the world. Karen knew that cycling here was going to be tough. Thinning air and headwinds made it tougher, and as their food supplies dwindled the little party toiled painfully upwards with gritted teeth.

At the summit of the pass, Karen paused to catch her breath. She had made it. The bitingly cold wind discouraged her from lingering but she acknowledged her achievement. Then she abandoned herself to the euphoria of the descent, as the road snaked its way downwards through thrilling hairpin bends into the Indus Gorge.

The exhilaration of the mountains was something that Karen had yearned and grieved for since her fall. Now she realised that her paralysis did not exclude her from that sense of joy. The only threat to her freedom had been in her mind.

In the ten years after her ride up the Karakoram Pass, Karen took on a series of new challenges, each one an adventure in itself: hand-cycling the length of Japan; kayaking from Canada to Alaska; crossing Greenland by sit-ski. Understandably, she was still reluctant to contemplate a return to climbing. She learned, however, that sometimes people appear in your life for a reason. Her partner, Andy Kirkpatrick, who was a talented and dauntless climber, began restoring Karen's confidence through practice. He taught her to climb with ascenders, a mechanical device which allows a climber to pull herself up a rope by degrees. This technique is often used for smooth walls where there are few handholds and footholds.

When 2007 arrived, Karen was staring up at the granite face of El Capitan. There can be no more daunting rock face in the world than this 3,000-foot monolith in California's Yosemite National Park. Karen had seen it first when she was on holiday with her parents at the age of ten. She had marvelled at the climbers, looking like tiny dots clinging to the vastness of its surface, and she had promised her parents that one day, she too would climb it.

Just to arrive at the point where she could consider ascending El Capitan, Karen had to revisit memories almost too painful to bear. As she practised on rock faces closer to home, she forced herself to confront her worst fears. Should she even consider it? Was it not demanding too much of herself, not to mention her family, who had nearly lost her once before? The ascent of El Capitan had been beyond her capabilities even when she was fully mobile. It was a mad idea. On the other hand, said the insistent voice inside her, who would she be if she didn't try?

Andy was already an experienced climber of El Capitan. He led the way up the pitches, while Karen and the other two team members took turns to follow. They camped on portaledges, lightweight sleeping platforms that can be suspended from a cliff face when an ascent takes several days. Time and again, as she stepped off the platform into the yawning abyss, Karen felt a knot in her stomach and talked silently to herself to calm her nerves. She was safe. What could go wrong? Then on the fourth day her ropes tangled, preventing any movement upwards or downwards. She was helpless, and dangling thousands of feet above the ground. She wept with fear.

As the panic subsided, reason returned. To free herself, Karen had to unclip her safety rope and spin herself around to release the tangle. Her companions watched, silently willing her to act. Nobody could help her. The rescue had to come from within.

She forced herself to breathe and focus on each individual movement. Many endless minutes later, she was being grabbed by the arms
and hauled up onto a ledge.

Karen finished the climb of El Capitan in the dark, under a starry
sky. A storm was threatening, and the team knew that time was of
the essence. At the summit, as she lay in her sleeping bag on the cold,
unyielding granite, she felt utterly at peace. The fear that had been
torturing her for years had finally gone.

Today, Karen is perhaps better known as a Paralympic athlete,
having competed in London (2012) and Rio (2016). Her clutch of
medals, including a Gold from the Women's Time Trial H1-3 in
Brazil, bear witness to her talent and dedication. She has set up a
company offering coaching for individuals who wish to attain their
own life goals, and she is a motivational speaker in schools, organisations and businesses around the world. As she continues to explore
the world, she seeks to convince others of the wisdom she has gained
herself: that life's hardest challenges can bring the greatest gifts.

> If we can know ourselves better, we can explore our abilities,
> and achieve all manner of things we may previously have thought
> impossible.

All references in this chapter from www.karendarke.com by Karen Darke,
reproduced with permission

CRAIG MATHIESON

Polar explorer
Born: 13th March 1969 (Elderslie)
§
Royal Scottish Geographical Society's
first Explorer in Residence (2014)

When I was dropped off in Antarctica I spent ages looking around, drinking it in. I remember taking that first footstep South, knowing my life was about to change forever.[1]

WHEN CRAIG MATHIESON was twelve, he knew he wanted to be a polar explorer. All his spare time was spent outdoors, camping wild in the country around his hometown of Buchlyvie in Stirlingshire. He would catch fish and rabbits and cook them over a camp fire, dreaming of the journeys he would make.

This was not mere childhood fantasy; it was preparation. Craig devoured Apsley Cherry-Garrard's *The Worst Journey in the World*, which tells the harrowing story of Robert Falcon Scott's ill-fated Antarctic expedition, and Scott became one of his all-time heroes. He loved the way in which Cherry-Garrard wrote, which was honest and free of ego. One snowy day he built a sledge and dragged it all the way to Aberfoyle, pretending that he was trekking to the South Pole. Then he phoned his Mum from a call box and asked her to come and pick him up.

While his beloved primary school teacher, Jimmy Brown, believed in him, Craig found that others did not. When he was sixteen, he explained to a guidance teacher that he wanted to be a polar explorer and was told that he had no chance of doing that kind of thing. He was going to have to find out about it himself, plan it himself, and do it himself. That was fine with Craig, who is quietly spoken but fiercely determined.

Robert Falcon Scott had been a naval man, so Craig decided to follow his example. At the military careers office in Glasgow, he asked simply, 'Do you go to Antarctica?' The affirmation was enough. Within three weeks he was accepted, and bound for training in Plymouth. Craig served in the Gulf War and was then sent south for patrol duty on board a ship in the Falkland Islands.

In the South Atlantic, the proximity to the routes taken by Scott and Shackleton inevitably fascinated him. When his ship visited the islands of South Georgia, he pleaded with his captain for time off to retrace the steps of Shackleton, Crean and Worsley in May 1916, when they made a desperate march across the island to find help at the whaling station of Stromness. With permission granted, Craig went ashore for three memorable days, walking along the route they took and visiting Shackleton's grave. His ambition struck him afresh; he knew he needed to go to the South Pole.

The dream remained dormant a few more years. Discharged from the Navy, Craig married and started a family. He found a 'proper' job in accountancy, and fed his passion for the outdoors by climbing in Scotland's mountains. While exciting in itself, this was not his ultimate ambition, and in 2002 Craig knew he could wait no longer. He was more than ready; military training as well as expeditions in Greenland had given him the skills to survive, and he had been mentally preparing for the challenge for over twenty years. Just getting to the Antarctic requires specialist support, however. A few days after he telephoned the logistics company to arrange the transport, an invoice for a down payment of $80,000 dropped through his letterbox. It was, says Craig, the most positive thing he had ever been given.

Symbolically, it had been a hundred years since William Speirs Bruce set sail on the *Scottish National Antarctic Expedition*. Determined to lead the first dedicated Scottish expedition to the South Pole, Craig approached companies for sponsorship. He found a willing listener in Chris Tiso, head of the chain of outdoor shops, who could see the potential beneath Craig's nervousness. Without hesitation, he agreed to be a major sponsor.

With the support of the Royal Scottish Geographical Society, the planning for Craig's expedition got under way. He started training in earnest and, like his childhood self, he read books that would help him get into the mindset of being an explorer.

> For me, the professionalism and attitude of Amundsen and Nansen shaped the way I would plan and train for expeditions, whilst the inspiration to achieve would come from the likes of Scott, Shackleton, Bruce, and of course Sir Wally Herbert.[2]

Craig would be hauling a 160lb sledge for a distance of 730 miles, so he planned his food intake for this extreme effort with great care. He would be expending around 10,000 calories per day, but physically he would only be able to consume half of that; it would be, as he puts it, a kind of controlled starvation. He deliberately bulked up to about 13 stone before setting out, aware that over the next two months he would lose more weight than he could possibly gain.

Knowing that he wanted his expedition to consist of two people, Craig found a companion in business colleague Fiona Taylor, who he believed had the right attitude for the trek. 'People with egos,' he says, 'are always the first to break down.'[3] The two trained intensively during the months beforehand and were excited about carrying the Scottish flag together to the South Pole. Unfortunately, when they reached the Antarctic in November 2004, fate took a different turn. With storms rolling in, conditions were particularly brutal from the outset and temperatures dropped to -51°C inside the tent. Fiona developed frostbite in her hands and after four days she was transferred to Patriot Hills Logistics Base for medical treatment. Craig decided to carry on alone.

The exceptionally cold temperatures persisted as Craig battled across 50 miles of sastrugi —snowfields that have been rippled and buckled by the wind – and struggled to pitch his tent on blue ice hard as rock. He navigated the simple way, using a watch and a shadow to gauge his position. He had occasional contact with his family via a satellite phone, and every day he felt that he could hear the voices of his children egging him on as he skied ever closer to his goal. On Christmas Day he opened their card which he had been carrying, and found drawings and a wine gum secreted inside it. He unwrapped their gift, which turned out to be a box of chocolate mini-rolls. There were four other people attempting to ski to the South Pole at the same time as Craig, and he skied over to greet them with a feast that made them feel like millionaires.

On the morning of 28th December Craig noticed a black dot on the horizon and realised that it was the South Pole base station. At last, this was the culmination of his dream. As he stood and gazed, every hope and every memory that had led him to this point seemed to pour through his head in a tumult of images. It was an overwhelming experience. He broke down and gave way to the flood of emotion. Tears, however, freeze instantly in the Antarctic, and the last 11 miles were still in front of him. He brushed the ice from his face and waited for the other skiers to catch up, so that they could arrive at the Pole shoulder to shoulder.

Coming home, Craig remembers, was a strangely unnerving experience. He was overjoyed to be reunited with his family but when he turned on the television he was appalled by the superficial obsessions of the media. His first trip into a city almost killed him; unused to busy roads, he was nearly knocked down by the traffic. At a restaurant he was annoyed to hear people complaining about the food when he had survived for three months on simple rations. The world seemed to have no appreciation for what was important. He had only been away for two months and yet his perspective had completely changed. His reaction was to do something positive: he visited schools, and talked to students about his experiences. It was an impulse that sowed the seed of a great idea.

> Exploring, for me, is about sharing with others the privilege and knowledge gained, never kept to yourself.[4]

As his success was celebrated throughout Scotland, Craig was invited to the Scottish Parliament where he spoke to First Minister Jack McConnell. He voiced his concerns about some of the children he was meeting in schools. He could see that they had started out with aspirations but they were learning to abandon them because they were losing belief in themselves. Often overlooked by teachers because they were neither academically brilliant nor noisily disruptive, they were concluding that life might hold great things for some people, but not for them. Craig told McConnell that he could train such a student and prove that he or she could do the impossible. He would take them to the North Pole.

It was a daring idea, and McConnell was impressed. Craig's next task was to find the ideal student.

Chris Struthers from Falkirk was Craig's first ever pupil. He was fifteen, withdrawn, and extremely shy. He spent most of his time playing computer games, but when encouraged by Craig, he admitted that his secret wish was to be able to stand up in front of his family and tell them he had a place at university. What he lacked was the confidence to achieve, and Craig knew that he could help him find it. Chris's parents were initially doubtful, but Craig countered this by persuading them that they, too, had to believe in their son. When they saw Chris's enthusiasm they willingly gave their consent.

The months of training which Craig designed for Chris in preparation for his Arctic expedition were nothing less than gruelling. Together they walked for 40 miles over Rannoch Moor, dragged tyres across beaches, and spent hours on cross-trainers. The final stage of training was spent in Greenland, where Chris was taught survival techniques and skied for 20 miles around the coastline. He also had the privilege of sharing a meal with an Inuit family. A few weeks later, when they were dropped off by Russian helicopter on the Arctic ice sheet, Craig told Chris that, instead of being the participant, he was now the leader – such was the trust that Craig had helped to build in him, and which Chris now felt within himself. Their expedition unfolded seamlessly, and on 24th April 2006 they reached the North Pole.

The impact on Chris's life was immediate and far-reaching. He came home with new confidence, and he was respected by his peers. He applied the same determination and logic to his studies that he had devoted to his Arctic training with the result that, not only was he able to tell his family that he had been accepted at university, but he emerged four years later with a first class honours degree in geology. His parents, overjoyed at the transformation in their son, were inspired to pursue their own dreams.

Meanwhile, Craig had a decision to make. There were thousands of teenagers just like Chris, and he wanted to help them. His employer had just made him a partner, but he realised he had something more important to do. He quit his job and in 2013 he set up a charity, which he named the Polar Academy, to offer Arctic training and expeditions to youngsters who needed to rediscover their confidence. He knew very well that there would be plenty of bureaucratic hurdles to jump, not least in the field of health and safety, but he had already proved what he could do, and wanted to give young people an opportunity of a lifetime.

> I know these kids have greatness within them; they just need the catalyst to release it.[5]

Every year, the Polar Academy selects ten pupils from around Scotland and prepares them for an expedition to the Arctic. The rigorous two-day selection process, based at Glenmore Lodge in the Cairngorms, involves the parents as well as the candidates. When the team has been chosen, Craig trains them in the same way that he trained Chris, the way that Fridtjof Nansen trained, based on the principle that success is more about focus than fitness. Within a year they are elite athletes, ready to embark on an expedition to Greenland in the company of Craig and a small team of world-class, hand-picked experts.

In the Arctic, Craig is emphatic about the students' level of responsibility. They navigate, pitch the tents, cook the food, dig the latrines, and set up bear fences. He watches the transformation with pride. 'They seem to grow in confidence from hour to hour. I have a very slick professional team who achieve huge distances. Nothing scares them any more, but they have the common sense to understand risk.'[6]

The youngsters' responsibilities do not end when they come home. They are, in effect, ambassadors for the Polar Academy, because their role is now to visit schools and speak to hundreds of children, encouraging them to rediscover their aspirations by taking the same steps that they did. This they do with passion and enthusiasm. Not surprisingly, the demand for places at the Polar Academy is extremely high. From a financial viewpoint, it is expensive to send just one student to the Arctic, and Craig is responsible for all the fundraising. Fortunately, powerful sponsors are increasingly seeing the potential of the Polar Academy and giving their backing.

In 2014, Craig was invited to become the Royal Scottish Geographical Society's first Explorer in Residence, a role which he considers a great honour. He speaks about his life with modesty, but his eyes are alight with confidence and passion. He is, after all, inspiring the leaders and explorers of the future, and giving youngsters the confidence to pursue their dreams. 'I feel,' he says, 'as if I have got the best job on the planet.'[7]

---

1. Interview with author, April 2017

2. Craig Mathieson, from 'Inspiring People' on RSGS website www.rsgs.org

3-4. Interview with author, April 2017

5. Craig Mathieson, from 'Inspiring People' on RSGS website www.rsgs.org

6-7. Interview with author, April 2017

AFTERWORD

A T THE ROYAL SCOTTISH Geographical Society we believe that geography, in its role of explaining the world, its physical processes and human interactions, has never been more vital. Bearing this in mind, we have long since determined to promote geographical understanding on the bases of rational scientific evidence and debate. Recent political developments have persuaded me that this is more important than ever.

The world has undergone momentous change over the last two centuries. The study of geography not only helps to explain that change, but its leading lights have also shaped and even inspired its progress. The Society is privileged to include many of the most inspirational in its number: Council members, staff, speakers and medallists, with each becoming a vibrant thread in the tapestry of our history, and underlining our contemporary relevance, then and now.

From the highest mountain tops to the depths of the oceans, from the icy Poles to the widest deserts, and even to the Moon, the people featured in *The Great Horizon* have achieved many significant 'firsts'. Driven by a thirst for new knowledge and adventure, they have expanded the boundaries of human endeavour and added enormously to our scientific and cultural understanding. They left a great legacy too, of knowledge, research, humanitarian or environmental good, and ultimately of inspiration. The characters who inhabit the Society's history affirm the reach and impact of geography in the past, but I believe they also underline our contribution today.

Our Society is an academic institution, an educational charity, a membership body, and a policy-influencing organisation, but it is also part of an international network of such societies. Alongside these, by merit of its extensive archives, it has become a repository of the best adventure stories of the past 150 years, and it is part of our job to keep them alive. That is why I was so delighted to meet the inspirational Jo Woolf, whom we appointed Writer in Residence after she became captivated by our collections.

The book you now hold in your hands is the product of that meeting and of years of effort by Jo. I am immensely grateful to her for bringing these characters to life, and hope that in time we can go to work on the next fifty, and maybe the fifty after that. Meanwhile, we will continue to find and celebrate the modern-day Shackletons, Bruces, Birds and Starks, who will inspire future generations.

As a small charity with little funding, we must be creative with what are limited resources. To the many Society members and supporters who so generously subscribed to a copy before the book was even written, I owe a huge debt of gratitude. My thanks also go to our Treasurer Tim Ambrose, to The Patron's Fund, and to my friend Nick Hayes, the brilliant cartoonist who produced the stunning back cover image. This project would never have seen the light of day without all of these supporters, and without the assistance of Sandstone Press.

I hope you, like me, enjoy the insights this book provides into some of the most colourful and remarkable people of the last 150 years. Most of all though, I hope it will inspire you to explore in your own right, to set your own goals and adventures, and to help inspire others. If you are not a member and would like to help keep our heritage alive for future generations, please join us or visit our website to find out more about our work.

Mike Robinson
Chief Executive of the
Royal Scottish Geographical Society
Lord John Murray House
15-19 North Port
Perth PH1 5LU
www.rsgs.org

SELECT BIBLIOGRAPHY

ICE

Fridtjof Nansen
Bain, J. Arthur, *Fridtjof Nansen: His Life and Explorations* (Partridge, 1897)
Huntford, Roland, *Nansen: The Explorer as Hero* (Abacus, 1997)
Nansen, Fridtjof, *Farthest North* (Newnes, 1898)

Robert Peary
Herbert, Wally, *The Noose of Laurels* (Hodder & Stoughton, 1989)
Peary, Robert E., *The North Pole* (Stokes, 1910)
Weems, John Edward, *Peary, the Explorer and the Man* (Tarcher, 1967)

Robert Falcon Scott
Fiennes, Ranulph, *Captain Scott* (Hodder & Stoughton, 2003)
Huxley, Elspeth, *Scott of the Antarctic* (Weidenfeld & Nicholson, 1977)
Scott, Robert Falcon, *The Voyage of the Discovery* (Nelson, 1905)
    with foreword by Sir Peter Scott, *Scott's Last Expedition – the Journals* (Methuen, 1983)

Teddy Evans
Evans, E. R. G. R., *South With Scott* (Collins, 1924)
(See also Robert Falcon Scott)

Sir Ernest Shackleton
Huntford, Roland, *Shackleton* (Abacus, 1989)
Mill, Hugh Robert, *The Life of Sir Ernest Shackleton* (Heinemann, 1923)
Shackleton, Ernest, *The Heart of the Antarctic* (Heinemann, 1909)
―――― *South* (Macmillan, 1920)

William Speirs Bruce

Rudmose Brown, R. N., J. H. H. Pirie and R. C. Mossman, *The Voyage of the Scotia* (Blackwood, 1906)

Speak, Peter, *William Speirs Bruce* (NMSE Publishing, 2003)

Speirs Bruce, William, *Polar Exploration* (1911)

Roald Amundsen

Amundsen, Roald, *My Life as an Explorer* (Amberley, 2008)

Bown, Stephen R., *The Last Viking – the Life of Roald Amundsen* (Da Capo, 2013)

Sir Wally Herbert

Herbert, Kari, *The Explorer's Daughter* (Penguin, 2004)

Herbert, Wally, *Across the Top of the World* (Longman, 1969)

———— *The Noose of Laurels* (Hodder & Stoughton, 1989)

———— *The Polar World: The Unique Vision of Sir Wally Herbert* (Polarworld, 2007)

Official website: wallyherbert.com

Sir Ranulph Fiennes

Fiennes, Ranulph, *Mad, Bad and Dangerous to Know* (Hodder & Stoughton, 2007)

———— *Cold: Extreme Adventures at the Lowest Temperatures on Earth* (Simon & Schuster, 2014)

———— *Fear: Our Ultimate Challenge* (Hodder & Stoughton, 2016)

Official website: ranulphfiennes.co.uk

Børge Ousland

Ousland, Børge, *Alone to the North Pole* (1994)

———— *Alone across Antarctica* (1997)

———— *The Great Polar Journey: In the Footsteps of Nansen* (2009)

Official website: ousland.no

Ice Legacy – crossing the world's 20 largest glaciers: icelegacy.com

VOYAGERS

Tim Severin
Severin, Tim, *The Jason Voyage* (Hutchinson, 1985)
—— *The China Voyage* (Little, Brown, 1994)
—— *The Brendan Voyage* (Abacus, 1996)
Official website: timseverin.net

Isobel Wylie Hutchison
Hoyle, Gwyneth, *Flowers in the Snow* (University of Nebraska, 2001)
Wylie Hutchison, Isobel, *On Greenland's Closed Shore* (Blackwood, 1930)
—— *North to the Rime-ringed Sun* (Blackie, 1934)
—— *The Aleutian Islands* (Blackie, 1943)

Isabella Bird
Bird, Isabella, *A Lady's Life in the Rocky Mountains* (Murray, 1879)
—— *The Yangtze Valley and Beyond* (Murray, 1899)
Ireland, Deborah, *Isabella Bird: A Photographic Journal of Travels Through China 1894-1896* (Ammonite Press, 2015)
Stoddart, Anna M., *The Life of Isabella Bird* (Murray, 1906)

Sir John Murray
Murray, John and Laurence Pullar, *Bathymetrical Survey of the Freshwater Lochs of Scotland* (1910)
—— *The Depths of the Ocean* (Macmillan, 1912)
Online at the National Library of Scotland nls.uk

Mary Kingsley
Frank, Katherine, *A Voyager Out: The Life of Mary Kingsley* (Corgi, 1988)
Kingsley, Mary, *Travels in West Africa* (Macmillan, 1900)

Sven Hedin
Hedin, Sven, *Trans-Himalaya – Discoveries and Adventures in Tibet* (Macmillan, 1909)
—— *Southern Tibet* (1917)

―――― *My Life as an Explorer* (Cassell, 1926)

The Sven Hedin Foundation: svenhedinfoundation.org

Freya Stark

Fletcher Geniesse, Jane, *Passionate Nomad* (Modern Library, 2001)

Stark, Freya, *The Valleys of the Assassins* (John Murray, 1934)

―――― *A Winter in Arabia* (John Murray, 1972)

Bertram Thomas

Thomas, Bertram, *Alarms and Excursions in Arabia* (George Allen & Unwin, 1931)

―――― *Arabia Felix: Across the Empty Quarter of Arabia* (Jonathan Cape, 1932)

Robert Ballard

Ballard, Robert D., *The Discovery of the Titanic* (Madison, 1987)

Ballard, Robert D., with Will Hively, *The Eternal Darkness* (Princeton, 2000)

Ocean Exploration Trust: oceanexplorationtrust.org

Michael Palin

Palin, Michael, *Pole to Pole* (BBC Books, 1997)

―――― *Sahara* (Weidenfeld & Nicolson, 2002)

―――― *Himalaya* (Weidenfeld & Nicolson, 2004)

Official website: palinstravels.co.uk

HEAVEN AND EARTH

Sir John Lubbock (Lord Avebury)

Hutchison, Horace G., *The Life of Sir John Lubbock* (Macmillan, 1914)

Lubbock, Sir John, *The Pleasures of Life* (Macmillan, 1890)

―――― *The Use of Life* (Macmillan, 1895)

Sir Archibald Geikie

Geikie, Archibald, *Class-book of Geology* (Macmillan, 1891)

——— *Scottish Reminiscences* (James Maclehose, 1904)

——— *A Long Life's Work* (Macmillan, 1924)

Sir Francis Younghusband

French, Patrick, *Younghusband: The Last Great Imperial Adventurer*
(HarperCollins, 1994)

George Mallory

Gillman, Peter and Leni Gillman, *The Wildest Dream* (Headline
Publishing, 2000)

Mallory, George, *Climbing Everest* (Gibson Square, 2012)

Frank Kingdon Ward

Kingdon Ward, F., *The Land of the Blue Poppy* (Cambridge Uni-versity
Press, 1913)

——— *A Plant Hunter in Tibet* (Jonathan Cape, 1934)

Cox, Kenneth, Kenneth Storm Jr and Ian Baker, *Frank Kingdon Ward's
Riddle of the Tsangpo Gorges* (Antique Collectors' Club, 2001)

W. H. Murray

Murray, W. H., *Mountaineering in Scotland* (Dent, 1947)

——— *Undiscovered Scotland* (Dent, 1951)

——— *The Evidence of Things Not Seen* (Baton Wicks, 2002)

Sir Edmund Hillary

Hillary, Edmund, *View from the Summit* (Doubleday, 1999)

Hunt, John, *The Ascent of Everest* (Hodder & Stoughton, 1953)

Johnston, Alexa, *Sir Edmund Hillary: An Extraordinary Life* (Penguin,
2006)

Sir Chris Bonington

Bonington, Chris, *I Chose to Climb* (Gollancz, 1969)

——— *Everest the Hard Way* (Hodder & Stoughton, 1976)

——— *Chris Bonington – Mountaineer* (Baton Wicks, 1996)

Official website: bonington.com

Sir Alan Cobham
Cobham, Alan J., *A Time to Fly* (Shepheard-Walwyn, 1978)

Neil Armstrong
Hansen, James R., *First Man: The Life of Neil Armstrong* (Simon & Schuster, 2005)

MISSIONARIES AND MAVERICKS

David Livingstone
Jeal, Tim, *Livingstone* (revised ed., Yale, 2013)
Livingstone, David, *Missionary Travels and Research in South Africa* (John Murray, 1857)
Tomkins, Stephen, *David Livingstone: The Unexplored Story* (Lion, 2013)
Online resource: livingstoneonline.org

Henry Morton Stanley
Jeal, Tim, *Stanley: The Impossible Life of Africa's Greatest Explorer* (Faber & Faber, 2008)
Stanley, H. M., *The Autobiography of Sir Henry Morton Stanley* (Low, Marston, 1909)

Joseph Thomson
Thomson, J. B., *Joseph Thomson, African Explorer* (Sampson Low, Marston & Co, 1897)

Fanny Bullock Workman
Workman, Fanny Bullock, *In the Ice World of the Himalaya* (Cassell, 1900)
Workman, Fanny Bullock, and William Hunter Workman, *Sketches Awheel in Modern Iberia* (G. P. Putnam's Sons, 1897)
——— *Algerian Memories: a Bicycle Tour over the Atlas to the Sahara* (Fisher Unwin, *c.*1905)

Annie Taylor

Carey, William, *Adventures in Tibet* (Baker & Taylor, 1901)

Taylor, Annie, *Pioneering in Tibet* (Morgan & Scott, 1895)

Lord Kitchener

Arthur, George, *The Life of Lord Kitchener* (Macmillan, 1920)

Mildred Cable, Eva and Francesca French

Cable, Mildred and Francesca French, *Through Jade Gate* (Hodder & Stoughton, 1939)

——— *The Gobi Desert* (Hodder & Stoughton, 1943)

——— *Something Happened* (Hodder & Stoughton, 1944)

Frederick Marshman Bailey

Bailey, Frederick Marshman, *Mission to Tashkent* (Oxford University Press, 1992)

Marion Newbigin

Maddrell, Avril, *Complex Locations: Women's Geographical Work in the UK 1850-1970* (Wiley-Blackwell, 2009)

Newbigin, Marion, *Modern Geography* (Williams & Norgate, *c*.1911)

——— *Frequented Ways* (Constable, 1922)

Withers, Charles W. J. and Hayden Lorimer (editors). *Geographers: Biobibliographical Studies* Vol 28 (Bloomsbury, 2015)

Rosie Swale Pope

Swale Pope, Rosie, *Just a Little Run Around the World* (HarperTrue, 2009)

Official website: rosieswalepope.co.uk

VISIONS FOR CHANGE

John George Bartholomew

Fleet, Christopher, Margaret Wilkes and Charles W. J. Withers, *Scotland: Mapping the Nation* (Birlinn, 2012)

Online historical resource: johnbartholomew.com
National Library of Scotland: digital.nls.uk/bartholomew

Sir Patrick Geddes

Kitchen, Paddy, *A Most Unsettling Person* (Saturday Review Press, 1975)
Stephen, Walter, *Think Global, Act Local: The Life and Legacy of Patrick Geddes* (Luath, 2015)
Tyrwhitt, Jaqueline, *Patrick Geddes in India* (Lund Humphries, 1947)
Geddes' Collège des Ecossais in Montpellier, France:
metagraphies.org

Sir Hubert Wilkins

Nasht, Simon, *No More Beyond: The Life of Hubert Wilkins* (Birlinn, 2006)

Thor Heyerdahl

Heyerdahl, Thor, *Kon-Tiki* (Rand McNally, 1950)
——— *Fatu-Hiva: Back to Nature* (George Allen & Unwin, 1974)
——— *The Ra Expeditions* (George Allen & Unwin, 1971)

Wangari Maathai

Maathai, Wangari, *Unbowed* (Arrow, 2008)
——— Wangari, *The Challenge for Africa* (Arrow, 2010)

Dick Balharry

Laughton Johnston, J. and Dick Balharry, *Beinn Eighe: The Mountain above the Wood* (Birlinn, 2001)

Sir David Attenborough

Attenborough, David, *The Living Planet* (Little, Brown, 1984)
——— *The Trials of Life* (Collins/BBC, 1990)
——— *The Life of Birds* (BBC Books, 1998)
——— *Life on Air* (BBC Books, 2003)

Sir David Hempleman-Adams

Hempleman-Adams, David, *Walking on Thin Ice* (Orion, 1999)

———— *At the Mercy of the Winds* (Bantam, 2001)
———— *No Such Thing as Failure* (Constable, 2014)
Official website of Polar Ocean Challenge: polarocean.co.uk

Karen Darke
Darke, Karen, *If You Fall* (Winchester, 2006)
———— *Boundless: An Adventure Beyond Limits* (Akreative, 2012)
Official website: inspireandimpact.com

Craig Mathieson
The Polar Academy: thepolaracademy.org
Official website: mathiesonexplorer.com

General exploration and history

Allen, Benedict (editor), *Faber Book of Exploration* (Faber & Faber, 2002)
Hanbury-Tenison, Robin and Robert Twigger, *The Modern Explorers* (Thames & Hudson, 2013)
Hopkirk, Peter, *Foreign Devils on the Silk Road* (John Murray, 2006)
———— *The Great Game: On Secret Service in High Asia* (John Murray, 2006)
Pakenham, Thomas, *The Scramble for Africa* (Abacus, 1992)
Mills, William J., *Exploring Polar Frontiers: A Historical Encyclopaedia* (ABC-CLIO, 2003)

Women explorers

Herbert, Kari, *Heart of the Hero: The Remarkable Women Who Inspired the Great Polar Explorers* (Saraband, 2013)
Miller, Luree, *On Top of the World: Five Women Explorers in Tibet* (Mountaineers Books, 2000)
Morris, Mary, with Larry O'Connor, *The Virago Book of Women Travellers* (Virago, 1996)
Robinson, Jane, *Unsuitable for Ladies: an Anthology of Women Travellers* (Oxford, 2001)
Russell, Mary, *The Blessings of a Good Thick Skirt: Women Travellers and their World* (Flamingo, 1994)

INDEX

Note: Entries in **bold type** indicate a chapter devoted to that person.

WITH GRATITUDE

Our thanks to the following RSGS members and supporters
who helped to make publication of this book possible:

Michael Adams
Thomas Agnew
Nick Allen
Iain Allison
Tim Ambrose
John Anderson
Nigel & Linda Armstrong
Mrs Susan Baillie
Gordon Ballantyne
Mary D Barr
Ivon Bartholomew
Linda & Steve Bassett
Anne Beeson
Martin Bell
Dr Edith Beveridge
Claire M Blackadder
Andrew Blyth
Alverne Bolitho
F David Bottomley
Hamish Breckenridge
Professor John Briggs
Mrs J Brown
Sheila Brown
Sheila & Alistair Brown
Colin & Sarah Brown
Barrie Brown
Finlay Bryden
Philip Bryers
Bob Byiers
Mary Cairncross
Dr John & Mrs Erica M
    Caldwell
James Callander
Hazel Buchan Cameron
Mrs Margaret Campbell
Peter Capewell
Avril Carroll
Scott Carswell
Dr Stephen J Carthew
Dr Kathleen Cartwright
Nicola & Sam Chakraverty

Rebecca Chambers
Mr Alan Chan
Aidan Christie
Mary Clarkson
Dr Vanessa Collingridge
Alan Colvill
Gordon Cooper
John & Margaret Craig
David Craig
Ian, Liz & Jenny Crisp
Professor Roger Crofts
Nicola Crosbie
Alastair Cruickshank
Sandy & Julie Cruickshank
Fraser & Meredith
    Cruickshank
Fiona Cuthbert
Norma P Cuthbertson
Fiona Cuthill
Norman Dalgleish
Andrew Dalgleish
Anne Daniel
Margaret Daniel
Linda Davidson
Caroline H Dawson
Simon W Dedman
Miguel del Monte
Richard and Jo Doake
Mrs Mary Doig
Irene Duncan
Kevin Dunion
Gary Dunion
Dr Margaret Dykes
Kevin J Edwards
Mark Evans
Maggie & Cammie Ewen
Andrew Fairbairn
Leonard J Findlay
Jess & Stuart Findlay
John Finney
Marc A Fleming

Isabelle Forteath
Ruth Fraser
Jacqueline Freeguard
Craig Galbraith
Liz & Ron Gellatly
Susan Gemmill
Mrs Muriel George
Lorraine & Andrew Gill
Todd Gillenwater
Gil Gillenwater
Jayne Glass
Jim Goodlad MA, FRSGS
Moira & Peter Goodman
Dave Gordon
Andy Gordon
Mrs Elizabeth A Gordon
Scott Govan
James A P Grant
Alison Grassick
Mike & Trish Gray
Floris Greenlaw
Rev Dr ADC Greer
Gerry Griffiths
Keith Griffiths & Fiona
    Smart
Mr John O'Mailley
Iain & Margaret-Anne
    Halliday
Hannah Ham
Hamish Hamill
Douglas James Hamilton
Jane Harker
Morna Hawksford
W J C Henderson, W.S.,
    F.R.G.S.
Alister Hendrie
Barry Hill
Jeremy Hopkins
Robbie Horne
Matthias Berghaus &
    Stefanie Hose

WITH GRATITUDE

Pamela Howat
Elma & John Innes
Wendy Jacques-Berg
Sue James
R A Jefferson
Dick Jennings
Gillean & Jonathan Joels
Sonia Johal on S.S. Salacia
Dr J V Johnson
Margaret Johnstone
Gillian Joiner
Ann & Ian Kellie
Dave Kelly
Miss Christine Kelt
Pam Kemp
N R Kermack
Matt & Ruth Kerr
Margot Kerr
R A Kirk
Patricia Knowles
Arthur F Kuebel
Sinclair Laing
Andrew P Leggate in
    memory of Geo. M
    Leggate & Roger M
    Leggate
John W Lewington
Colin Liddell W.S.
Katharine M E Liston
Mrs Jackie Littlechild
Margaret Lobban
James M Loughridge
Debbie Lyle
Jane Lyle
Richard Lyle
G J Macfarlane
Fiona MacInnes
John Mackay
Alex Mackenzie
Douglas & Moira
    Mackinnon
Iain Mackintosh
Kenny & Hazel Maclean
Matt & Marie
    Macpherson

Duncan & Edith
    MacQuarrie
George MacQuarrie
E Ann Mailer
John D Martindale
Chris Masterton
Marjory Maxwell
Eleanor M McArthur
Professor John
    McCutcheon
Gemma McDonald
Murdo McEwan
Mary V McEwan
Mr Martin McKay
Erica McKellar
David McVey
Mrs Lyndsey McWhirter
Ian & Amy Millar
Dave & Catherine Mitchell
Sue Moncrieff
Jill Moody
Gordon and Margaret
    Murdoch
Douglas Murray
Kelvin Murray
Dr A J Murray
Jean & Ross Nairn
Lorna Ogilvie
Tom Ogston
Helen Ord
Abigail & David Page
Andrew Parrott
Keith Paul
Angus Pelham Burn
Peter & Betty Philip
John Pocock
Catriona Prebble
Sally Quinn
Dr Fiona Reid
Kaye Ridge & Andrew
    Ridge
Hazel & Luke Robertson
Alexander Robertson
Jamie, Euan & Fergus
    Robinson

Mr I L S Rolfe
Freda Ross
Gordon & Teresa Ross
David Rowlands
Mary-Anne Scott
Kay & Len Seal
Anne & Dilip Shah
Colin Shannon
Paul Shaw
Margaret & Gordon Shiach
Derek G Sime
Professor Ian Simpson
Tony Simpson
Dorothy Sloan
Murray & Margaret Smith
Ian & Ann Snodgrass
Jean Sobecki
James Stephen
James R Stewart
Bob Stock
Jeffrey C Stone
Mrs Elisabeth Stowe
Britta and David Sugden
Kenneth Thompson
Kerr Thomson
Bob Thomson
Mike Todd
Hunter & Brodie Torrance
Dr Charles Warren
Maurice Watson
Susan N Watt
Roger & June Watts
John Wells
Olga West
Colin & Jay Whimster
Margaret Wilkes
Chris Wilkins
Irene Williamson
F W Wilson
Ian R & Mrs Mary C
    Wilson
Graham & Melanie Woolf
Pete Woolf
Jamie Wylie

and the many supporters who wished to remain anonymous.

413